American Zombie Gothic

CONTRIBUTIONS TO ZOMBIE STUDIES

White Zombie: Anatomy of a Horror Film. Gary D. Rhodes. 2001

The Zombie Movie Encyclopedia. Peter Dendle. 2001

*American Zombie Gothic: The Rise and Fall (and Rise)
of the Walking Dead in Popular Culture.* Kyle William Bishop. 2010

*Back from the Dead: Remakes of the Romero
Zombie Films as Markers of Their Times.* Kevin J. Wetmore, Jr. 2011

*Generation Zombie: Essays on the Living Dead
in Modern Culture.* Edited by Stephanie Boluk and Wylie Lenz. 2011

*Race, Oppression and the Zombie: Essays on Cross-Cultural Appropriations
of the Caribbean Tradition.* Edited by Christopher M. Moreman
and Cory James Rushton. 2011

Zombies Are Us: Essays on the Humanity of the Walking Dead.
Edited by Christopher M. Moreman and Cory James Rushton. 2011

The Zombie Movie Encyclopedia, Volume 2: 2000–2010. Peter Dendle. 2012

Great Zombies in History. Edited by Joe Sergi. 2013 (graphic novel)

Unraveling Resident Evil*: Essays on the Complex Universe
of the Games and Films.* Edited by Nadine Farghaly. 2014

"We're All Infected": Essays on AMC's The Walking Dead
and the Fate of the Human. Edited by Dawn Keetley. 2014

Zombies and Sexuality: Essays on Desire and the Walking Dead.
Edited by Shaka McGlotten and Steve Jones. 2014

American Zombie Gothic

The Rise and Fall (and Rise) of the Walking Dead in Popular Culture

KYLE WILLIAM BISHOP

Foreword by JERROLD E. HOGLE

CONTRIBUTIONS TO ZOMBIE STUDIES

McFarland & Company, Inc., Publishers

Jefferson, North Carolina

LIBRARY OF CONGRESS CATALOGUING-IN-PUBLICATION DATA

Bishop, Kyle William, 1973–
    American Zombie Gothic : the rise and fall (and rise) of the
walking dead in popular culture / Kyle William Bishop ;
foreword by Jerrold E. Hogle.
        p.   cm. — (Contributions to Zombie Studies)
    Includes bibliographical references and index.

    ISBN 978-0-7864-4806-7 (softcover : acid free paper) ∞
    ISBN 978-0-7864-5554-6 (ebook)

    1. Zombie films — History and criticism.   I. Title.
PN1995.9.Z63B52   2010
791.43'675 — dc22   2009050018

British Library cataloguing data are available

Cover image ©2010 Shannon Eberhard (after Grant Wood's
American Gothic)

Printed in the United States of America

McFarland & Company, Inc., Publishers
  Box 611, Jefferson, North Carolina 28640
    www.mcfarlandpub.com

For Rachel, Xander, and Sydney.
And also for VR Magleby

ACKNOWLEDGMENTS

I wish to thank those who have helped make this book happen: Peter Dendle, Charlie Bertsch, Maribel Alvarez, Jennifer Jenkins, Suresh Raval, Amy Parziale, Jay "Maggie" Jesse, James Wermers, and especially Todd Petersen. My deepest appreciation and gratitude go to Susan White, my wonderful and tireless dissertation director, and the other two members of my committee who worked so diligently with me on the early drafts of the manuscript: the great Gothic scholar Jerrold E. Hogle and the brilliant critical theorist Carlos Gallego. Everlasting thanks also go to the Pretenyrds of Southern Utah University — Jessica, Robin, Kurt, Ed, Charles, and Crazy Joe — along with my other colleagues in the Southern Utah University English Department.

My utmost thanks go once again to Dr. Hogle, who offered a much-appreciated foreword and invaluable liner notes. For assistance in obtaining my visuals and screen images, I thank Drs. White and Petersen, SUU Provost Rodney Decker and English Department Chair Kurt Harris, Jerry and Dollie at Jerry Ohlinger's Movie Material Store, Derek and Todd at Photofest Digital, and Shannon Eberhard, my illustrator. Most of all, I thank my patient and longsuffering family: my parents Kent and Bonnie, my devoted grandfather VR, and, of course, Rachel, Xander, and Sydney.

Some of the following material has been published previously (albeit in much abbreviated versions) in a variety of academic journals: part of the introduction appears in the *Journal of Popular Film and Television* as "Dead Man *Still* Walking: Explaining the Zombie Renaissance" (37.1 [2009]: 16–25, © Taylor and Francis), material from chapters 1, 2, and 3 can be found together in "Raising the Dead: Unearthing the Non-Literary Origins of Zombie Cinema" in the *Journal of Popular Film and Television* (33.4 [2006]: 196–205, © Taylor and Francis), the first half of chapter 2 is printed in *The Journal of American Culture* as "The Sub-Subaltern Monster: Imperialist Hegemony and the Cinematic Voodoo Zombie" (31.2 [2008]: 141–152, © Wiley Blackwell), and a portion of chapter 4 will soon be published in *The Journal of Popular Culture* in an article titled "The Idle Proletariat: *Dawn of the Dead*, Consumer Ideology, and the Loss of Productive Labor" (43.2 [2010], © Wiley Blackwell).

CONTENTS

FOREWORD
BY JERROLD E. HOGLE

It is my pleasure to help present a book long overdue: a thoroughly analytical and theory-based study of the whole development of the "zombie" film since the 1920s from its older Caribbean roots to the stunning "renaissance" of zombie cinema at the dawn of the twenty-first century. There have already been, to be sure, good professional articles and some helpful books on this unique genre of horror, all of which are duly acknowledged here. But none of them, from all I know, are as culturally probing, as broadly revealing, and as comprehensive overall as the following history and analysis by Kyle Bishop.

As he shows, zombie cinema has had increasingly important "cultural work" to do in the highly conflicted struggle among systems of belief in the modern and postmodern West. In the face of all that, no other study has exposed and explained so well the many deep cultural issues that zombie films have addressed and symbolized for their audiences, nor has any previous scholarship been as precise as Bishop's on how we can see this cultural work acted out in the visible and audible particulars of the most important zombie productions.

This study had its formal beginning as a doctoral dissertation at the University of Arizona, under the excellent direction of Professor Susan White, and I was honored to be a committee member there, along with Professor Carlos Gallego, adding my own limited expertise to the mix that helped this study come about. We all saw by this study's initial completion, though, just as we now see after some more recent revisions, that this was and is such a major and comprehensive account of its subject, so superior to most previous work on zombie films, that we knew it had to become a book almost immediately, and we are now quite proud to see that it has. It makes an unusually strong and thorough contribution to the study of a zombie phenomenon that has been understood only in bits and pieces — often the state of zombies themselves — until Bishop drew all this together and argued his case for its cultural meanings by closely examining the major zombie films in ways that will be

1

extraordinarily helpful to both the teaching and the further researching of this whole tradition.

Indeed, by doing so much to expand the reach of what some have called "zombie studies," Bishop has also revealed how a longer and more complex cultural history actually flows into this one as well, even as zombie cinema has changed the course of that history in the twentieth and twenty-first centuries. More than any other analyst in zombie studies, Dr. Bishop has detailed the relation of the zombie film from the start to the "Gothic" tradition in fiction, theater, and eventually film and video — or rather the *neo*–Gothic tradition that began in literature with Horace Walpole's novella *The Castle of Otranto: A Gothic Story*, first published in England in 1764.

In such works, which came famously to include Mary Shelley's original *Frankenstein* (1818) and Bram Stoker's novel *Dracula* (1897), figures and features left over from the Middle Ages (and "Gothic" in that sense) — among them supernatural ones such as ghosts, alchemy, vampires, ruins, and sites of burial — appear as looming vestiges of a waning past and are placed in conflict with more modern assumptions about the causes of earthly events, the progress of civilization, the problems of social equity, and the psychology of human beings. This juxtaposition both hollows out the remnants of older ideologies, making them all haunting ghosts of what is no longer firmly believed, and makes post–Enlightenment beings and actions react to those hauntings with a mixture of attracted fascination and terrified repulsion. As a result, the Gothic ghosts or monsters that convey the draw of the past, even the creatures in *Frankenstein* or *Dracula,* look back to what the ghosts or apparitions are in *The Castle of Otranto*: specters walking out of pictures or enlarged fragments of effigies, ghosts of old *representations* (rather than of bodies or grounded realities) no longer clearly rooted in past ways of thinking.

Walpole, after all, as in much later English and American Gothic, uses regressive figures and settings once grounded in a medieval Catholicism that he himself disavowed as a British Protestant and a Whig opponent of the most conservative and aristocratic Tory beliefs of his time. Consequently, his monstrous specters, the first "Gothic ghosts" in a long tradition, have much of their original significance scooped out of them. That vacancy allows the projection of much later and more modern concerns and quandaries, such as the conflict between aristocratic and middle-class attitudes for Walpole, *into* those now-emptied figures, which in *The Castle of Otranto* are largely silent and only awkwardly mobile in coming to suggest hidden primal crimes bound up with the efforts of the present to overcome or transform the persistence of past ideas.

Starting with the Caribbean revenants in the films of the early 1930s, zombies closely resemble these Walpolean specters. Zombies are empty figures of the dead usually lurching silently about and, as reworkings of age-old

Caribbean traditions, playing out their symbolic roles, at least initially, as manifestations of the enslavement and other victimizations imposed on native *or* transplanted peoples by present continuations of past outrages (such as the primal crime of slavery itself) in the history of the Western world.

As much as the most classic and original "Gothic" ghosts or monsters, then, zombies, though not as based on literary originals as the film adaptations of *Dracula* or *Frankenstein*, are figures uprooted from older schemes of mythology and legend that, because of their uprooting, can come to suggest very current cultural fears and uncertainties that were not all projected originally into the pre-cinematic zombie-figures of West Indian voodoo and folklore. Bishop here shows, in fact, that the progression of the zombie-figure in and after its initial forms on film allows it to be a very "floating signifier" (to use the linguistic terms of Ferdinand de Saussure and Jacques Lacan) that can become linked to, and thus become a repository for, *many* social and psychological meanings in the thought-patterns of Westerners as history moves between different eras of the twentieth and the current century.

Quite firmly now, because of what Bishop reveals, the zombie film, at least in its most symbolic and suggestive versions, is no longer "mere horror" or "sick fun" alone, a place in which to watch the predations of the living dead from a position of entirely theatrical safety (always an aspect of horror). It is also a symbolic field in the Gothic tradition calling forth and examining in a fictional guise some profound cultural debates and the fears and hopes about them over 70–80 years. Through Kyle Bishop's efforts and his building on the best work of his predecessors, zombie cinema can now emerge as the Gothic has over the last few decades: as the important subject of cultural, aesthetic, and historical study that it has been all along, especially in the hands of such writers and directors as Jacques Tourneur, Stephen King, Danny Boyle, and especially George Romero. In looking at zombies on film, as we do at Frankenstein's creature or at the human vampire in the wake of *Dracula*, we look at ourselves, albeit in a kind of distortion mirror, in the case of zombies as we struggle to deal with the contradictory emotions of being potentially mindless participants in an increasingly technological and cybernetic-cyberspace world unable to resolve its ongoing conflicts over gender, race, class, sex, economics, personal freedom vs. public order, and what the relationship really is between death and life.

As much as zombie cinema is popular culture, like the Gothic, it is also symbolic literature of immense import for its captivated audiences, and this book by Bishop show us how that is true in ways that no study has so fully recounted before. I therefore urge you to read this book in its entirety if you have any level of interest in zombies, horror, the Gothic, the modern mythologies of monsters, the folklore of the Americas, or film history as cultural history. The following pages provide remarkable illuminations in all of these areas, so much so that you, the reader once you have finished this, like me after I first perused what now follows, will never look at a zombie film or a Gothic-monster story or any kind of aesthetic horror in the same way again.

PREFACE

My mother continually wonders where she went wrong in my upbringing. "Why not musicals?" she asks. "Or romantic comedies? Why zombies, of all things?" Why indeed? I suffer from no debilitating trauma, have no deep-seated psychopathic impulses, feel no hunger for human flesh; yet I am fascinated by the singularity and longevity of zombie narratives and by the essential role such films play in our society.

My exploration into the realm of the walking dead began one innocuous day at lunch in the Southern Utah University food court a few years ago. My fellow professor Todd Petersen and I began brainstorming film genres that have no established antecedents in written literature, and, being the aficionado of horror films that I am, I proposed the zombie, a creature about which I knew little beyond the gut-wrenching action found in George A. Romero's landmark films. That conversation, and the many that eventually followed, unearthed the rather unique position the zombie holds in the pantheon of movie monsters — a creature born directly out of folklore, new to the twentieth century, and fundamentally American in its origins. My resulting enthusiasm for what I considered a relatively unplumbed topic developed first into a conference presentation at the 2005 Far West Popular and American Culture associations' annual meeting and eventually an article in the *Journal of Popular Film & Television*. My research — conducted extensively via Netflix and at my local multiplex — exposed me to a host of zombie films, and it wasn't hard to see that the majority of the movies had been produced during the twenty-first century.

Because the filmography of the infinitely useful *Zombie Movie Encyclopedia* (McFarland, 2001) ends with 1998, I contacted author Peter Dendle directly to see if he had any insights into what was going on with the movies produced by our post-millennial culture. We exchanged a series of e-mails discussing this "Zombie Renaissance," and my suspicions that zombie films indeed demonstrate an important cultural cathexis were confirmed. In fact, I began to view all recent zombie films in light of the terrorist attacks perpetrated against the United States on September 11, 2001, and another successful conference paper soon followed, this one presented at the 2006 Popular and American Culture associations' national conference in Atlanta. I soon realized I had a project with enough scope, depth, and relevance to justify a much longer investigation. As I was then preparing to pursue a Ph.D. in English and film studies, I knew I had the perfect dissertation topic to propose, although I recognized there would likely be some resistance from the more traditional quarters of academia.

However, to my great surprise and satisfaction, the University of Arizona strongly encouraged and supported my academic investigations into all things related to the zombie: folkloric origins, implicit ideology, post-colonial foundations, psychoanalytic and cultural-materialist implications, and the rich cinematic tradition itself. Under the invaluable guidance of Susan White, Jerrold E. Hogle, and Carlos Gallego, I began to shift my emphasis to focus on the place zombie narratives — particularly the zombie *invasion* narrative — have in the Gothic literary tradition. As I assembled my existing essays, articles, and drafts, I approached the project as a book manuscript modeled on the tone, style, and format of the texts I was reading for my research, books such as Gregory A. Waller's *The Living and the Undead* (University of Illinois Press, 1986), David J. Skal's *The Monster Show* (Faber and Faber, 1993), Gary D. Rhodes' *White Zombie* (McFarland, 2001), Kim Paffenroth's *Gospel of the Living Dead* (Baylor University Press, 2006), and Jamie Russell's *Book of the Dead* (FAB Press, 2006).

My research focuses largely on Romero's movies, as one would expect, but unlike some treatments of the subgenre, I also investigate the folkloristic origins of the zombie mythology, the early voodoo-based zombie films, and the more recent movies that depart somewhat from Romero's canonical framework. That said, I have in no way attempted to provide an overview of all zombie films ever made; my book is not a survey or a reference book like Dendle's *Encyclopedia*, Russell's *Book of the Dead*, Glenn Kay's *Zombie Movies: The Ultimate Guide* (Chicago Review Press, 2008), or the more recent *Zombie Holocaust* by David Flint (Plexus, 2009). These works have been essential and vital to my own research, and the scholarship they contribute is unmatched; however, my book, in contrast, offers more close readings of a limited number of films to argue for the zombie subgenre's place in the academy, especially as part of the Gothic tradition.

When I began this project four years ago, the market offered very few books about zombie cinema, but now a number of such texts exist. The most prominent critical work is Shawn McIntosh and Marc Leverette's landmark anthology *Zombie Culture: Autopsies of the Living Dead* (Scarecrow Press, 2008), a highly academic collection that provides a series of indispensible articles on zombie folklore, films, videogames, and other forms of narrative. Although McIntosh and Leverette offer more detailed investigations into the

Italian zombie film tradition, the world of zombie videogames, zombie body politics, and the feminist issues raised by Romero's movies than I do, my book provides a deeper look at zombie folklore and ideology and a broader overview of the cinematic subgenre as a whole, and I cast my entire argument in terms of the Gothic literary tradition. Needless to say, as my book and its predecessors demonstrate, the zombie phenomenon has yet to be plumbed to its depths by the academic and literary markets.

This book represents my attempts to understand a popular, if often much-maligned, cultural phenomenon. My love and respect for zombie cinema, along with my desire to explain both its singular origins and recent renaissance, have led me to champion the subgenre as a valuable and complex manifestation of contemporary concerns and repressed cultural anxieties.

The dead indeed continue to walk, and I hope they do so for a very long time.

Kyle William Bishop • January 2010

INTRODUCTION—THE ZOMBIE FILM AND ITS CYCLES

Zombies, man. They creep me out.—Kaufman, *Land of the Dead*

All great literary productions manifest what Stuart Hall calls "cultural identity," a revelation about our collective "one true self" that is both historical and ever-changing.[1] This shared identity can usefully reveal the darkness as well as the light, for as Tony Magistrale argues, all literature, both in print and on screen, addresses society's most pressing fears and is "nothing less than a barometer for measuring an era's cultural anxieties."[2] This cultural function of literature works to an even greater degree in Gothic fiction, which, as Jerrold E. Hogle has said, "helps us address and disguise some of the most important desires, quandaries, and sources of anxiety, from the most internal and mental to the widely social and cultural."[3] For example, wars, natural disasters, financial crises, and other political and social tragedies affect cultural consciousness as much as the blast from a high-yield explosive or a massive earthquake, and the ensuing shockwaves reach far and wide. One of the most reliable ways to recognize and understand these undulations is by analyzing the literature and dramatization of any particular era. For instance, the use of atomic weapons at the end of World War II ushered in nuclear paranoia narratives such as the films *Godzilla* (1954) and *Them!* (1954), and that era's fear of the encroaching Communist threat inspired alien invasion stories such as Jack Finney's *Invasion of the Body Snatchers* (1954) and the earlier *Invaders from Mars* (1953). The terrorist attacks of September 11, 2001, have unleashed perhaps the largest wave of paranoia and anxiety on American society since the Japanese attack on Pearl Harbor in 1941. From the beginning of the War on Terror that followed 9/11, the popular culture produced in the United States has been colored by the fear of possible terrorist attacks and the grim realization that people are not as safe and secure as they might have once thought. As in the past, perceptive scholars can quite readily recognize and understand this shift in the cultural consciousness through patterns in narrative fiction, and I ultimately want to argue that zombie cinema is among the most culturally revealing and resonant fictions of the recent decade of unrest.

Of course, Hans Robert Jauss has already emphasized how we cannot approach a cultural product simply through its historical context or its formal elements alone. Instead, the audience, those intended to receive a given work, prove essentially relevant, for "it is only through the process of its mediation that the work enters into the changing horizon-of-experience of a continuity in which the perpetual inversion occurs from simple reception to critical understanding."[4] In other words, the reception of a literary text, its popularity among consumers, is an important component of cultural studies. For example, big-screen zombie narratives have proven increasingly popular since their inception in the early 1930s, and in the years following September 11, the number of both studio and independent zombie movies has risen dramatically. Although interest in the subgenre had noticeably decreased during the halcyon days of America in the 1990s, Hollywood has since re-embraced the genre with revisionist films such as *28 Days Later* (2002), video game-inspired action movies such as *Resident Evil* (2002), big-budget remakes such as *Dawn of the Dead* (2004), and even romantic comedies such as *Shaun of the Dead* (2004). Even now, the zombie craze shows no signs of slowing down, with 2007 seeing the theatrical releases of *Planet Terror*, *28 Weeks Later*, and *Resident Evil: Extinction* — the Sundance Film Festival even featured two zombie films that season[5] — and with a remake of *Day of the Dead*, George A. Romero's own *Diary of the Dead*, and *Zombie Strippers* all coming out in 2008. David Oakes' *Zombie Movie Data-Base* website confirms this increased interest in zombie cinema, with data showing a marked swell in all kinds of zombie narratives over the past ten years, with 41 titles listed for 2008 alone.[6] And 2009 proved to be an even greater banner year for the screen zombie, with titles such as *Dead Snow*; *Romeo & Juliet vs. The Living Dead*; *Silent Night, Zombie Night*; *Yesterday*; *Zombieland*; and Romero's sixth zombie movie, *Survival of the Dead*, to name just a few of the titles listed on *The Internet Movie Database* website.[7] In a recent interview I conducted with Peter Dendle, Pennsylvania State University professor and an expert on zombies, he observed how the number of amateur zombie movies has "mushroomed considerably" since 2000, with fan filmmakers spending thousands on digital video and fake blood. Although the quality of many of these backyard, straight-to-video and internet-based productions remains a matter of debate, a clear surge in the subgenre's popularity among fans and filmmakers cannot be denied.

Such an array of films and narrative genres has thus addressed the social and cultural anxieties stemming from recent terrorist attacks, and I want to

A host of gold-seeking Nazi zombies (lead by Örjan Gamst) pursues hapless vacationers across the snows of Norway in Tommy Wirkola's *Dead Snow* (IFC, 2009; Photogest Digital).

show that they do so because of a foundation on which they build. The fundamental generic conventions of Gothic fiction in general and zombie cinema in particular make the subgenre the most likely and appropriate vehicle with which to explore America's post–9/11 cultural consciousness. During the latter half of the twentieth century, for example, zombie movies repeatedly reacted to social and political unrest, graphically representing the inescapable realities of an untimely death (via infection, infestation, or violence) while presenting a grim view of the modern apocalypse in which society's supportive infrastructure irrevocably breaks down. The twenty-first-century zombie movies are not much different from their historical antecedents, but society itself has changed markedly since the World Trade Center towers were destroyed, making cinematic zombies and their accompanying narratives all the more timely and affecting. Scenes depicting deserted metropolitan streets, abandoned human corpses, and gangs of lawless vigilantes have become more common than ever, appearing on the nightly news as often as on the movie screen. Because the aftereffects of war, terrorism, and natural disasters so closely resemble the scenarios depicted by zombie cinema, such images of death and destruction have all the more power to shock and terrify a population that has become otherwise jaded to more traditional horror films. The most telling barometer of this modern age, therefore, is to be found not in the romanticized undead protagonists of vampire melodramas such as Stephenie Meyer's *Twilight* series (2005–2008) or with the nihilistic sadists torturing victims in the latest *Saw* movie (2004–), but in the unstoppable hoards of the zombie invasion narrative. That is why many now speak, and speak correctly, of a current "zombie renaissance."

The Developmental Cycles of Zombie Cinema: Bringing on the Renaissance

Since the occupation of Haiti by the United States in the early decades of the twentieth century, the word *zombie* has become a fixture in American culture. It can be used ethnographically, referring to the victim of voodoo magic or hypnosis — "a soulless corpse said to have been revived by witchcraft" — or metaphorically, describing "a dull, apathetic, or slow-witted person."[8] The term also appears in bars and taverns, referring to an exotic mixture of rum and fruit juices, and, in recent years, we have seen the creation of such sinister concepts as "zombie banks" and "zombie computers."[9] As far as narrative fiction is concerned, however, the word *zombie* conjures up images of unnatural creatures that have risen from the dead in search of human flesh. This latter conceptualization is perhaps the most familiar to readers, as the zombie has become a common staple of popular horror movies, especially since Romero first shocked the movie-going public in 1968 with *Night of the Living Dead*. This low-budget film sensationally reinvents the almost-forgotten specter of the voodoo zombie, fusing the dumb automatons of Haitian folklore with the masses of bloodthirsty dead from films such as Ubaldo Ragona and Sidney Salkow's *The Last Man on Earth* (1964). Yet in the last few years alone, the so-called "walking dead" have transcended B-movies, escapist graphic novels, and ultraviolent survivalist video games to become a tenacious part of mainstream American culture, appearing in one form or another on the radio waves, at rave parties, all across the internet, in parades, on television, and — somewhat belatedly — in popular novels. In fact, in just under 100 years' time, the icon of the zombie has both invaded and inundated American culture. But where did the monster really come from, and why should it be considered an essential part of the monster tradition?

Not only is the zombie a fundamentally *American* creation, but it is also perhaps the most unique member of the monster pantheon; that is, although creatures such as ghosts, werewolves, vampires, and reanimated corpses were also born in the depths of folk tradition, the zombie is the only supernatural foe to have almost entirely skipped an initial literary manifestation, "pass[ing] directly from folklore to the screen."[10] Almost every vampire movie owes something of its mythology to Bram Stoker, and the reanimated dead have clear ties to Mary Shelley, especially when the creatures share more in common with the living than they do the dead. The zombie, however, has no germinal Gothic novel from which it stems, no primal narrative that established and codified its qualities or behaviors. Even though vague and inconsistent zombie references could be found in some nineteenth-century travel narratives and non-fiction anthropological texts, it took the publication of William B. Seabrook's sensational travelogue *The Magic Island* in 1929 to bring the zombie out of the misunderstood superstitions of Haiti and into the light of mainstream America. Since the release of Victor Halperin's *White Zombie* in 1932, Americans have regularly enjoyed the horror, terror, and at times excessive violence of many successful zombie movies, most departing drastically from the creature's humble and ethnographic origins. Yet while some critics are ready to dismiss these films as mindless entertainment or B-reel schlock, the zombie creature retains an uncanny ability to make audiences think while they shriek.

Zombie cinema has been around in one form or another for over 70 years now, and like other genres, it has gone through developmental periods of both feast and famine. In fact, the frequency of these movies has noticeably increased during periods of social and political unrest, particularly during wars such as those in Vietnam and Iraq (see "Frequency of Zombie Film Production by Year").[11] The initial wave of zombie films, beginning with the landmark *White Zombie* and including Jacques Tourneur's *I Walked with a Zombie* (1943), reveals imperialist anxieties associated with colonialism and slavery. By allowing native voodoo priests to enslave white heroines, these inherently racist movies terrified Western viewers with the thing they likely dreaded most at that time: slave uprisings and reverse colonization. Similar films followed in the wake of World War II and well into the Cold War, although hostile interstellar aliens replaced the voodoo sorcerers in movies such as Edward L. Cahn's *Invisible Invaders* (1959) and Terence Fisher's *The Earth Dies Screaming* (1964). Nevertheless, the key anxieties revealed by these science-fiction variations remained the same: loss of freedom and autonomy.

Then, just when the cinematic zombie seemed destined to be relegated to campy parodies and low-profile cameos, a new kind of zombie was born, one both infectious and cannibalistic, with the release of *Night of the Living Dead*. Romero's film did away with the puppet master entirely, focusing instead on a massive horde of zombies that operated more or less independently, driven only by their own insatiable hunger — admittedly similar to vampires, but without the ubiquitous finesse of speech and high-class dress. Furthermore, *Night of the Living Dead* established a firm narrative scenario

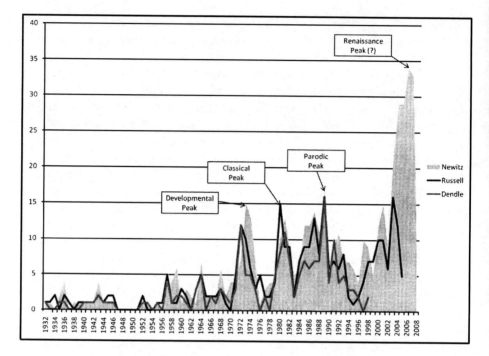

Frequency of Zombie Film Production by Year.

by focusing on a motley group of survivors, led by an unconventional African-American hero named Ben (Duane Jones), who must spend the night in a besieged country house, waiting for the authorities to arrive. The movie also restored a seriousness and gravitas to the subgenre, for when the county militia finally does show up in the final reel, their first response is to shoot and kill Ben, the only survivor of the film's supernatural abattoir. The violence and grotesque images were unprecedented at the time, aiding this low-budget horror film in its function as an allegorical condemnation of the atrocities of Vietnam, violent racism, and the opposition to the civil rights movement. Called "hippie Gothic" by film theorist Joseph Maddrey,[12] *Night of the Living Dead* protested the war by graphically confronting audiences with the horrors of death and dismemberment and by openly criticizing those who use violence to solve their problems. The politically subversive film captured a cult following and went on to make over $30 million worldwide.[13]

Recognizing the potential market and profitability of such movies, other filmmakers began to experiment with the storyline — with little-known films such as *Garden of the Dead* (1972), *El ataque de los muertos sin ojos* (aka *Return of the Evil Dead*) (1973), and *El buque maldito* (aka *Horror of the Zombies*) (1974) — with Romero himself releasing *Dawn of the Dead* in 1978. This critically acclaimed follow-up, now focusing on a group of reporters and SWAT team members stuck for weeks in an abandoned shopping mall, also acts as a scathing cultural allegory, this time lampooning capitalism and rampant consumerism. *Dawn of the Dead* proved even more successful than its predecessor, particularly in Europe, and it was almost immediately followed by Lucio Fulci's unofficial sequel *Zombi 2* (1979), an exploitation film about a global zombie infestation originating on a exotic Caribbean island. These two films firmly defined and established the formula, ushering in a rich and lucrative "classical" period for the subgenre. *Dawn of the Dead* became a huge mainstream hit, grossing $55 million worldwide,[14] and it spawned a veritable surge of imitative zombie movies both in the United States and abroad, such as Marino Girolami's *Zombie Holocaust* (1980), Fulci's *Paura nella città dei morti viventi* (1980),[15] and such lesser-known titles as *Night of the Zombies* (1981), *La mansión de los muertos vivientes* (aka *Mansion of the Living Dead*) (1982), and *Wu long tian shi zhao ji gui* (aka *Kung Fu Zombie*) (1982).

In spite of such proliferation and success on B-reel screens, cinematic narratives featuring infectious, cannibalistic zombies seemed already to have played themselves out by the early–1980s, especially with the arrival of Michael Jackson's *Thriller* video in 1983. The producers clearly tried to make this campy short film uncanny and frightening, but once the walking dead start to dance and jive with the King of Pop, zombies become little more than a joke. Although Romero attempted to revitalize the genre in 1985 with *Day of the Dead*, in which the metaphor this time addresses Cold War fears and paranoia, the cycle was unavoidably entering the death throes of its parodic phase. *Day of the Dead* failed miserably at the box office, and Maddrey supposes "audiences in the carefree, consumer-friendly 1980s apparently did not feel the need for such a serious examination of personal and societal values."[16] Instead, young audiences demanded more comedic films such as Dan O'Bannon's *The Return of the Living Dead* (1985), a lowbrow punk movie that flagrantly abuses Romero's generic rules by featuring zombies that can talk and by introducing the now ubiquitous eating of human brains. In such unmemorable films as *Zombie Brigade* (1986), *I Was a Teenage Zombie* (1987), and *Redneck Zombies* (1987), budgets plummeted and camp took the place of serious scripting.

Historically, zombie cinema had represented a stylized reaction to the greater cultural consciousness — primarily social and political injustices — and America in the 1990s settled perhaps into too much complacency and stability to warrant serious, classical zombie narratives. The Cold War was over, the Berlin Wall had fallen, Ronald Reagan's Star Wars defense system had been proven unnecessary, and George H. W. Bush's Gulf War had seemingly been resolved. In fact, aside from some skirmishes in third-world countries, Americans were largely insulated from global warfare. It was suddenly the Clinton decade, a time when sexual impropriety took the headlines away from global genocide and tyrannical massacres. With nothing specific to react to or to protest against, cinematic versions of the zombie subgenre declined steadily throughout the '90s, and not even Romero could keep his brainchild afloat. Tom Savini's remake of *Night of the Living Dead* failed at the box office in 1990, despite a new script penned by Romero himself, and no studio was interested in backing Romero's proposed fourth zombie film. One of the few bright spots at the end of the twentieth century occurred in New Zealand, where Peter Jackson released *Braindead* (1992), an outlandish farce that provided viewers some fresh ideas by exploiting a micro-genre commonly called "splatstick" comedy, in which excessive blood and guts become the primary comedic medium. Nevertheless, almost no new or original stories were produced in the 1990s, although Dendle observes that no-budget, direct-to-video films continued to be released.[17]

Yet even though zombies were no longer a source of terror on the silver screen, a largely sedentary youth culture found renewed interest in zombies via violent video games. In 1993, id Software released a revolutionary first-person-shooter called *Doom*, which features zombified Marine soldiers; however, these basically two-dimensional foes use guns instead of teeth, and the game's plot is more science fiction than horror. While zombies continued to play bit parts in other games, the first true zombie video game did not come until 1996 with Capcom's *Biohazard* (since renamed *Resident Evil*). This game takes its central premise directly from Romero's movies, requiring players to explore an isolated country manor while shooting reanimated corpses and trying to avoid being eaten — although unlike Romero's movies, the game understandably features a lot more "fight" than "flight." Nevertheless, the terror and action of zombie movies translates quite logically from the big screen to the video screen, and a non-traditional form of narrative thus incubated the genre until it was ready to reemerge in theaters in 2002 with the release of two new mainstream movies.

By returning to the classical form of Romero's films, British director Danny Boyle officially kicked off the "zombie renaissance" with the first truly frightening zombie movie in years. Riding high from his *Trainspotting* (1996) success, Boyle created a new version of the zombie story in England with *28 Days Later*, a terrifying vision of the apocalypse in which a man wakes from a coma to find London abandoned and full of decaying corpses. Many fans might have debated the film's technical designation as a zombie movie — as Boyle introduced faster, more feral zombie creatures, and he kept the monsters alive rather than dead — but audiences responded as if the subgenre were new, instead of just newly re-visioned. Boyle saw his movie's scant $8 million budget eventually pay off with a more than $82 million gross worldwide.[18] At the same time, Hollywood was also attempting to kick start the subgenre, capitalizing on the popularity of the video game circuit with Paul W. S. Anderson's *Resident Evil*, an action-packed, science-fiction movie that was admittedly more video game than narrative. A host of big-budget and mainstream films has since followed, including two *Resident Evil* sequels (in 2004 and 2007); remakes of *Dawn of the Dead* (2004), *Night of the Living Dead* (2006), and *Day of the Dead* (2008); Edgar Wright's revisionist comedy *Shaun of the Dead*; and the return of Romero with 2005's *Land of the Dead*, 2008's *Diary of the Dead*, and 2009's *Survival of the Dead*.

The popularity of the zombie has continued to flourish in other media as well. The shooting-gallery nature of zombie survival — the more you kill, the more keep popping up — still spawns new video games every year in which players become part of the action. For instance, *Land of the Dead* inspired the game *Land of the Dead: Road to Fiddler's Green* (2005), the *Biohazard* series now has over a dozen game titles, and Electronic Arts has just released *Left 4 Dead* (2008), a multiplayer game that even allows players to control zombie avatars.[19] The zombie narrative has also maintained a healthy presence in the world of graphic novels, most notably with Steve Nile's *George A. Romero's Dawn of the Dead* (2004), Jason's minimalist *The Living and the Dead* (2007), and Robert Kirkman's ongoing epic series *The Walking Dead* (2004–). Zombies can be found outside of visual fiction as well, the most well-known example being the humorous, yet strangely eerie *Zombie Survival Guide*, which came out in 2003. In this parody of popular survivalist handbooks, Max Brooks makes a straight-faced, seemingly non-fiction attempt to prepare the public for an actual zombie infestation. Furthermore, the zombie craze has even been adopted by some as an alternative lifestyle, similar to the vampire-inspired Goth movement, with a number of hard-rock bands also embracing the zombie philosophy, as in the case of Zombie Ritual and their 2004 album *Night of the Zombie Party*.

However, in spite of this evidence establishing a clear resurgence in the popularity of the zombie monster since 2002, no one formally recognized the trends as an official "renaissance" until early 2006. Steven Wells ran a piece in the *Guardian* reacting to Showtime's made-for-TV movie *Homecoming* (2004), in which "Americans killed in Iraq rise from their flag-draped coffins and slaughter their way to the polling booths so they can vote out a warmongering president."[20] Wells demonstrates an even broader impact, claiming "there were zombies everywhere in 2005," from an all-zombie production of *Romeo and Juliet* to online zombie blogs to a zombie appearance on *American Idol*.[21] Zombies even show up in the later Harry Potter novels, if only for brief cameos. This appearance of zombies in print media other than graphic novels is perhaps the most notable evidence of a renaissance within the mainstream public. According to Don D'Auria, executive editor of Leisure Books, "Until three years ago [zombies] were really unseen. Then they just seemed to pop up everywhere."[22] In a 2006 *New York Times* article, Warren St. John provides just a few examples of the zombie literary invasion: Brian Keene's *The Rising* (2003), a novel about "smart zombies"; David Willington's *Monster Island* (2004), an online book about a zombie infestation in Manhattan; and *World War Z: An Oral History of the Zombie War* (2006), another faux-non-fiction creation from Brooks.[23] In addition, Stephen King, the unequivocal master of modern literary horror, finally released a full-blown version of the zombie story with his novel *Cell* (2006), a chilling morality tale in which unnamed terrorists turn the majority of Americans into enraged cannibals by brainwashing them with a mind-scrambling cell phone signal.

While the zombie renaissance is basically a given to zombie scholars and fans, such mainstream journalistic coverage as *The New York Times* gives Wells' observations a greater semblance of credibility as well as publicity. The return of the zombie, most obviously and prolifically in film, has finally come to the attention of the masses generally, as box office receipts and related merchandising show. St. John summarizes the renaissance quite simply: "In films, books and video games, the undead are once again on the march, elbowing past werewolves, vampires, swamp things and mummies to become the post-millennial ghoul of the moment." All this evidence points to one unavoidable fact: "Zombies are back."[24] Furthermore, this saturation of American popular culture by the walking dead justifies and even demands a critical investigation into both the narratives themselves and their remarkable, if perhaps initially mystifying, appeal. The sheer volume of zombie narratives in popular film, television, and other media indicates the presence of something more compelling and complex than mere entertainment; like other, more established Gothic monstrosities including vampires and reanimated golems, the zombie must be doing valuable cultural work, providing viewers much needed catharsis while revealing *and* disguising repressed fears and anxieties, if they are reappearing as much as they are. Our first step, therefore, is to break down and analyze the protocols of this singular subgenre to find out what makes these dead creatures come back from the grave to terrorize us again and again.

The Primary Characteristics of Zombie Cinema: Understanding the Subgenre

The twenty-first century has clearly been experiencing a zombie renaissance, as we see in the tremendous increase of big-budget Hollywood productions, the relatively low cost for fans to make their own such splatterfest films on video and online, and the popularity of zombies in a variety of other media beyond film. Yet before I present any explanation for this phenomenon or propose a way to understand the post–9/11 social and cultural relevance of zombie cinema, I must first outline the essential characteristics of such films and establish how this subgenre differs from other types of supernatural horror. Unlike many other tales of terror and the supernatural, the classic zombie story — i.e., the apocalyptic invasion of our world by hordes of cannibalistic, contagious, and animated corpses — has remarkably specific conventions that govern its plot and development. These generic protocols include not only the zombies themselves and the imminent threat of a violent death, but also a post-apocalyptic backdrop: the collapse of societal infrastructures, the resurgence of survivalist fantasies, and the fear of other surviving humans. All of these plot elements and motifs have been included with surprisingly few variations in most zombie films since *Night of the Living Dead*, but they have become even more relevant to a contemporary and post–9/11 audience.

Of course, a number of culturally relevant and important films explored both zombiism and the reanimation of dead bodies prior to Romero's retooling of the subgenre in 1968. In fact, the first half of the zombie subgenre in history deals not with contagious infection or the eating of human flesh but rather with voodoo, hypnotism, and scientific experimentation. These "voodoo-inspired" zombie films have more to do with folklore, ethnography, and imperialist paranoia than they do with the strictly supernatural. Therefore, the basic narrative structure of films such as *White Zombie*, George Terwilliger's *Ouanga* (1936), and *I Walked with a Zombie* more closely follow the model established by such Gothic melodramas as Tod Browning's *Dracula* (1931) and James Whale's *Frankenstein* (1931), films in which a single menacing figure threatens the safety of a helpless female character. Indeed, the "monsters" of the voodoo-themed zombie films are not even the zombies but rather the sinister priest or master pulling their strings. The zombie films of the 1950s are little different, following the same basic structure of the voodoo films: an evil threat — this time usually a mad scientist or alien race (read: Communist) — turns human corpses into a slave army designed to invade and conquer. Movies such as Don Siegel's *Invasion of the Body Snatchers* (1956) best illustrate this variation on the voodoo theme, even though the film's "pod people" merely resemble zombies with their vacuous stares and slow movements. Yet this threatening concept of mass enslavement clearly paved the way for Romero's innovations, and it would prove quite easy for him to split up the creature into a new taxonomic development between "enslaved" zombies and "infected" zombies (see "The Taxonomy of the Dead").

Regardless of the basic natures of the different zombies — enslaved or infected, dead or alive — the most conspicuous feature of zombie movies is naturally the zombies as creatures, both what they *are* and, perhaps more importantly, what they are *not*. Because the "living dead" developed by Romero have proven to be the most popular and lasting subspecies of zombie, I will focus primarily on establishing and categorizing their place in the larger group of supernatural monsters, noting especially their fundamental nature, their viruslike reproductive process, and their particular limits. For starters, audiences fear these ghouls for a number of obvious reasons; primarily, they are corpses raised from the dead — more significantly, they are the corpses of the *known* dead, what horror scholar R. H. W. Dillard calls "dead kindred."[25] In addition, the zombies pursue living humans with relentless, tireless dedication and kill people mercilessly by eating them alive. Because zombies are technically "dead" rather than the more romantic "undead" (i.e., vampires) — thus occupying a separate place in the continuum of monsters (see "The Scale of the Living and the Dead") — they possess only a rotting brain and have no real emotional capacity.[26] To that end, zombies cannot be reasoned with, appealed to, or dissuaded by logical discourse — or repelled by superstitions such as garlic or crosses, for that matter. The other supernatural foes devised by authors and other Hollywood filmmakers are generally conscious and thinking figures, at least somewhat. In fact, in recent years, traditional supernatural monsters have become sympathetic protagonists and misunderstood heroes, such as the ghosts in *The Sixth Sense* (1999) or *The Others* (2001), the vampires in Anne Rice's "Vampire Chronicles" (1976–2003) or Meyer's *Twilight* series, and characters on television such as Angel and Spike in *Buffy the Vampire Slayer* (1997–2003) and *Angel* (1999–2004). Without dramatic alterations to the zombie's essential identity, such a re-casting of the walking dead seems to remain an illogical impossibility for creators of zombie tales and films.[27]

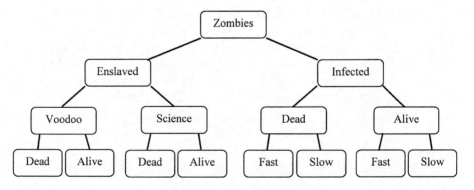

The Taxonomy of the Dead.

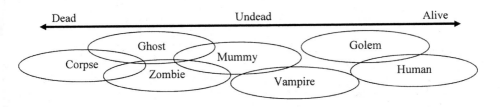

Dead   Undead   Alive

Corpse   Ghost   Mummy   Zombie   Vampire   Golem   Human

The Scale of the Living and the Dead.

On top of all this — and in additional contrast to other supernatural or undead creatures — the zombie directly manifests the visual horrors of death: unlike most ghosts and vampires, zombies are in an active state of decay. Cinematic ghosts either take on the appearance of the living, replicating their idealized selves or their human condition prior to death, or they retain the horrific wounds that caused their demise, as in both *The Shining* (1980) and *Beetle Juice* (1988). Yet even when ghosts have the look of the dead, they also have static appearances, since these figures are merely remnant images of the physical beings they once were. Vampires, as "undead" creatures, even more thoroughly resemble living humans; in fact, they are usually depicted as not only hale and healthy on the surface, but even suave, sexy, and desirable, most notably in romanticized movies such as the *Underworld* series (2003–2009) and the graphic novels and films in the *Blade* franchise (1973–). Zombies, on the other hand, never transcend their essential identity as dead, decaying bodies. In the afterword to Kirkman's *Miles Behind Us* graphic novel (2004), Simon Pegg, co-writer and star of *Shaun of the Dead*, observes, "Metaphorically, this classic creature embodies a number of our greatest fears. Most obviously, it is our own death, personified. The physical manifestation of that thing we fear the most."[28] It is thus no coincidence that the modern cinematic zombie cycle began "on the eve of the Tet offensive in Vietnam,"[29] when the general populace was being exposed to graphic images of death and violence regularly on the nightly news. In addition, the inescapable realities of mortality ensure that everyone both fears and can relate to the zombie; although no one expects to rise from the grave as a cannibalistic ghoul, everyone will ultimately die.

Indeed, as audiences have become more familiar with special effects and more accustomed to images of violence, cinematic depictions of zombies have had to become progressively more naturalistic and horrific in their recreation of corporeal dissolution and decay. In *Night of the Living Dead*, for example, the ghouls are basically just pasty-faced actors, and even the scenes of cannibalistic acts are rendered somewhat less shocking because of the black-and-white cinematography. By *Dawn of the Dead*, however, the zombies become much more realistic (yet strangely blue), and scenes of death and dismemberment are shockingly graphic and naturalistic — thanks for the most part to the special effects wizardry of Savini, who claims that "much of my work for *Dawn of the Dead* was like a series of portraits of what I had seen for real in Vietnam."[30] Romero and Savini push the envelope of decency even further into the graphically realistic with *Day of the Dead*, as they confront audiences with grotesque autopsies and exposed internal organs. Now, after even more exposure to global warfare and bloodshed, the twenty-first-century audience, largely desensitized by violent video games and other media, demands an upping of the ante. In response, *28 Days Later* and *Land of the Dead* feature zombies with missing limbs, decaying flesh, and only partially constituted heads and faces; even the rather light *Shaun of the Dead* (a self-proclaimed "romantic comedy" zombie film) has some exceedingly gruesome ghouls and nauseating dismemberment scenes.[31]

Of course, even though zombies are certainly uncanny and frightening by themselves — as both hostile threats to the safety of the human protagonists and as more symbolic *memento mori* figures — such monsters would not prove much of a threat if actualized in the modern-day world; most probably the police or military could quickly exterminate these aberrations. However, zombie movies are almost always set during (or shortly after) the apocalypse, where those reassuring infrastructures cease to exist. In *Night of the Living Dead*, the zombie infestation seems limited to just one backwoods county, but over the course of *Dawn of the Dead*, scanty media reports give the rather clear impression that the walking dead have overrun the country. Romero's feckless survivors must hole up in a shopping mall for an indeterminate amount of time, waiting in vain for the resumption of informative broadcasts and for military help that never arrives. The zombie war has clearly been over for a very long while by the time of *Day of the Dead*, for the few soldiers and scientists hiding in their underground bunker are desperately seeking their own solution to the zombie plague instead of waiting for rescue. Things haven't improved much in the narratives of the current renaissance, with *28 Days Later* being based on the premise that all of the UK has been devastated in just under a month. *Land of the Dead* offers an even bleaker scenario: this film is set in a zombie-dominated world, where Pittsburgh has been set up as a city-state unto itself. In all of these scenarios, the virus, plague, or infestation has been so rapid and complete that cities are quickly overrun, buildings abandoned, posts deserted, and the air waves silenced.

One of the greatest — or at least the most detailed — literary imaginings of the apocalypse is King's *The Stand* (1978), a novel with admittedly no zombies but with most of the other zombie motifs. After all, it explores both the utter fall and eventual resurrection of America following a devastating global viral pandemic.[32] King's novel blames the end of modern society on the governmental military complex and models the deterioration of America's infrastructure on William Butler Yeats' description of the end of the world: "Things fall apart; the center cannot hold."[33] This poignant image is central to zombie cinema as well; Brooks describes this "new world order" in his *Zombie Survival Guide*:

> When the living dead triumph, the world degenerates into utter chaos. All social order evaporates. Those in power, along with their families and associates, hole up in bunkers and secure areas around the country. Secure in these shelters, originally built for the Cold War, they survive. Perhaps they continue the façade of a government command structure. Perhaps the technology is available to communicate with other agencies or even other protected world leaders. For all practical purposes, however, they are nothing more than a government-in-exile.[34]

Apocalyptic narratives, then, particularly those featuring zombie invasions, offer a worst-case scenario for the collapse of all American social and governmental structures. Once people start to die at an uncontrollable rate, panic rages through all levels of the government and the military — a literal "dog eat dog" world — and most are more interested in saving themselves and their families than simply doing their jobs.[35]

This terrifying breakdown of social order leads to one of the more curious allures of zombie films: their ability to fulfill survivalist fantasies. Those obsessed with the survivalist credo hoard foodstuffs and ammunition in their isolated mountain cabins and basement bunkers, just hoping for the day when society will collapse and their paranoia will finally be justified. Numerous survival manuals and websites, like those Brooks' book parodies, encourage and direct such behavior, and apocalypse narratives allow proponents of survivalism some cathartic enjoyment. Furthermore, as we see in such movies as *The Omega Man* (1971) and *Night of the Comet* (1984), the end of the world means the end of capitalism, where everything is free for the taking — at least until supplies run out. As a matter of survival, then, looting becomes basically legal, or, at the very least, there is no law enforcement presence to prevent wanton theft. Anyone can own a Porsche, wear the latest Paris fashions, or go on an unbridled shopping spree. Perhaps the best depictions of this contradictory "fun amidst the terror" are found in both the 1978 *Dawn of the Dead* and the 2004 remake by Zach Snyder. Both films take place primarily in shopping malls, locations that afford both security and sustenance. In the '78 version, Romero presents a light-hearted montage showing the four remaining survivors playing basketball, eating exotic foods, and putting on make-up and expensive clothes — what horror scholar David J. Skal calls "consumerism gone mad."[36] Snyder's film continues this critique with a similar montage: finding themselves relatively safe from everything but boredom, the survivors play games, try on expensive clothes and shoes, watch movies on big-screen televisions, and even play golf. In a sick way, the mall becomes the ultimate vacation resort. The guests just cannot go outside — ever.

Such sequences show that once the survivors take both the law and their protection into their own hands, establishing some kind of defensible stronghold — a farmhouse, a shopping mall, a military bunker, an apartment complex, or even a neighborhood pub — the zombies cease to be much of a direct threat. Instead, the real fear comes from the other human survivors, those who can still think, plot, and act. As Dillard points out, "The living people are dangerous to each other, both because they are potentially living dead should they die and because they are human with all of the ordinary human failings."[37] In most zombie films, therefore, the human protagonists eventually establish unequal hierarchies and begin to argue, fight, and even turn against one another; cabin fever can make those inside the strongholds more dangerous than the zombies on the outside.[38] In addition, the journey from survivor to vigilante is a short one; with the total collapse of all governmental law-enforcement systems, survival of the fittest becomes a very literal and grim reality. Some groups begin to reinstate their own self-serving sense of law and order, and those with power, weapons, and numbers simply take whatever they want. However, in the new zombie economy, everything is already free — except other humans, of course. For lawless renegades, the only real sport left is slavery, torture, rape, and murder, the enactment of base appetites that cannot be satisfied by simply going to the mall.

Since zombies don't think or plan or scheme, they are mere animals to be avoided; other survivors, however, are more calculating and dangerous.[39] In the 1978 *Dawn of the Dead*, the peaceful haven of the shopping mall is destroyed by the violent arrival of a vigilante biker gang. These bandits, whose primary aim is to loot the stores, disrupt the careful balance established between the zombies and the remaining survivors in hiding; as a result of their intrusion, more people die, and all security is lost. In *28 Days Later*, this vigilante scenario is all the more frightening because the primary threat comes from the military, from men who are supposed to protect citizens, not abuse them. In a misguided attempt to repopulate the world, the soldiers threaten the female protagonists with rape, and Jim (Cillian Murphy) narrowly escapes execution for defending them. By contrast, *Land of the Dead* depicts a dystopian world where the wealthy elite literally hold the power of life and death over the heads of the impoverished masses. Dennis Hopper's Kaufman, the materialistic fascist who rules Pittsburgh, openly oppresses the people living beneath him, and he proves more than willing to kill anyone who stands in his way. The symbolic threat of the zombies remains a fundamentally frightening part of these films, but because the threats of bodily harm, rape, and murder are real-world potentialities, both in and beyond the zombies, such scenes become all the more terrifying by being inescapable in supposedly escapist movies.

The Twenty-First-Century Zombie: Explaining the Renaissance

The most obvious explanation for the Zombie Renaissance is largely economic — zombies sell, so demand is understandably increasing supply — and that's why reception theory provides an insightful approach to understanding the recent increase in zombie-based narratives. As I investigate them, I am largely following Jauss' admonition regarding literary history, one that calls for "the removal of prejudices of historical objectivism and the grounding of the traditional aesthetics of production and representation in an aesthetics of reception and influence."[40] Because zombie narratives represent popular cultural commodities, a purely formalist or historical approach fails to address all the complexities of the phenomenon. Of essential import to my argument is not merely why zombie narratives came into being or why they achieved a measure of relevance in the past, but also why those same stories have returned — from the dead, as it were — to enjoy similar success and popularity in the twenty-first century. According to Jauss, "A literary past can return only when a new reception draws it back into the present, whether an altered aesthetic attitude willfully reaches back to reappropriate the past, or an unexpected light falls back on forgotten literature from the new moment of literary evolution, allowing something to be found that one previously could not have sought in it."[41] I argue that both processes are at play today: zombie narratives have been reconditioned to satisfy a new aesthetic, but they have also returned to prominence because the social and cultural conditions of a post–9/11 world have come to match so closely those experienced by viewers during the civil unrest of the 1960s and '70s.

Furthermore, because of the subgenre's remarkable ability to adapt to changes in cultural anxiety over time, zombie cinema must also be viewed as part of the larger Gothic tradition. For example, the zombie narratives of today perform the same task Horace Walpole was attempting when he developed the Gothic back in the eighteenth century. According to E. J. Clery, "Walpole wanted to combine the unnatural occurrences associated with romance and the naturalistic characterization and dialogue of the novel."[42] Films such as *Night of the Living Dead* certainly achieve such a blending of the romantic with the realistic, confronting recognizable "everyman" characters in very real and ordinary contemporary environments with overwhelming supernatural forces. Furthermore, zombie narratives manifest the predominant cultural anxieties of their times, anxieties usually repressed or ignored by the mainstream media. Steven Bruhm identifies this revelatory function of Gothic literature, calling it "a barometer of the anxieties plaguing a certain culture at a particular moment in history."[43] Since the Second World War, for example, these key anxieties and horrors include "the fear of foreign otherness and monstrous invasion," "the technological explosion," "the rise of feminism, gay liberation, and African-American civil rights," and "the heightened attack against Christian ideology and hierarchy as that which should 'naturally' define values and ethics in culture."[44] Once again, such Gothic concerns are readily identifiable over the course of Romero's films and in more contemporary examples such as 28 Days Later and the Dawn of the Dead remake.

Nevertheless, the majority of post–9/11 zombie invasion films remains remarkably true to the subgenre's original protocols. Although the zombies are not always literally dead as in Romero's films, hordes of cannibalistic creatures, various forms of large-scale apocalypse, and the total collapse of societal infrastructures remain central and telling features. In addition, the subgenre tends to emphasize certain end-of-the-world metaphors, including infectious disease, biological warfare, euthanasia, terrorism, and even rampant immigration. Although Romero's version of the subgenre is now 40 years old, these concepts resonate more strongly with modern-day Americans than ever before, given such events as September 11, the war in Iraq, and natural disasters like Hurricane Katrina providing the media with the most extreme forms of shocking ideas and imagery. In a post–9/11 climate, then, the zombie film works as an important example of the contemporary Gothic, readdressing "the central concerns of the classical Gothic," such as "the dynamics of family, the limits of rationality and passion, the definition of statehood and citizenship, the cultural effects of technology."[45] In addition to exposing such repressed cultural anxieties, Fred Botting emphasizes how Gothic narratives "retain a double function in simultaneously assuaging and intensifying the anxieties with which they engage."[46] In other words, zombie narratives always stand out as telling and valuable cultural indicators, recreating — hopefully cathartically, yet perhaps more destructively — the scenes and images that horrify a populace that has become otherwise desensitized to lesser representations of death, destruction, and other terrorist activities.

The end of the world is understandably the ultimate societal fear, one that has become even more of a potentiality with current weapons of mass destruction and the increasingly unstable governments of countries possessing nuclear weapons. Hence Snyder's remake of Dawn of Dead actually depicts this apocalypse on screen through a sequence of shocking events most movies only suggest. Ana (Sarah Polley), the film's protagonist, wakes one morning to find the world she knew collapsing around her. Her husband tries to kill her, neighbors shoot one another with handguns, and explosions of unknown origins rock the skyline. The chaos, disorientation, fear, and destruction she witnesses have a tone disturbingly similar to the initial news footage broadcast on September 11, 2001, and Snyder recreates Ana's terrifying experiences through jerky, hand-held camera work and documentary-style film quality. Boyle's *28 Days Later* is similarly disturbing and topically familiar. Although Jim wakes from his coma after the British apocalypse is essentially over, the film nevertheless presents a disturbing sequence of cinematic images by showing a metropolitan London void of all human presence. At the time of its conception, this moment in the screenplay was probably intended to simply shock audiences with its uncanny foreignness, but after the events of September 11, the eerie street scenes take on new meaning.

Although the screenplay for *28 Days Later* was written and filming had begun before September 11, Boyle and screenwriter Alex Garland had already drawn from other international crises and disasters for their apocalyptic images. The scene in which Jim picks up stray pound notes off the empty streets of London was directly inspired by journalist footage from the "killing fields" of Cambodia during and after the reign of Pol Pot, and the street billboard displaying hundred of photos and notes seeking missing loved ones, which has such a direct tie to 9/11 now, was based on an actual street scene following a devastating earthquake in China. The abandoned city, overturned buses, and churches full of corpses were scenes all founded on existing moments of civil unrest and social collapse.[47] Such images of metropolitan desolation and desertion certainly resonate more strongly with contemporary audiences because, according to Brooks, "People have apocalypse on the brain right now.... It's from terrorism, the war, [and] natural disasters like Katrina."[48] In fact, during and after the collapse of the World Trade Center towers in New York, numerous journalists and bystanders commented on how the events seemed unreal—like something out of a movie.[49] Hurricane Katrina had a similar effect: nightly news clips showed the deserted streets of New Orleans as if the city were a film set, with abandoned cars, drifting newspapers, and stray dogs.

Romero's movies, like all great imaginative texts, have always been critical allegories, and the great twenty-first-century zombie films have continued in this vein. According to Andy Coghlan of *New Scientist Magazine*, "Infectious diseases are indeed the new paranoia that's striking Western society,"[50] and *28 Days Later* unabashedly addresses the risks of an unstoppable pandemic, in this case a blood-borne virus that can wipe out the entire United Kingdom in just under a month's time. Boyle's characters refer to the raven-

Ben (Cillian Murphy) is overwhelmed by the apparent abandonment of London in Boyle's *28 Days Later* (Fox Searchlight Pictures, 2002; Photofest Digital).

ous monsters as *infecteds*, not *zombies*; the creatures are not technically dead, after all, just hapless people infected with a neurological virus that makes them ultra-aggressive and violent. This kind of zombie is more frightening than the traditional fantasy monster. Thus, instead of just being a horror movie, *28 Days Later* crosses the genre into science fiction: it *could* happen. In fact, Boyle calls the movie "a warning for us as well as an entertainment."[51] This viral plague is most easily a reference to AIDS, but it could just as well reference cholera, smallpox, anthrax, or the avian or swine flus. In fact, in an unsettling irony, England experienced a devastating outbreak of foot-and-mouth disease during the filming of *28 Days Later*, resulting in the slaughter of millions of livestock.[52] Similarly, the *Dawn of the Dead* remake was shot during the SARS epidemic of 2003, and Snyder immediately noticed the alarming parallels between his film and the nightly news, as both were fraught with panic and misinformation.[53] This widespread fear of infestation and other biohazards is hardly less significant today; it's hard to view either film — or any zombie movie, for that matter — without thinking of recent threats from avian influenza, anthrax, tainted toys from China, or the H1N1 (swine) flu.

This idea of a terminal, debilitating illness or infection even leads to the less obvious metaphor present in almost all recent zombie movies: euthanasia. As many films since the original *Dawn of the Dead* have asked, is it better to murder diseased loved ones or to allow them to become something monstrous? In Romero's *Land of the Dead*, those bitten by zombies are usually given the choice between being killed immediately or being left alone to die gradually and turn into zombies themselves. Like a terminally ill patient, those infected by the zombie virus have time to say goodbye, put some affairs in order, and determine the method of their own death in a kind of morbidly poignant "living will."[54] In *28 Days Later*, however, anyone infected must be killed at once — and often brutally because the virus takes only 20 seconds to manifest its insanity fully. This evolution to the transformative process not only does away with the clichéd "goodbye scene" of other monster movies; it also greatly reduces the choices of the protagonists. For example, when Selena's (Naomie Harris) traveling companion Mark (Noah Huntley) is bitten in a zombie attack, she immediately hacks off the injured limb and butchers him with a machete. In an even more pathetic scene, young Hannah (Megan Burns) gets barely the chance to say goodbye to her father (Brendan Gleeson) before the British military shoots him. The slaughter of the infected living becomes an essential form of mercy killing. The choices of the zombie landscape are hard ones because survival is the top priority.

All of these narrative motifs and cinematic images naturally resonate strongly with modern viewers of the zombie movie, but the primary metaphor in the post–9/11 zombie world is of course terrorism itself. According to St. John, "It does not take much of a stretch to see the parallel between zombies and anonymous terrorists who seek to convert others within society to their deadly cause. The fear that anyone could be a suicide bomber or a hijacker parallels a common trope of zombie films, in which healthy people are zombified by contact with other zombies and become killers."[55] The transmission of the zombie infection is a symbolic form of radical brainwashing, as in the enslaved automatons of some early zombie films. Because anyone can become infected (i.e., conditioned) at any time, everyone is a potential threat; paranoia, therefore, becomes a crucial tool for survival. Those bitten often hide the injury, so even friends and family members cannot be fully trusted. In fact, the first zombie encountered in Snyder's remake of *Dawn of the Dead* is a young girl (Hannah Lochner), and her apparent innocence makes her violence all the more unexpected and shocking.

Land of the Dead adds to such shocks by confronting issues of economic and social disparity, and class division becomes more critical in its storyline than in those of other zombie films. Romero designed his fourth zombie movie to depict a post-zombie apocalypse society, a world where humanity has already lost the conflict and been forced to retreat into the cities, where the enemy is literally at the gates. Tenacious survivors have converted Pittsburgh into an island stronghold, with rivers and electric fencing keeping the zombie plague out and the residents locked safely in. The upper class lives an opulent lifestyle in a luxurious high-rise while attempting to ignore the problem; the commoners, however, must face reality while living in the slums below. In Marian Mansi's documentary about the making of *Land of the Dead*, Romero comments, "Thematically, what the film is about is a bunch of people trying to live as though nothing has changed. Or at least that's what the administration believes. The protagonists understand that the world has completely changed."[56] To keep the wealthy properly fed and supplied, the poor and industrious are forced to risk their lives by venturing outside the city's fortifications, scavenging the countryside in an ever-widening radius. They see the grim horrors of death and infection every day, much like soldiers on the front line of combat.

The wealthy elite who live in the Fiddler's Green skyscraper are literally isolated from the bleak situations that make their lifestyle possible — i.e., both the zombie infestation and the oppression of the poor masses. To insure such a status quo, Kaufman enforces the world's most excessive form of border security: blown up and barricaded bridges make the rivers impassable, and electric fences and armed guards protect an isolated neck of land from any intrusion. In a severe depiction of xenophobia, the soldiers guarding the human city shoot any intruders on sight. These forms of "immigration control" have become even more jarringly familiar with recent and ongoing debates about erecting a fortified wall between the United States and Mexico and with the recent redeployment of National Guard troops by George W. Bush to guard the country's southern border. *Land of the Dead* is certainly not subtle in its critique of modern American foreign policy; in fact, Romero himself goes so far as to identify the fascist Kaufman as Donald Rumsfeld and the Fiddler's Green tenants board as "the Bush administration."[57] Supposedly like Americans in the years immediately after the 9/11 terrorist attacks, the residential population in *Land of the Dead* is ironically asked by their selfish and misguided leaders both to continue their lives as if no real threat existed and to toe the line because of the threat that *does* exist.

Aside from some understandable updating and obvious changes in allegorical references, the defining protocols of the zombie invasion subgenre have remained largely unchanged since the original *Night of the Living Dead*. Yet the reception of such narratives, like all good Gothic fiction, *has* changed; that is, the relevance of zombie cinema for viewers has become all the more poignant. In other words, a post–9/11 audience can hardly help but perceive the characteristics of zombie cinema through the filter of terrorist threats and apocalyptic reality. In my interview with Dendle, he emphasized that the problem is "sorting out whether the movies really are doing something different in the post–9/11 world, or whether it's simply that audiences can't help but see them differently now." Most twenty-first-century zombies are faster and more deadly than their cousins from the initial years of the subgenre's development, and their symbolism has become increasingly transparent, but otherwise the films are doing exactly what Romero started back in the 1960s. However, these movies *are* fundamentally different now, at least from this all-important perspective of reception. As Dendle also told me, "We all view the world differently now, and ... filmmakers and audiences alike are inherently attuned to read themes and motifs through different lenses than they would have before." The films may reflect society's greatest anxieties and concerns back upon us, but they must vary their approach because we have irrevocably changed ourselves.

Dead Man Still *Walking*

Over the course of the last century — and particularly in light of the increased cinematic, literary, and multimedial productivity of the early twenty-first century — the zombie narrative has proven itself to be just as popular, lasting, complex, and revealing as other, more established Gothic traditions. My intention with this detailed critical investigation into the cultural history of the zombie, in fact, is partly to make a case for the creature's historical and literary importance, based on its formal elements, its cultural contexts, and its reception(s) by mass audiences. On the one hand, the zombie is curiously unique because it began its infamous career in folklore, drama, and cinema — not in literature, like vampires, ghosts, werewolves, and golems. The zombie is also a singular and important figure in American historical and cultural studies, as it is the only canonical movie monster to originate in the New World. On the other hand, zombies and the narratives that surround them provide critics an important lens through which they may discern the prevailing attitudes, tendencies, concerns, and anxieties of the society or generation that produced those narratives, as in the great narratives and films about ghosts and vampires as well. As I demonstrate in the following chapters, the zombie functions primarily as a social and cultural metaphor, a creature that comments on the society that produced it by confronting audiences with fantastic narratives of excesses and extremes. By forcing viewers to face their greatest fears concerning life and death, health and decay, freedom and enslavement, prosperity and destruction, the zombie narrative provides an insightful look into the darkest heart of modern society as it is now or as it might quickly become.

Essentially, then, zombies and the narratives that surround them function as part of the larger Gothic literary tradition, even as they change that tradition as well. Teresa Goddu emphasizes how "the gothic is not a transhistorical, static category but a dynamic mode that undergoes historical changes when specific agents adopt and transform its conventions."[58] The zombie can therefore be seen as part of this dynamic adaptation, a new monster for a New World that has facilitated the Gothic's ability to remain relevant in a post-industrial, cyberspace era. Unnatural death is now more horrific, pervasive, and far-reaching than Walpole ever could have imagined, and the zombie works as a dramatic manifestation of this ever-present anxiety. In many ways, the contemporary Gothic — especially the Gothic narratives of zombie cinema — works more effectively now than the classical Gothic ever did because the "real world" of the twenty-first century, particularly the post–9/11 world, is more horrific, more violent, and more traumatic than the nineteenth and early twentieth centuries ever were, at least on English and American soil. Furthermore, as Botting argues, "Gothic figures" represent anxieties associated with turning points in cultural historical progress, usually in "fearful form," so much so that "supernatural demons, natural forces ... and most recently technological powers have successively assumed a predominant role in Gothic representations of cultural anxieties."[59] The unleashing of the atom bomb on Hiroshima and Nagasaki, the disastrous Tet Offensive and the fall of Saigon, the collapse of the World Trade Center towers, the rise in terrorist activities, unexplained pandemics, and natural disasters: each of these human catastrophes mark such cultural "turning points." The zombie creature, therefore, represents a logical "form" for anxieties related to such moments of "cultural historical progress," a supernatural creature, often the result of misguided technology, that is nonetheless essentially natural in its appearance.

In my first chapter, I explore the ethnographic origins of the zombie figure, emphasizing Haitian folklore and the mythologies of the voodoo religion. I also start making a case for the historical value of the zombie as cultural artifact, showing the legendary figure to be a popular manifestation of the long-standing conflicts that have arisen from imperialism, oppression, and slavery. Even before the creature made its way into the mainstream consciousness via the silver screen, it turns out, the zombie worked as an allegorical figure, functioning as an oppressive ideological apparatus in Haiti and other colonial nations by instilling both black and white populations with fears regarding enslavement and the loss of individual sovereignty. In this initial chapter, I provide a detailed look at the cultural history of Haiti in general and voodoo in particular by building on such books as Alfred Métraux's 1959 study *Voodoo in Haiti* and Joan Dayan's *Haiti, History, and the Gods* from 1995. I also trace the literary origins of the zombie creature through ethnographic texts, such as Seabrook's travelogue *The Magic Island* and Zora Neale Hurston's *Tell My Horse* (1938), before outlining the manner in which the zombie made its way from the mythologies of the West Indies into the popular fictions of the United States.

Chapter 2 investigates how the zombie came to establish itself as part of the Hollywood entertainment industry. I use postcolonial theories — particularly those established by Aimé Césaire, Frantz Fanon, Edward W. Said, and Gayatri Chakravorty Spivak — to analyze the most influential and important of the voodoo-based zombie pictures, particularly Halperin's *White Zombie* and Tourneur's *I Walked with a Zombie*, films in which the terror comes from being turning *into* a zombie instead of being killed *by* one. I argue that Halperin's film, while admittedly bringing the zombie to the attention of America filmgoers, unfortunately presents a dated and ultimately negative view of black society and culture. Although the movie might effectively frighten white viewers with the terrible possibility that black nations could indeed threaten the safety and autonomy of white women — in effect reversing the oppressive mechanisms of colonialism — *White Zombie* does so by relying on offensive stereotypes and an inaccurate sensationalizing of Haitian folklore and culture. *I Walked with a Zombie*, on the other hand, provides audiences with a more accurate and culturally sensitive view of West Indian society, and Tourneur does so with a greater cinematic aesthetic and finesse. Nonetheless, the film never fully transcends the stereotyping that it and other voodoo-based films of the 1930s and '40s exploit to encourage its viewers' anxieties concerning black cultures. In the end, none of the early zombie movies manages to rise above racial paranoia and cultural ignorance, but they remain important historical artifacts, nevertheless, for their ability to capture and reveal these deep-seated fears and anxieties of earlier decades.

My third chapter focuses exclusively on Romero's synthetic creation of the more current zombie invasion narrative with *Night of the Living Dead*. I establish the genealogy of this new kind of zombie and trace the developmental process Romero followed to create such an unexpected and fresh subgenre. Rather than designing his version of the "living dead" from nothing, the young filmmaker drew upon a long lineage of horror cinema, including not only the voodoo-based zombie films of the 1930s and '40s, but also the alien invasion films of the 1950s and '60s. Furthermore, Romero borrowed themes, tropes, and images from other narratives, including John W. Campbell, Jr.'s 1938 story "Who Goes There?," Alfred Hitchcock's film version of Daphne Du Maurier's *The Birds* from 1963, Siegel's movie version of *Invasion of the Body Snatchers*, and, most importantly, Richard Matheson's 1954 novella *I Am Legend*. Using Freud's foundational essay on the uncanny (1919), I provide a largely psychoanalytical interpretation of Romero's first film, emphasizing the power his screen zombies have over viewers to exploit their most repressed, yet deeply familiar, fears concerning mortality and death. In a dramatic departure from the earlier zombie movies, Romero's creatures are both contagious and cannibalistic; in this way, they more closely resemble vampires than the earlier, voodoo-based zombies, but because of their large numbers and ceaseless attacks, they constitute a full-scale invasion. Furthermore, *Night of the Living Dead* openly embraces the Gothic literary tradition that is such a fundamental influence on zombie cinema, using both terror and horror to frighten audiences and testing the limits of its human protagonists by confining them to an isolated, antiquated space. At the same time, Romero's film forever changes the course of the subgenre by offering revealing insights into cultural concerns regarding the Vietnam War, the Civil Rights Movement, and changes in American family dynamics.

In my fourth chapter, I follow the course of the zombie invasion narrative through its developmental stage and into its classical phase with the arrival of Romero's masterpiece, *Dawn of the Dead*. This film constitutes a high mark for the fledgling subgenre, illustrating both the artistic and allegorical possibilities of zombies and the apocalyptic stories that surround them. I take a largely cultural-materialist approach to the movie, building on existing criticism to offer my own reading of *Dawn of the Dead* as a powerful critique of 1970s consumer culture. Romero's second zombie film famously exploits its location in a suburban shopping mall to present a scathing metaphor that

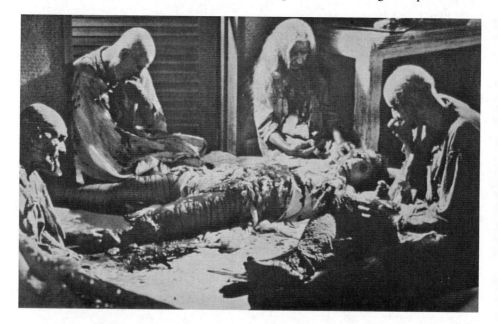

Thanks to Romero, zombies have become voracious cannibals, as in films such as Fulci's *Zombi 2* (Variety Film Production, 1979; Jerry Ohlinger).

aligns humans with zombies and vice versa. Here we are almost all mindless and voracious monsters, driven by an irresistible hunger to do little beyond consume. However, *Dawn of the Dead* tells a complicated story of dependency and loss that transcends the more sensational frame-narrative of the zombie infestation. The movie's extended middle section paints a grim picture of the then newly-invented "mall culture" and portrays the shopping center as a depressing Gothic space, one in which people are more haunted by the past and by empty consumption than they are comforted by material possessions. Furthermore, the film depicts an empty society in which life has been reduced to use alone. The survivors hiding in the mall no longer have a need to work or to produce on their own, and, as a result, they lose those self-fulfilling activities that make them subjective individuals, which Marx calls "species beings." In addition to its insights into ongoing cultural tension regarding race and gender roles in our culture, *Dawn of the Dead* also proposes a bleak look at modern society in general, one in which the individual runs the risk of being consumed by the overpower forces of capitalism.

My final investigation into the course of the zombie narrative, Chapter 5, looks at the gradual decline of the subgenre — a descent from the heights of sophisticated allegory into the depths of exploitation, visual excess, and lowbrow comedy — and its triumphant return in the renaissance at the dawn of the twenty-first century. On the heels of *Dawn of the Dead*'s success, many low-budget imitators quickly followed, and a variety of directors in both the United States and Europe were ready to present their own visions of the zombie narrative. Unfortunately, most of these films rely more on sex, violence, nudity, and gore to amuse their young audiences than they do metaphor and cultural criticism. Even though Romero did his best to maintain the complexity of the subgenre with *Day of the Dead*, I show how viewers appeared to be more interested in riotous comedies such as *The Return of the Living Dead*. The subgenre as Romero had established it went into a marked decline in the 1990s, thriving only in video games and graphic novels, before it emerged newborn and revitalized, particularly in the wake of September 11. However, I argue that the most important development in the subgenre during these two decades lies in the increased interest both directors and fans have shown in zombie evolution and subjectivity. Following a lead established by vampires in their ever-popular narratives, Romero and others have been exploring stories featuring zombies that can think and learn and act on their own desires, and I investigate the ramifications of *Day of the Dead*'s single "zombie protagonist" and the zombie-centric storyline at the heart of *Land of the Dead*. In other words, the recent years of the zombie renaissance have proven that the zombie subgenre will likely continue to be a popular and important form of horror entertainment — and that the future of the narratives lies in increased zombie subjectivity and the exploration of other contagion narratives.

The zombie subgenre, be it in films exploring the horrible limits of enslavement or those depicting an apocalyptic, infectious invasion, has clearly proven itself as a timely, popular, and relevant narrative form. Because such films so overtly and directly deal with the trauma associated with enslavement, infection, death, and decay, they operate as revealing lenses turned upon the heart of our social and cultural anxieties. Initially, zombie movies shocked audiences with their unfamiliar images; today, however, they are even more shocking because of their familiarity. In fact, fans of horror films, particularly such apocalypse narratives as Romero-style zombie movies, may find the inverse to be true. Over the summer of 2005, Dendle was approached by a law student who had survived the horrors of September 11 first-hand. Although the experience was understandably shocking, this student claimed he had been emotionally prepared for the tragedy, not by his family, community, or government, but by the zombie movies of which he had been a long-time appreciator. Perhaps, then, zombie cinema is not merely a reflection of modern society, but a type of preemptive panacea, and that protective potentiality alone gives the subgenre both great cultural significance and lasting social value.

Chapter 1

RAISING THE LIVING DEAD
The Folkloric and Ideological Origins of the Voodoo Zombie

> They are not men ... they are dead bodies! ... Zombies! The living dead. Corpses taken from their graves who are made to work in the sugar mills in the fields at night. — Coach Driver, *White Zombie*

Before the raging armies of the dead made popular by filmmakers such as Romero and movies such as his *Night of the Living Dead*, the zombie was a thing of mythology and folkloristic ritual, a much maligned and little understood voodoo practice primarily from the West Indian nation of Haiti.[1] In fact, zombies are more than just mindless monsters bent on the destruction of humanity and global social culture; they are also important ethnographic and anthropological creatures, embodying both folkloristic and ideological beliefs and traditions.

Zombie mythology actually has ties to science and biology (since they are one of the only supernatural monsters that actually exists in some real-world form), and the ideology connected to them is directly linked to the political and social life of postcolonial Haiti. The zombie is thus a complex and relevant cultural artifact, a fusion of elements from the "civilized" New World and mystical ancient Africa. Indeed, it is a creature born of slavery, oppression, and capitalist hegemony and in that way a manifestation of collective unconscious fears and taboos.

To begin to comprehend this much-misunderstood creature, I want first to establish a working theoretical framework with which to approach the zombie as a product of folkloristic mythology. I will then examine the historical and scientific environment that created such a monster, consider the ideological ramifications of its application in both traditional and popular culture, and trace the journey of the zombie from ethnography to cinematic narratives.

Unearthing the Origins of the Zombie

As I have already said, the two most unique and interesting qualities of the cinematic zombie narrative are, first, the virtual lack of a true literary antecedent and, second, its firm connection with the colonized Americas of the western hemisphere. Zombies, in fact, made the leap from mythology to cinema with almost no previous literary tradition.[2] Rather than being based on creatures appearing in novels or short stories, zombie narratives have developed instead directly from their folkloristic, ethnographic, and anthropological origins. By contrast, Count Dracula, perhaps the world's best-known supernatural monster, arrived on the screen via Browning in 1931 as an adaptation of Stoker's 1897 novel, F. W. Murnau's film *Nosferatu, eine Symphonie des Grauens* (1922), and Hamilton Deane's 1927 stage play *Dracula*—all of which look back all the way to John Polidori's *The Vampyre* of 1819. In addition, Dr. Frankenstein's animated golem, sensationalized by Whale's 1931 movie, was similarly based on a stage play (Peggy Webling's *Frankenstein* of 1927), which was of course an adaptation of Shelley's 1818 novel. Other fantastic creatures such as ghosts, evil spirits, and demons have even longer pedigrees, appearing in novels, stories, and folk songs for centuries. The zombie, on the other hand, had made only minor appearances in travel narratives, non-fiction accounts of the Caribbean, and voodoo-themed stage productions before being transferred to the screen, as we will see, in 1932.

The other singular characteristic of the zombie as a Hollywood movie monster is its undeniable and unique connection with the colonial history of the Americas. Vampires, reanimated corpses, ghosts, and even werewolves have folkloristic and mythological origins similar to those of the zombie, but these creatures can be found in almost every cultural history of Europe, Asia, and even Africa. While those monsters have such cross-cultural mythologies, the zombie remains purely a monster of the Americas, born from imperialism, slavery, and —most importantly—voodoo magic and religion.[3] More precisely, the zombie, as rendered by filmmakers in the 1930s, '40s, and after, comes from the social, cultural, and religious beliefs of Haiti. When recognized in this light, the zombie monster can be seen as truly belonging to the Americas, being built on the relatively new folklore of the Caribbean, and having essential ties to colonialism, slavery, and ancient mysticism. These exceptional characteristics also make an investigation of the anthropological roots of the zombie an essential part of understanding this particular sub-genre of horror.

Because any analysis of the cinematic zombie must therefore be founded on an investigation into the cultural and mythological origins of the monster itself, the primary task of this chapter is to create a traceable genealogy of the zombie and to attempt to establish the creature's cultural and ethnographic authenticity. Such an academic approach is vital to most folkloristic inquiries, as has been discussed at length by the leading authority on "authenticity," Regina Bendix. In the introduction to her *In Search of Authenticity* (1997), Bendix emphasizes how "processes of authentication bring about material representations by elevating the authenticated into the category of the noteworthy."[4] This passage illustrates why the verification of a cultural artifact's authenticity becomes so essential: without the establishment of that authenticity, the object, event, or practice simply lacks any credibility or cultural value. In addition, Bendix points out how this authenticity is recognizable only once the scholar establishes an "external simplicity of form."[5] Part of my task in this chapter is to establish the singularity of the zombie monster a part of twentieth-century American culture, and, because authenticity is indelibly linked to a codifiable form, I will illustrate the patterns found in the zombie phenomenon in my later analysis of the existing literature to verify this sense of the "authentic" zombie narrative.

Another folklore theorist essential to this investigation is Barre Toelken, who defines folklore as "culturally constructed communicative traditions informally exchanged in dynamic variation through space and time."[6] This paradigm will prove useful in investigating the zombie, for although this figure is rooted in voodoo traditions and practices, the variations exhibited by different ethnographers establish the critical investigation of the zombie as the purview of folklore studies. Because zombie legends and mythologies are irrevocably tied to a particular "folk group,"[7] moreover, an examination of that culture is necessary before considering the variations occurring within those traditions. In fact, the study of voodooism and zombies is more akin to what Barbara Kirshenblatt-Gimblett designates as the study of *folklife*, which "preserves the concerns of statistics and geography in the specificities of locale, habitat, and material culture."[8] Because zombie legends and practices are so clearly tied to a particular folk group (i.e., the practitioners of voodoo in Haiti), any scholarly investigation must be concerned with the social, religious, and even geographic environment that produced the zombie mythology, rather than merely the oral traditions and artistic productions emphasized by most mainstream folklore.

However, zombie narratives are not generally produced by the folk group that actually believes in the reality of voodoo ritual and zombification, but rather by those who have studied or experienced that culture second hand. As I will later demonstrate, many people living in Haiti do not consider the creation of a zombie, along with other mystical voodoo practices and beliefs, a matter of mythology or the thing of fairy tales; those who embrace the tenets of the Vodoun religion accept zombies as a terrifying reality. This

Voodoo paraphernalia, Port-au-Prince, Haiti (photograph courtesy Doron, 2002; used by permission according to the GNU Free Documentation License, Version 1.2).

inevitable fissure — the scholar's folklore versus the folk's reality — is addressed by Kirshenblatt-Gimblett. She reveals how "folklore is not only a disciplinary subject and disciplinary formation (we use one and the same term for both), but also a mode of cultural production. ... folklorists *produce* folklore through a process of identification and designation."[9] Because ethnographers have traveled to Haiti to document and theorize the living, breathing cultural system that exists there, the zombie has been transformed into a thing of *folklore*, rather than simply an aspect of Haitian *folklife*, and it should therefore be approached as both a disciplinary subject and the resulting product of such academic investigations.

With the scholarship of folklore thus in mind, my investigation begins by asking where the zombie actually comes from. What is the antecedent of this creature, a monstrosity that has become so familiar and even commonplace in contemporary American society? A recent documentary produced for The History Channel by Jon Alan Walz, *Fear Files: Zombies* (2006), attempts to address this issue for a popular audience. Walz maps out the mythological roots of the zombie in cultures that predate Haiti. For instance, his documentary traces the tradition of raising the dead from Gilgamesh to the so-called "hopping corpses" of China to Jesus Christ's raising of Lazarus in the Bible.[10] Perhaps the most relevant pre–Haitian quasi-zombie legend comes from Tibet and the legend of the *ro-langs*. According to anthropologist Turrel V. Wylie, Tibet has an established oral tradition of dead corpses brought back to life by both human and demonic means. These ro-langs resemble the zombies of Haiti in that they are reanimated human bodies, but the force behind their apparent resurrection is that of demonic possession rather than the insidious actions of a priest or magician.[11] Similar myths concerning the risen dead can be found in other cultures as well, but none can be tied directly to the cinematic monster as clearly as the zombies of the West Indies.

An ethnographic study carried out by Hans W. Ackermann and Jeanine Gauthier in 1991 provides the most detailed investigation of the zombie to date. In addition to surveying and summarizing the major discoveries and beliefs regarding Haitian zombies, Ackermann and Gauthier also establish their ties to other cultural traditions and mythologies, particularly those of Africa. These scholars have documented accounts of reanimated corpses in Benin, Zambia, Tanzania, and Ghana; in most of these African legends, witches resuscitate the dead to create slaves and servants, and some mythologies allude to large communities of zombies residing atop mountains.[12] In addition, Ackermann and Gauthier establish similar folkloristic beliefs and parallels throughout the Caribbean, especially in Jamaica, Surinam, and Martinique, although it remains unclear which culture influenced which first.[13] Ultimately, and of the most importance for their investigation, Ackermann and Gauthier conclude that the Haitian zombie is not an indigenous creation, but rather "an immigrant to the West Indies,"[14] an observation that underscores the essential role played by imperial colonization and slavery in the creation of the modern-day zombie.

Nevertheless, as I will detail later, the American popular perception and conceptualization of the zombie comes directly from Haiti, regardless of the creature's more elaborate genealogy. Because the very idea of the zombie was brought to the attention of mainstream America via ethnographers of the Caribbean and United States military officials, my study will consider the folkloristic zombie of Haiti as the definitive source of the Hollywood cinematic zombie. Although many similarities can be established between voodoo folklore and the ritual beliefs and legends of other, related cultures, filmmakers of the 1930s latched onto the sensational tales carried by other Americans who had visited Haiti in person. However, to understand the relationship between the originating folklore and the resulting populist entertainment thoroughly, a more academic and disciplined investigation of the origins of the zombie is required, particularly if the more modern-day iteration of this supernatural monster is to be properly analyzed. The best place to begin such an investigation is therefore with Haiti itself and the voodoo religion that governs the belief-systems of its people.

The Historical and Cultural Environment of Haiti

As a former French colony, Haiti is a complex land of synthesis and hybridity, a liminal space where Western Christianity fused (albeit irregularly) with ancient African ritual and mysticism. The resulting religious system came to be known in the West as *voodoo*, an often misrepresented and misunderstood set of beliefs and rituals that deals directly with death and the spirit world. Alongside potions, love charms, and voodoo dolls, the zombie — the "living dead" — came to be a source of both fear and fascination to white Westerners, and the movies produced by Hollywood, in the 1930s and '40s especially, exploited both exoticism and romanticism to draw large crowds to the theaters. To provide readers with a concise historical framework for a detailed discussion of the zombie in twentieth-century American film culture, I rely heavily on three quintessential books concerning Haiti, voodoo, and zombiism. The first is Métraux's *Voodoo in Haiti*, one of the most comprehensive texts about Haitian history, voodoo practices and rituals, and the origins of the zombie. A similarly authoritative and important book is Dayan's *Haiti, History, and the Gods*, one of the definitive texts on Haitian history and culture. Dayan's book investigates not only the historically significant events in Haiti's variegated past, but also considers the impact of voodoo on Haitian culture and literature. Finally, I am indebted to Gary D. Rhodes of Queen's University in Belfast for important historical background and a detailed analysis of the first feature-length zombie movie. In his 2001 book *White Zombie: Anatomy of a Horror Film*, Rhodes presents a thorough overview of the development of the zombie narrative from exotic folklore to mainstream Hollywood entertainment.

Haiti, the second oldest independent nation in the Western Hemisphere, has a complex and violent history, founded primarily on the mixing of black slaves of diverse African cultural origins with European imperialists and Christians. In his 1971 introduction to Métraux's book, anthropologist Sidney W. Mintz summarizes the colonial events leading up to the establishment of the "Black Republic." As he says, the Spanish annihilated the indigenous population of the Caribbean island they called Española to make way for experiments in plantation production. After the more lucrative discovery of mineral resources on the mainland, Española was basically abandoned to "anti–Spanish vagabonds, religious and political refugees, deserters, and runaways" until the Treaty of Ryswick in 1697, which gave the western third of the island to the French.[15] Over the next century, Saint Domingue, as the French renamed their end of Española, became one of the cruelest and most profitable of the slave-based plantation colonies. Mortality rates were high, and slaves were replaced at a prodigious rate more by "new stock" from Africa than by procreation. The resulting slave population was therefore less creolized and more connected to African traditions and resistance than the slaves of other Caribbean colonies.[16]

By the end of the eighteenth century, the black slaves of Saint Domingue far outnumbered the French colonists, and a revolution was almost inevitable. According to Dayan, the fight for Haitian independence officially began with a solemnly performed voodoo ceremony on the night of August 14, 1791.[17] Over ten years of brutal violence followed, during which the three great Haitian military leaders — Toussaint-L'ouverture, Henry Christophe, and Jean-Jacques Dessalines — battled Napoleon Bonaparte's beleaguered soldiers and their general, Victor-Emmanuel Leclerc. Finally, in 1804, Saint Domingue became the "only locale in history for a successful slave revolution," resulting in the first "Black Republic." Dessalines created a new flag by removing the white from the French tricolor and called the new nation "Haiti" from the original Amerindian word for the island that meant "mountainous lands."[18] Dessalines made himself the "first president and emperor of Haiti" and tried to establish a progressive society in which former slaves were considered free and where national identity was tied to one's "blackness."[19] Dessalines's policies ended up encouraging an inevitable racist backlash because he refused to acknowledge whites and mulattos as "true Haitians"; he denied property rights to those with suspicious ancestry, which probably helped lead to his brutal assassination in 1806.[20]

After the death of Dessalines, decades of political turmoil and social unrest followed. In 1807, Haitians elected Alexandre Sabès Pétion president, but tensions between the *noirs* in the north and the *jaunes* in the south and west resulted in a divided republic. Christophe became president of the north in 1807 and crowned himself King Henry I in 1811. In 1818, Petion died and was replaced by Jean-Pierre Boyer, who reunited Haiti after the suicide of Christophe in 1820.[21] Although Boyer established Haiti as a refuge for freed and emancipated slaves, offering land to blacks emigrating from the United States, his long rule became unpopular because of his *Code Rural,* which essentially reduced the majority of Haitians to slave laborers who toiled just to support the extravagant lifestyles of the military and civic leaders.[22] Boyer abdicated his presidency after the 1843 revolution, and another uprising occurred just one year later. Four more presidents followed in quick succession until 1849, when President Faustin Soulouque followed Dessalines's example and crowned himself Emperor of Haiti.[23] Soulouque abandoned the throne in 1859 to be replaced by President Fabre Nicholas Geffrard, who remained in power until the 1915 invasion and occupation of Haiti by the United States Marines.[24] Their overt goal, according to Rhodes, was to modernize the island — building roads, hospitals, and schools — and to establish a stable democratic government. However, the locals resented this imperialist presence (seeing as most of the improvements undertaken by the US Marines relied on forced native labor), and the United States' presence was largely gone by 1929.[25]

The political landscape of Haiti is thus one of revolution,

Jean-Jacques Dessalines (1760–1806) (image courtesy Quartier Latin 1968, Wikipedia Commons).

civil wars, and coups, and the religious environment reflects a similar tension. Yet, whereas political strife in "The Black Republic" has often been solved by violence, potential religious conflicts have been ameliorated by dialectical synthesis. Hurston, in her extensive ethnographic study of the Caribbean, *Tell My Horse*, emphasizes the dual nature of Haiti, for although it is nominally (as well as officially) a Catholic country, in reality "it is deeply pagan."[26] The religion embraced and practiced by most Haitians, especially the lower classes, is voodoo. Métraux defines *voodoo* as "a conglomeration of beliefs and rites of African origin, which, having been closely mixed with Catholic practice, has come to be the religion of the greater part of the peasants and the urban proletariat of the black republic of Haiti."[27] Hall calls this cultural situation a paradox of difference and continuity, for the pagan gods of Africa survived, albeit in an "underground existence," as Catholic saints, and former slaves from a variety of home countries were brought together through this unifying religious amalgamation.[28] Furthermore, Catholicism was the religion of the imperialists, and voodoo was the belief system of the slaves; when Haiti gained its independence, the two disparate influences rapidly converged.

As more and more native Africans were brought from the Gulf of Guinea as slaves, in fact, the local practice of voodoo received a constant influx of tribal rituals and beliefs, resulting in a new "syncretic religion" that drew heavily from "the ancient religions of the classical East and of the Aegean world."[29] Métraux suggests that some of the slaves were inevitably priests or "servants of the gods" who knew the old rites and rituals and were able to resurrect them in exile.[30] The European overlords tried to stem the influx of these pagan beliefs, but even though an official decree in 1664 made the baptism of all slaves in the colonies mandatory, "no religious instruction was given to the slaves."[31] As a result, most Haitians were devout Catholics in name only, going through the outward motions in church, but preferring to perform their own ceremonies and follow their own traditions at home. Although the average peasants were aware of Jesus Christ and the canon of saints, they were far more intimate with the *loa* (or gods) of the voodoo pantheon. In Métraux's words, "Voodoo is for [the Haitian] a familiar personal religion, whereas Catholicism often shares the cold nature of the cement chapels which crown the crests of the hills."[32]

Yet rather than being at constant odds, the two belief systems synthesized into a new, dialectical faith. The resulting Vodoun religion quickly became an important part of daily life in Haiti, and after the revolution against the French ended in 1804, voodoo was allowed to grow and develop more freely without constant influence from colonial Catholic priests.[33] Later, when Western ethnographers began to visit and investigate Haiti, voodoo became a source of confusion and consternation for European and American Christians. The recorded rituals were ancient and elaborate, but the contemporary practices had obviously been heavily influenced by Catholic liturgy, as well.[34] Most Westerners could not reconcile the seemingly conflicted and ambiguous relationship between the pagan and the Christian. According to Métraux, "The equivocal reputation which Voodoo has acquired is in fact due to just this very syncretic quality by which it mixes together, in almost equal proportions, African rites and Christian observances."[35] As mention by Hall above, the point of greatest contention is likely the use of Catholic iconography in voodoo ritual.

Practitioners of Haitian voodoo include images of Catholic saints and even the Virgin Mary in their ceremonies and on their altars. Early ethnographic scholarship assumed the saints had been scandalously re-appropriated by the voodooists, but Hurston takes pains to show this view is a misreading. Rather than actually worshipping the images of Catholic saints, the devout would simply use the pictures and statues as approximations of their own *loa*, the voodoo spirits tenaciously held over from the pagan African faith systems.[36] Because "no Haitian artist has given them an interpretation or concept of the loa,"[37] and since most of the iconographic saints share similar features and attributes with specific *loa*, the adoption of one for the other was a logical move; for instance, Damballah Ouedo is usually represented by St. Patrick or Moses because they all share the symbol of a serpent.[38] Voodooists also maintain dedicated shrines to individual *loa*, presenting them with food, money, and other sacrifices.[39] Some of the more elaborate rituals even require blood sacrifices,[40] a seemingly barbaric ritual that would be seen as conflicting with mainstream Catholic teachings despite the dogma of transubstantiation and the Eucharistic drinking of wine as the blood of Christ.

The political, social, and religious histories of Haiti, particularly during the tumultuous nineteenth century, therefore represent a complicated web of converging powers, influences, and ideologies. Control of the country has shifted from European imperialists to local freedom fighters to militaristic despots to ambitious capitalists — and often back again. Such multifarious forces have created a heterogeneous and hybrid culture, visible primarily through the observation of ancient voodoo rituals. This very religion constitutes a delicate liminal space that fuses recognizable aspects of mainstream Catholicism with pagan rites and powerful mythologies, and this hybridization of both culture and religion is of primary interest to an investigation of the zombie legend. On the one hand, the voodoo zombie leaves its African roots and pagan origins largely behind except in two key regards: the understanding of the human soul as something tangible that can be captured and manipulated by black magic and the zombie's allegorical function as a metaphor for enslavement. On the other hand, the zombie mythology has obvious ties to Christian theology and iconography as well, particularly in the resurrection of the dead. In fact, the local folk stories of the "living dead" represent not only an important cultural artifact but also an ideological apparatus used by those in power to maintain social control; therefore, a detailed look at the zombie as a figure of folklore will pave the way for my analysis of the accompanying ideologies.

The Zombie as Folkloristic Artifact

A direct result of the limited U.S. occupation of Haiti at the beginning the twentieth century was increased Western awareness of and greater curiosity about and fascination with voodoo rituals and zombie practices. Tales of reanimated corpses used by local plantation owners to increase production were of singular interest to visiting ethnographers, and the zombie quickly became a focal point for the investigation of the folklore of Haiti. In Toelken's discussion of the processes that create folklore, after all, he claims the study of a culture's folklore begins with the registering of a "cultural metaphor, a shared awareness that a word or phrase has meanings that go beyond apparent manifest of lexical content."[41] This non-canonical significance provides a subtext not readily understood by those outside of the cultural unit, and the zombie is a prime example of such a phenomenon. Although white westerners may have certain preconceived associations with the word *zombie*, the folkloristic implication for native Haitians is far more complex.

According to ethnobotanist Wade Davis, the modern English word *zombie* most likely derives from the Angolian Kimbundu term *nzúmbe*, which means "ghost" or "spirit of a dead person."[42] Ackermann and Gauthier provide an even more detailed etymological investigation of the term, showing significant ties to the Congo and African terms referencing a "corpse" or a "body without a soul."[43] These eerie concepts were brought from Africa to Haiti with the slave trade and, like the pagan origins of the voodoo religion itself, eventually synthesized with the West through the Creole word *zôbi*, later *zombi*, which was finally modernized as *zombie* by American English. In contemporary United States vernacular, the word is often used to describe a boring, drugged-out person, a corporate automaton, or even an exotic mixed drink, but as far as the traditional cinematic monster is concerned, the designation of *zombie* is reserved for the walking dead: people brought back to life to serve — and in later films, to devour — the human race.

Long before any horror films were made by enterprising Hollywood directors, however, the zombie was simply a terrifying part of Haitian folklife. As anthropologists began to return to the United States to publish their findings, the facts and realities of the zombie phenomenon began to be codified. Hurston provides a chillingly succinct definition of the creatures: "They are the bodies without souls. The living dead. Once they were dead, and after that they were called back to life again."[44] In their much later ethnographic account, Ackermann and Gauthier describe the physical appearance of a zombie as a "resurrected individual [who] is deprived of will, memory, and consciousness, speaks with a nasal voice, and is recognized chiefly by dull, glazed eyes and an absent air."[45] These explanations summarize the initial impressions that non–native people have had of the zombie, whose original purpose was relatively straightforward: to become the slave of the sorcerer who zombified the victim.[46]

More than any other author, Seabrook is credited with bringing exotic tales of voodoo to a mass American audience.[47] After a fact-finding trip in 1924 to Arabia, Seabrook traveled to Haiti to perform a first-hand ethnographic investigation into voodooism. He learned Haitian Creole and even lived with a native "sorceress" named Maman Célie, attempting to immerse himself fully in the local culture.[48] Seabrook was exposed to the creation of *ouanga* charms, potions, and powders, and he took active part in a number of authentic voodoo ceremonies and rituals. One night, according to Seabrook in *The Magic Island*, he talked at length with Haitian farmer Constant Polynice about the supernatural creatures rumored to inhabit the countryside. Although such monsters as werewolves, vampires, and demons were familiar to him from European folklore, the concept of the zombie was new to Seabrook, and it sounded "exclusively local."[49] His interest was piqued, and American readers would soon be exposed to the zombie in Seabrook's chapter on "Dead Men Working in the Cane Fields."

Seabrook presents the following detailed description of the mythical creature:

> It seemed ... that while the *zombie* came from the grave, it was neither a ghost, nor yet a person who had been raised like Lazarus from the dead. The *zombie*, they say, is a soulless human corpse, still dead, but taken from the grave and endowed by sorcery with a mechanical semblance of life — it is a dead body which is made to walk and act and move as if it were alive. People who have the power to do this go to a fresh grave, dig up the body before it has had time to rot, galvanize it into movement, and then make of it a servant or slave, occasionally for the commission of some crime, more often simply as a drudge around the habitation or the farm, setting it dull heavy tasks, and beating it like a dumb beast if it slackens.[50]

Seabrook then records Polynice's story of a local zombie. Allegedly, a worker for the Haitian-American Sugar Company (Hasco) named Ti Joseph brought a troupe of nine zombies to work one morning, registering them to labor in the sugar fields. They were kept hidden in the countryside, away from suspicious eyes, and sustained on bland, tasteless fish, for, according to Polynice, zombies cannot taste salt or else their master will lose his hold over them. On Saturday, Joseph would return to the factory to claim the weekly wages for all ten of them, but he would naturally not share the money with the poor brutes. Eventually, Joseph's wife took pity on the creatures and tried to placate them with some *tablettes* candy. The nuts used to make the confections had been salted, however, and, upon ingesting the food, the zombies rose, let out dreadful cries, and fled to the cemetery. There the pitiable zombies collapsed and "died," finally to be reburied by their loved ones.[51]

After hearing such a phantasmagoric tale, Seabrook insisted on seeing some zombies himself, and Polynice arranged a meeting for his American friend. Consequently, Seabrook chillingly narrates the encounter he had with three of the creatures, describing them as dumb workers, "plodding like brutes, like automatons.... The eyes were the worst.... They were in truth like the eyes of a dead man, not blind, but staring, unfocused, unseeing. The whole face, for that matter, was bad enough. It was vacant, as if there was nothing behind it."[52] Seabrook was even bold enough to shake hands with one of the zombies, confirming the physical existence of the creature and leading him to surmise a non-supernatural explanation for the phenomenon. In his written account of the event, Seabrook tries to rationalize the phenomenon as cases of mistaken identity or doubling—the so-called zombies simply *look* like missing or dead relatives, but they are really other people entirely—and he refuses to concede a supernatural cause.[53] Regardless, the American public was probably less interested in the science anyway and more enamored by the spectacle; Seabrook's book became a huge success, forever establishing the idea of the "living dead" in the imaginations of the West.

Although Hurston's 1938 book about her own ethnographic trip to Haiti follows the first appearance of zombie movies in America, her record of her first-hand experiences with the living dead is as useful as Seabrook's in establishing the cultural realities of the monsters. Hurston states frankly, "I know that there are Zombies in Haiti."[54] In *Tell My Horse*, she presents a detailed account of the zombification ritual, at least from the perspective of local mythology and folklore. According to her sources, plantation owners could "buy" zombie labor from practitioners of black voodoo sorcery. The priest, or *Bocor*, would then perform the proper ceremony, visit the home of the intended victim, suck his soul out through a crack in the door, and wait for the body to die. After the funeral, the *Bocor* would approach the tomb, call the dead out by name, and restore the captured soul to its body by passing it under the dead man's nose for a few seconds. Finally, the newly reanimated zombie would be paraded past his own home, insuring that he could not later recognize it and leave the service of the *Bocor*.[55] After all these steps are followed, the zombie "will work ferociously and tirelessly without consciousness of his surroundings and conditions and without memory of his former state."[56]

After presenting readers with a number of documented zombie cases, Hurston relates her personal encounter with Felicia Felix-Mentor at the hospital at Gonaives. According to official records, Felicia had allegedly died in 1907 and was soon largely forgotten by the community. Then, in 1936, she was found wandering aimlessly through the Haitian countryside, naked, confused, and muttering about her father's farm. She was taken to the local hospital and reluctantly identified by her husband.[57] Hurston met the young woman a few months later, and she describes her appearance as "dreadful. That blank face with the dead eyes. The eyelids were white all around the eyes as if they had been burned with acid.... There was nothing that you could say to her or get from her except by looking at her, and the sight of this wreckage was too much to endure for long."[58] Hurston managed to get a photograph of the young woman, but no one would provide any details of her case nor could anyone speculate on what had happened to her or who had killed her.[59]

Like Seabrook, Hurston sought a more rational explanation for the zombie phenomenon. She surmises in *Tell My Horse* that zombification is most likely the result of a powerful drug, one that "destroys the part of the brain which governs speech and will power."[60] Just such an explanation is proffered by Davis, probably the world's leading authority on the zombification ritual. As a Harvard University graduate student, he traveled to Haiti in 1985 in search of exotic new medicinal drugs. Davis recorded his weird experiences and botanical research in the book *The Serpent and the Rainbow*.[61] According to this primarily anthropological text, a limited number of powerful and unorthodox voodoo priests, which Davis renders as *bokors*, possess a keen knowledge of natural drugs and sedatives and have created a "zombie powder"—called *coup poudre*—that renders its victims clinically dead: no movement, no breath, and no discernible pulse.[62] Davis' interest in the drug is purely scientific at first, but he soon realizes that zombies are real creatures within the Vodoun religion. And the method of creating such a dangerous substance is naturally a closely guarded secret, controlled by the secret societies of Haiti.[63]

Those well versed in the administration of this powder could conceivably create the illusion of raising the dead, thus giving the zombie legend credibility. The most potent poison included in the *coup poudre* comes from a specific kind of puffer fish, a nerve agent called tetrodotoxin.[64] This drug "induces a state of profound paralysis, marked by complete immobility during which time the border between life and death is not at all certain, even to trained physicians."[65] All major life functions are paralyzed for an extended period, and those suffering from the effects of the drug run the real risk of being buried alive. If the powder is too strong or mixed incorrectly, the victim might die immediately — or suffocate slowly in the coffin.[66] Unfortunately, even those victims lucky enough to be rescued from the grave in time would inevitably suffer brain damage from the lack of oxygen; they would be understandably sluggish and dim-witted.[67] For Davis, therefore, zombification isn't a mysterious of supernatural occurrence but rather the result of pharmacology, the careful administration of powerful neurotoxins.

Although Davis's account of the Haitian zombie was well received by a popular audience, scholars such as Ackermann and Gauthier challenge many of his conclusions and question the overall method of his investigation. To begin with, they discount Davis's primary theory of the *coup poudre*, claiming inconsistencies in the samples of zombie powder brought back to the United States. In fact, tetrodotoxin failed to appear in most of Davis's samples, and the amounts that were present were too minimal to cause any physiological reactions.[68] These investigators challenge the "poison theory" entirely, claiming instead mental illness and vagrancy as better explanations for the most documented cases of zombification in Haiti. A great deal of Davis's research assumes the truth of the literal zombification of a man named Clairvius Narcisse, whom Ackermann and Gauthier are quick to discredit because of the singularity of the case and the unreliability of hospital records.[69] In the end, Ackermann and Gauthier attempt to present a more plausible, anthropological explanation of the Haitian zombie phenomenon, seeking their answers in folklore and myth rather than pharmacology and science.[70]

These ethnographic and scientific accounts of the zombie fulfill Toelken's "Twin Laws" of folklore. On the one hand, they show *conservatism* because in them zombie tales retain certain specific "information, beliefs, styles, customs, and the like" and attempt to pass those materials on from one generation to the next.[71] The recorded stories of the zombie all feature an apparently dead victim and the reported (and often documented) return of that victim to the world of the living. Yet the varied recounted stories also exhibit *dynamism*, for the stories are rarely identical but instead exhibit variation and drift.[72] Sometimes the zombie is created by magic, sometimes by poisoning; some zombies are employed by greedy capitalists, and others are created for revenge. Of particular note is not only how these stories are channeled through the eyes of a white ethnographer, but also how additional stories are told *by* those white ethnographers. In other words, instead of simply relating the tales of the indigenous folk population, those performing the fieldwork have become part of the tradition. As often happens with the ethnographic research of any culture, those investigating the folklore of zombiism practice both conservatism and dynamism in the recording of their own zombie legends.

Clearly, the ethnographic and folkloristic realities of the zombie are more complicated than the often pedantic versions of the creatures presented by the American popular entertainment industry. First-hand accounts provide a record of a diabolical mythology that plays on deep-seated fears about death and, perhaps more importantly, enslavement. Regardless of variations in the legends, the fundamental characteristic of the zombie phenomenon is the mystical interference with the natural processes of life and death, interferences rendered all the more plausible because of the ancient folk beliefs of the native people. Yet the mythology also taps into fears associated with Christian dogma, for zombification represents a violation of God's laws, a process by which one's eternal rest is interrupted and whereby one's autonomy is exchanged for a new existence of slave labor and isolated pain. The risk of becoming one of the living dead, therefore, constitutes the greatest fear of the voodoo-practicing Haitian; being forced to work as a virtually mindless slave represents a fate far worse than death itself.

The Zombie as Ideological Apparatus

In a country such as Haiti, then, the almost universal acceptance of voodoo by the common populace requires scholars to consider its social influence in terms of an ultimately repressive ideology, not merely as an innocuous system of religious beliefs. Voodoo represents ties between postcolonial Haitian society and the people's ancestral heritage from Africa, so these pagan practices are concrete manifestations of a history and a social culture that transcend the pervasive influences of the European imperialists. In a 1961 interview with Fernande Bing, Métraux emphasized how, most importantly, voodoo gave hope to the Haitians—first to the slaves, and later to the poor.[73] Voodoo allowed the slaves to organize and rebel, and voodoo united — and continues to unite — the common people against the central government and the prevailing economic system. Although my investigation cannot possibly consider the full scope of voodoo ideology, I will attempt to analyze and consider the ideology specifically associated with indigenous zombie mythology before moving on to consider its role in the context of United States popular culture. Ultimately, the threat of zombification in Haiti acts as a powerful controlling force applied by various agents in society to exert control and maintain stability across political, social, and economic strata.

The folkloristic belief in both the zombie creature and the process (and potential threat) of zombification represents an ideology of fear in Haiti that has affected and continues to affect most members of that society. In fact, the voodoo religion played an active ideological role in Haiti even when it was a French colony. Métraux points out how early French plantation owners in the eighteenth century lived in a constant state of fear and how "it was the witchcraft of remote and mysterious Africa which troubled the sleep of the people in 'the big house.'"[74] The rites and rituals practiced in the slave camps represented not only a disconcerting and foreign culture but also constituted a direct (if perhaps only perceived) threat. Hurston relates the pervasiveness of this threat in the postcolonial, twentieth-century Haitian society: "No one can stay in Haiti long without hearing Zombies mentioned in one way or another, and the fear of this thing and all that it means seeps over the country like a ground current of cold air. This fear is real and deep."[75] In a society where monsters such as zombies are accepted as real, any mythology associated with their existence and creation carries tremendous weight.

To understand the impact of the zombie paradigm on the population of Haiti, one must first recognize the differences between the voodoo zombie and the Hollywood zombie. Davis illustrates the most essential contrast between the living dead created by voodoo ritual and the cannibalistic ghouls of the movie screen: "In Haiti, the fear is not of being harmed by zombis; it is fear of becoming one."[76] In other words, the indigenous locals aren't afraid of the zombies themselves but of those individuals who have the power to create them. In the voodoo mythology, the mindless victims of zombie enslavement pose no direct threat to anyone (the ethnographic accounts present them as anything but hostile), but they represent a threat that is far more insidious. In fact, in Seabrook's discussion of the zombie, his friend Polynice claims the first reaction one has to a zombie is not fear, but rather intense pity.[77] The poor victim of a zombification ritual is a tragic figure, one who has had her identity and autonomy stripped from her, being converted to nothing more than an enslaved cipher.

In Haiti, the pervasive belief in zombification, and the fear resulting from that accepted potentiality, constitutes a powerful ideological force. For Terry Eagleton, ideology functions on two levels: what is said and what is implied. In other words, "ideology is less a matter of the inherent linguistic properties of a pronouncement than a question of who is saying what to whom for what purposes."[78] For those who believe in zombies, a vocalized threat from a powerful voodoo priest to capture one's soul constitutes more than just idle words. The threat represents a real possibility. Eagleton goes on to show how "ideologies are often seen as peculiarly *action-oriented* sets of beliefs, rather than speculative theoretical systems."[79] Once again, the Haitians who accept zombification as a grim potentiality are not so much concerned about the theoretical implications of the threat *as* threat; they are fundamentally fearful of the actions that could result from acts of zombification. The hybridized nature of Haitian culture in general, and in the voodoo religion in particular, makes this ideology all the more repressive: practitioners of voodoo believe zombies are real because of the pagan side of their belief system, and they find the fate all the more frightening and abhorrent because of their Christian faith in agency and a life after death (i.e., heaven).

The ideology of the zombie — or rather, the ideology of *becoming* a zombie — affects Haitian society on multiple levels and via multiple agents. In his essential discussion of Marxism, Louis Althusser clarifies a division in a society's superstructure that appears as the power of the state itself, on the one hand, and the power of "the ideological State apparatuses," on the other. These ISAs, as Althusser calls them, are separate from apparatuses of the state that wield power directly — such as the government, the army, the police, the courts, and the prisons — which he designates as the "Repressive State Apparatus."[80] The ISAs work on other levels, including religious, educational, familial, and cultural ones.[81] According to Althusser, these ISAs "function massively and predominantly *by ideology*, but they also function secondarily by repression, even if ultimately, but only ultimately, this is very attenuated and concealed, even symbolic."[82] In other words, societal institutions other than those under the direct purview of the government act to exert control over the populace. In Haiti, the ISA of the zombie threat can be seen working on political, social, and economic levels.

Eagleton proposes a broad definition of ideology as "a kind of intersection between belief systems and political power."[83] This very juxtaposition of the zombie mythology with both public and private life can be readily found in Haitian society. For instance, after Seabrook had his own first-hand encounter with a zombie, he sought a scientific explanation for the phenomenon from one Dr. Antoine Villiers. Although Seabrook presents Villiers as a rational man of science, the doctor admits there might be some truth to the zombie legends. As proof, he draws Seabrook's attention to Article 249 of the Haitian *Code Pénal* (Criminal Code):

> Also shall be qualified as attempted murder the employment which may be made against any person of substances which, without causing actual death, produce a lethargic coma more or less prolonged. If, after the administering of such substances, the person has been buried, the act shall be considered murder no matter what result follows.[84]

The mere presence of this law shows how ingrained the belief in zombification is in the minds of Haitians, regardless of the veracity of the legends; clearly enough such attempts were made to warrant preventative legislation. By supporting a law whose language can only sustain the perpetuation of the myth, the Haitian government actively encourages and maintains the fears associated with zombification.

The open acknowledgement of the zombie ritual by the Haitian legal system, if not the supernatural causes and effects, fuels the country's paranoia, and this fear becomes manifest in the daily life and rituals of the people. Polynice insists that zombies are real, and he tells Seabrook the practice is allowed to continued out of fear: "We know about them, but we do not dare to interfere so long as our own dead are left unmolested."[85] When it comes to zombies and the threat of zombification, people become understandably selfish. Hurston illustrates how people will try to prevent the zombification of their friends and loved ones. Embalming is, of course, the most sure-fire prevention, but as the practice is not common among the poor, more radical steps are necessary. For instance, family members will watch the gravesite for thirty-six hours, cut the body open before burial, or inject powerful poisons directly into the heart of the corpse.[86] Of course, in the case of a coma or other misdiagnosed death-like states, such precautions have deadly consequences.

Yet the zombie myth is not maintained merely to control or subjugate the masses; even the educated and upper classes are wary of vengeful *Bocors* and the potential risk of zombification, thus allowing the ISA to *combat* oppression as well. Hurston emphasizes how the paranoia is not limited to the poor or peasant class; the elite of Haiti fear zombification as well — perhaps more so, for they have more to lose:

> The upper class Haitians fear too, but they do not talk about it so openly as do the poor. But to them it is a horrible possibility.... It is not good for a person who has lived all his life surrounded by a degree of fastidious culture, loved to his last breath by family and friends, to contemplate the probability of his resurrected body being dragged from the vault — the best that love and means could provide, and set to toiling ceaselessly in the banana fields, working like a beast, unclothed like a beast, and like a brute crouching in some foul den in the few hours allowed for rest and food. From an educated, intelligent being to an unthinking, unknowing beast.[87]

For the elite classes, the threat of zombification poses a potential assault on their very way of life, challenging the social and class system they enjoy. For the wealthy and affluent, nothing could be worse than a half-life of toil and labor alongside the peasants. In fact, the initial series of zombie films produced by Hollywood prey upon this very fear: the fear that the imperialists will become the slaves of their own colonized people.

In an ethnographic study, Michael T. Taussig exposes how a folkloristic mythology can relate to and function within the capitalist economic framework of a postcolonial society. In his book *The Devil and Commodity Fetishism in South America* (1980), Taussig documents a hybridized native mythology similar to the one found in Haiti. During a four-year visit to Colombia, Taussig uncovered a local religion that has turned out to be "a dynamic complex of collective representations — dynamic because it reflects the dialectical interplay of attribution and counterattribution that the distinct groups and classes impose on each other."[88] As happened in Haiti, the religion practiced by the native, peasant classes of Colombia stemmed from a blending of the pagan deities of the original, indigenous population with the concept of the Christian devil brought by European imperialist.[89] The resulting belief system encourages a cultural practice in which workers make contracts with the devil to increase their productivity.[90] According to Taussig's research, male sugarcane laborers secretly meet with a devilish sorcerer to create a *muñeco* (an analogue to the Haitian voodoo doll), which is subsequently ensorcelled and hidden in the cane fields. The worker then believes he will enjoy greater production without having to work any harder than normal. The belief is so strong that laborers become unproductive, relying on the power of their *muñecos* to do their jobs for them, and supervisors and administrators must be on the constant lookout for any such dolls hidden in their fields.[91]

A similar intersection between folk superstitions and capitalist economics occurs in Haiti as well. Since zombies are, by definition, the cheapest of slave laborers, their existence — or at the very least, the *belief* in their existence — perpetuates and supports the economic ideological apparatus. Métraux emphasizes that, for the people of Haiti, there was always an implied cause-and-effect relationship between "sorcery and success."[92] Those who practice the ancient voodoo rites and have access to the blessings of the *loa* enjoy more success. Hurston emphasizes this connection as well, for many Haitian peasants, she says, told her about individuals who would willingly make grave pacts with local *Bocors* to insure financial prosperity. Like the peasants in Taussig's Colombia, desperate Haitians would broker deals with powerful priests, exchanging the souls of their loved ones for prosperity. The downside of such Faustian bargains was the eventual conversion of their sacrificed family members (and ultimately themselves) to zombies.[93] These legends and folk tales emphasize the relationship between zombies and the proletariat, whether those who create zombies prosper by supernatural means or by the direct labor of the zombies themselves.

The peasant class of Haiti consists largely of physical laborers, and the zombie represents the ultimate manifestation of such strenuous toil. If the propagated myth has any basis in truth, the zombie is therefore a worker who struggles all day for no recompense, blindly and loyally serving those who have either created it or purchased it. No average employee, or honest landowner, could possibly compete with such a workforce; for that reason, the threat of the zombie contributes indirectly to the economic system as well. Those who fail to produce or show results run the risk of being replaced by (or worse, turned into) cheaper zombie workers. This macabre labor structure illustrates Althusser's claim that "all ideological State apparatuses, whatever they are, contribute to the same result: the reproduction of the relations of production."[94] The poor, proletariat workers must either labor *like* zombies or run the risk of *becoming* zombies. Thus this monster becomes the most

The maniacal *Bocor* Gaston (Badja Djola) threatens to execute the heroine Marielle (Cathy Tyson) in Craven's *The Serpent and the Rainbow* (Universal Pictures, 1988; Jerry Ohlinger).

literal of postcolonial allegories. As I will discuss in more detail in Chapter 2, the zombie ideologically (and physically) represents the ultimate slave: unthinking, unspeaking, and lacking in all forms of inner will and autonomy.

A distinct connection clearly exists between the creation of zombies and the need to excel at agricultural production, yet Ackermann and Gauthier question the logic of this motivation, for physical labor has always been relatively cheap in Haiti. Instead, they side with Davis in his explanation of the cause for zombification, seeing it as a punishment meted out to those who are socially undesirable, heinous criminals, or offenders of the local *Bocor*.[95] This suspicion is supported by Hurston as well, who describes how zombies are often needed for more than merely work and are employed to be thieves or to threaten others to take some action.[96] In this regard, zombies become a more literal sign of one's social and cultural power. Eagleton emphasizes how ideology is not merely linked to a particular belief-system but to the question of power. More specifically, he emphasizes how ideology "has to do with *legitimating* the power of a dominant social group or class."[97] In Haiti, the dominant social class is not necessarily the established central government but rather the regional authorities and, most importantly, the leaders of voodoo cells and secret societies throughout the population.

In his search for the elusive zombie powder, Davis made contact with numerous voodoo priests and organizations. Along the way, he uncovered a complex system of *Bizango*, secret voodoo societies possessing their own organizational hierarchies, leadership, and judicial systems. Davis recounts his experiences with these "shadow governments" in *The Serpent and the Rainbow*, showing numerous times how control of voodoo ritual and, more importantly, punishment remained in the hands of these secret societies. Davis says it this way:

> I knew from my own research that in at least some instances the zombi powder was controlled by the secret societies, and a knowledge of poisons and their complex pharmacological properties could be traced in direct lineage ... to the secret societies of Africa. There was no doubt that poisons were used in West Africa by judicial bodies to punish those who broke the codes of the society.[98]

Davis cites Hurston's experiences as well, for she too had encountered underground organizations that enjoyed the power to judge members of the voodoo community and impose punishment as they saw fit.[99]

Davis's investigation consequently led him to a meeting with Jean-Jacques Leophin, a powerful figure and president of one of the five major *Bizangos* of Haiti. Davis there learned that the *Bizango* can be traced back to the days of the revolution and to the pre-revolutionary leaders of the rebellious Maroon bands.[100] According to Leophin's testimony, the *Bizango* exist to protect the people and to enact judgment against those who have committed crimes against members of the society. Those found guilty of violating one of the seven transgressions are properly punished; specifically, the guilty party can be sold to the society.[101] In addition, the official government works with the *Bizango* and must respect their regional authority: "The people in the government in Port-au-Prince must cooperate with us," Leophin claims. "We were here before them, and if we didn't want them, they wouldn't be where they are."[102] The *Bizango* societies clearly possess enough power and authority to keep those within their jurisdiction in line. Because of the pervasive cultural memory Haitians have of being a literally enslaved people, the threat of being made a zombie (i.e., "sold" into an even more repressive form of slavery) is generally enough to deter any upstart.

Whether the zombie mythology of Haiti is grounded in an actual voodoo practice or merely the rumor of such a possibility, the legend has a great deal of ideological power. The poor and wealthy alike possess a healthy fear of the folk tales, recognizing that it is better to be cautious and open-minded than the victim of such a punishment. The ideology of the zombie — or, more specifically, the threat of zombification — represents a pervasive and repressive ideological apparatus present in the legal system, the vernacular religious practices, and the agrarian economic structure of Haiti. Most importantly, the zombie is a folkloristic manifestation of a colonial or postcolonial society's greatest fear: subjugation, marginalization, and enslavement. Once travelers from the United States became aware of the folk tales and local legends, it was only a matter of a few years before the mythology was appropriated by the Hollywood entertainment industry. The creature that had been used for generations to terrify and subjugate the Haitian people was ready to scare a completely new population, and although many of the themes would remain the same, the Americanized zombie would become a decidedly different figure in the end.

Zombies "Invade" the United States

The very concept of the voodoo zombie, and, perhaps more importantly, the process of zombification itself, functions in Haiti as a repressive ideological apparatus primarily because of the fear it instills in the faithful peasantry. Because of both their hybridized belief system and their cultural history of imperial repression and enslavement, native Haitians readily fear zombie mythology and folklore, seeing it as both the potential return to slavery and as a violation of the Christian ideal of personal agency. That this cultural mythology would prove similarly terrifying in the United States and to a

Hollywood film audience should come as no surprise. On the one hand, the United States was once a colonial entity itself, now an autonomous country that cherishes freedom and equality above all else. On the other hand, slavery had been an essential part of the United States economic and social system for many years, and the wounds of the Civil War and a largely failed attempt at reconstruction would have still been fresh and sensitive at the beginning of the twentieth century. Like the imperialist forces who feared most the uprising of their repressed colonials, the mainstream public in the United States — especially the *white* mainstream public — would find the enslavement of white Christians by dark-skinned natives extremely abhorrent. Furthermore, because the victims of voodoo sorcery are most often female in these early, largely racist narratives, tales of the zombie would prey upon deep-seated social paranoia. In other words, a kind of collective social guilt, along with cherished national and religious tenets and racial- and gender-based fears, paved the way for zombies to "invade" the United States in the form of ethnographic accounts, literary narratives, and, eventually, feature films.

Not surprisingly, nonfictional accounts of voodoo practices and zombification, as we have seen, constitute the initial literary documentation of Haitian folklore by European and American scholars. According to both Rhodes and Métraux, the first detailed description of Haiti written for a Western audience was *Sketches of Hayti: From the Expulsion of the French to the Death of Christophe* by W. W. Harvey. This 1827 text presents a rather negative account of the perceived "savagery" of the rebellion of 1804 but does not directly discuss the presence of voodoo and pagan ritual practices. The first major American writer to examine Haiti was Spenser St. John, whose 1884 *Hayti; or, The Black Republic* is even harsher than Harvey's account, emphasizing the savagery of both voodooism and cannibalism.[103] In fact, most nineteenth-century literary documents concerning Haiti are decidedly negative and one sided, focusing on primitive and taboo behavior; it wasn't until 1907 that a sympathetic text, *Haiti: Her History and Her Detractors*, was published by J. N. Léger. Léger's book champions voodoo as an important social and cultural ritual, helping to define the people of Haiti in terms of their African heritage and traditions.[104]

Of greater interest to the narratological investigation of the zombie itself might be what results from etymological tracking of the term *zombie*. According to Patrick Polk, lecturer in world arts and culture at UCLA, the first use of the term *zombi* by a European occurred in the 1697 play *Le Zombi du Grand Pérou de La Comtesse de Coragne* by Pierre-Corneille Blessebois.[105] Rhodes, however, claims the first recorded use of the word *zombie* in print did not appear until 1792 in a text by Frenchman Moreau de Saint-Méry, who defines it as a "Creole word that means spirit, revenant."[106] However, the term was more often used in the 1800s to describe the voodoo snake god or to refer to the Haitian revolutionary Jean Zombi.[107] It was not until 1912 that the word *zombie* became associated with the living dead; an essay by Judge Henry Austin in *New England Magazine* refers to a Haitian poison that causes a comatose state in a victim that could be mistaken for death.[108] Also in 1912, Stephen Bonsal published *The American Mediterranean*, which documents the account of a Haitian man who was found tied to a tree in a zombie state days after his confirmed death and burial.[109] Nevertheless, although these two sources make reference to the condition of the living dead, it took Seabrook's 1929 travelogue *The Magic Island* to link the phenomenon directly with the term *zombie*.

Rhodes also mentions a number of fictional predecessors to Halperin's 1932 film *White Zombie*, most of which emphasize voodooism in general rather than zombiism in particular. According to Rhodes, one of the first works of fiction in English to address the subject of voodoo is Captain Mayne Reid's *The Maroon: A Tale of Voodoo and Obeah* (1883). This novel, set on a Jamaican sugar plantation, features an *Obeah* witch doctor — *Obeah* referring to the specific form of voodoo folk magic practiced in Jamaica — who brings his *own* corpse back from the dead. Although the term *zombie* is absent from the text, Reid does combine the notion of the "living dead" with voodooism.[110] The

Another image from *The Serpent and the Rainbow*, this one, showing Christophe (Conrad Roberts) and the skeletal remains of an old crone, illustrates the sensationalism Hollywood would impart to the folklore of Haiti (Universal Pictures, 1988; Jerry Ohlinger).

first major English play to exploit the exoticism of voodoo is Henry Francis Downing's *Voodoo* (1914), which concerns English Barbados in the late 1600s and features the first use of a voodoo chant, which is later featured prominently in Alice Calland's poem "Voodoo" of 1926.[111] Voodoo officially came to the United States with Natalie Vivian Scott's play *Zombi*, produced the same year Seabrook's book was published. Set in New Orleans, the play features the character of Marie Laveau but uses *zombi* as a reference to voodoo in general, not the reanimated dead.[112] Artistic experiments with voodoo narratives were not limited to literature, however; Walter Futter was the first filmmaker to experiment with the visual allure of zombies, producing a short film called *Curiosities* in 1931. A brief segment of this film shows "corpses being taken from the graves and prodded into life" to work in the rice fields.[113]

In spite of all these earlier ethnographic, non-fictional, and fictional accounts of Haiti, voodoo, and zombiism, though, it was Seabrook's travelogue that galvanized authors and artists to produce narratives focusing directly on the living dead. In 1932, three disparate fictional tales of voodoo and zombies came out almost simultaneously — a novel, a play, and a film. First, H. Bedford-Jones published *Drums of Damballa*, a novel that focuses primarily on the atrocities of voodooism but also features a detailed description of a zombie encounter that is reminiscent of *The Magic Island*. The book is surprisingly detailed and true to Haitian folklore, more so than any fictional text appearing prior to 1932.[114] The second major fictional piece produced in 1932 is Kenneth Webb's play *Zombie*. Rhodes claims its production must have followed the publication of Seabrook's book, for the play clearly shows its predecessor's influence. Although the play failed miserably in New York, it signifies an important landmark in the development of zombie narratives; for the first time, audiences actually saw zombies lumbering across the stage in the half-live, half-dead fashion that has come to be so essential to visual depictions of the walking dead.[115] Perhaps even more importantly, Webb's insistence on exhibiting this play sporadically across the United States brought it ultimately to Hollywood and the certain attention of the film production team of Victor and Edward Halperin.

I will discuss the Halperins' landmark film *White Zombie* in detail in the following chapter, but it must be noted, given all that we have just seen, how this transition of the zombie phenomenon from a creature of folkloristic ethnography to commodified Hollywood movie icon marked the shift the zombie went through from *folklore* to *folklorism* or "fakelore."[116] According to Hans Moser, *folklorism* describes "secondhand folklore," cultural artifacts that have been alienated from their true source. This adulteration occurs primarily when traditional performances take place "outside that culture's local or class community" or when folk motifs are playfully imitated by other social strata.[117] Although folklorism has occurred in the past between social classes, Moser emphasizes how it can occur most alarmingly in modern times when folklorism is "primarily commercially determined and deeply anchored in the tourism and entertainment industries."[118] The cooption of the zombie by Hollywood manifests what Métraux calls "the shameless prostitution of religion,"[119] casting the sacred (if terrifying) tenets of the Vodoun religion as a matter for tourism and exploitation. This shift away from the true antecedent of the zombie creates a disturbing parallel between the entertainment industry and colonial imperialism, a shift that becomes all too important when the voodoo-themed zombie films of the 1930s and '40s are examined through the critical lens of postcolonial theory.

Furthermore, Toelken makes a helpful parallel between folklore and biology, emphasizing how "variation affects every sort of characteristic, structural or functional, and occurs at every stage of life, in animal and plant life as in tradition."[120] The folklore of the zombie has experienced this variation not only within its own folk group but also, more pervasively, outside it. With the appropriation of the zombie into American popular culture, the film industry has created a new kind of "lore." Moreover, as the following chapters will show, that folklore is constantly growing and expanding, following Toelken's twin laws of conservatism and dynamism, as different filmmakers try both to preserve and to reinvent the zombie narrative. Filmmakers may have begun with the voodoo zombie in the initial years of the subgenre, but as the first decade of the twenty-first century has proven, the variations possible within the lore of the zombie are almost limitless. Even modern and contemporary zombie narratives must therefore be viewed as examples of folklore — be they examples of folklorismus or "fakelore" — because, as Richard M. Dorson sees it, folklore is a contemporary subject: "Mass culture uses folk culture. Folk culture mutates in a world of technology."[121]

By these means, then, the exotic and mysterious rituals and religious beliefs of voodoo were eventually discovered by the movie studios of the United States, and the conversion of the zombie from revered folklore to popular entertainment was inevitable and swift. Although the zombie began its methodical invasion of the United States through ethnographic and other nonfictional writings, other more sensational documents soon paved the way for exploitive Gothic narratives on both stage and screen. Essentially, Hollywood filmmakers immediately divorced the zombie from its religious and cultural roots the moment they appropriated the creature for mainstream entertainment. Nevertheless, many of the ties between the zombie and its ethnographic origins remain in the myriad of film variations that have arisen over the past century, and the next chapter will explore the postcolonial ramifications of such ongoing cultural connections.

Chapter 2

THE RETURN OF THE NATIVE
Imperialist Hegemony and
the Cinematic Voodoo Zombie

You don't think she's alive — in the hands of natives?
Better dead than that! — Neil, *White Zombie*

With the popular success of the first talkie horror films, Hollywood of the 1930s was anxious to find the next big-screen monster. As I have shown, the creative efforts of visionary filmmakers led them not only to the usual mythologies of Europe but also to exotic Caribbean travel literature. Sensational non-fiction books, such as Seabrook's *The Magic Island*, had begun to draw the American public's attention away from the Old World and towards the New, specifically to the island of Haiti and the exoticisms of the West Indies. Mainstream Americans were becoming increasingly aware of voodoo, African mysticism and ritual, and the legends about native priests who were able to kill their enemies and bring them back from the dead as mindless servants — the so-called *corps cadavres*, also known as the "walking dead."[1] This violation of the taboos of death piqued people's interest in what had been a previously unknown horror: the zombie. It didn't take long for this Caribbean monstrosity to make the jump from folklore to popular entertainment, with the first true zombie movie arriving in 1932 with Halperin's *White Zombie*. Loosely inspired by both Seabrook's travelogue and Webb's lackluster play *Zombie*,[2] and based on the stylistic model of Browning's *Dracula*, this germinal film presented audiences with the exoticism of the Caribbean, a fear of domination and subversion, and the perpetuation of the imperialist model of cultural and racial hegemony.

Although zombies would have to wait for Romero's *Night of the Living Dead* to reach the level of the bankable franchise — such as Dracula, Frankenstein's monster, and the Wolf Man — Rhodes insists "*White Zombie* had achieved enough success in 1932 to significantly impact the evolution of the horror film cycle."[3] Hoping to repeat Halperin's unexpected $8 million gross at the box office,[4] other filmmakers attempted to capitalize on the voodoo zombie in a number of moderately successful horror films such as *Ouanga, Revolt of the Zombies* (1936), *King of the Zombies* (1941), *I Walked with a Zombie, Zombies of Mora-Tau* (1957), and *The Plague of the Zombies* (1966). During the atomic age of the 1950s, zombies also appeared in Hollywood via such science fiction narratives as *Creature with the Atom Brain* (1955), *Invasion of the Body Snatchers*, the infamous *Plan 9 from Outer Space* (1959), *Invisible Invaders*, and *The Earth Dies Screaming*. Of all these representative films, Val Lewton's *I Walked with a Zombie* enjoyed perhaps the most critical attention and success, mostly because of its cinematic quality — thanks primarily to the direction of Tourneur — and the story's loose but undeniable connections to the literary tradition via Charlotte Brontë's *Jane Eyre* (1847). Jamie Russell succinctly sums up the cultural impact of this later film: "Lyrical, creepy and thoroughly unsettling, *I Walked with a Zombie* single-handedly thrust the living dead into the canon of critically acclaimed cinema."[5]

White Zombie and *I Walked with a Zombie* both use the exotic setting of the postcolonial Caribbean to entrance eager viewers, while accentuating the prevailing stereotypes of the "backwards" natives and Western imperialist superiority. In fact, *White Zombie* anticipates the socio-political theories and criticisms of Césaire, Fanon, and Said, emphasizing a type of Hegelian master/slave dialectic as well as the dominance of one culture (embodied in the voodoo master) over another (that of the zombie slaves). However, casting the natives in the position of power over their peers allows *White Zombie* to present a more complicated view of a postcolonial society, one in which the Western model of colonial imperialism has been adopted by the new nation's cultural apparatus. In this light, the film may also be critiqued as cultural discourse through the theoretical lens of Spivak, for the new "sub-subaltern" class of the zombie is literally silent, enslaved, and unable to connect with the dominant culture through any liminal space of discourse. Tourneur's film, on the other hand, is far less stereotypical in its presentation of native, black culture; Gwenda Young asserts that unlike *White Zombie*, *I Walked with a Zombie* "does not patronize its audience. Voodoo is not reduced to 'mumbo-jumbo' superstition, its practitioners are not portrayed as evil or childlike. The realism with which voodoo is portrayed encourages the audience to keep an open mind."[6] In other words, *I Walked with a Zombie* treats its subject almost in the manner of an ethnographic documentary, albeit a somewhat moody and melodramatic one.

Of course, for a Western, white audience, the real threat and source of terror in these early, voodoo-themed zombie films are not the political vagaries of postcolonial nations, the plights of enslaved native zombies, or even the dangers posed by menacing armies of the walking dead, but rather the risk that the white protagonists — especially the *female* protagonists — might be turned into zombies (i.e., slaves) themselves. In other words, the true horror in these movies lies in the prospect of a Westerner becoming dominated, subjugated, symbolically raped, and effectively "colonized" by pagan representatives. This new fear — one larger than merely death itself— allowed the voodoo zombie to challenge the pantheon of cinematic monsters from Europe, becoming the first thoroughly postcolonial creature from the New World to appear in popular horror movies.[7] Yet, in spite of recent critical acclaim from film scholars such as Rhodes, *White Zombie* remains a fundamentally negative portrayal of race differences and class struggle; the movie ultimately re-presents negative stereotypes of the native by propagating the imperialist paradigms of the West. *I Walked with a Zombie*, on the other hand, manages to demonstrate a rather evenhanded treatment of Caribbean and voodoo culture; however, even though it does attempt to present the realities of Haitian culture through a less racist lens than *White Zombie*, Tourneur's film nonetheless exploits racial and cultural difference to instill its audience with the terrors of a misunderstood and menacing (post)colonial Other.

The Zombie as Exotic, Postcolonial Terror

Because the very concept of the "walking dead" originated in Caribbean cultures that were once the colonies of imperialist nations, films that explore voodoo in general and zombies in particular need to be considered as examples of racial exploitation and romanticization, and they must also be investigated from a postcolonial theoretical perspective. On the one hand, Hollywood filmmakers likely found the exotic locales of such narratives appealing for a number of reasons: the Caribbean not only provided viewers with a romantic landscape — exotic, yes, but closer to home than the craggy peaks and ancient ruins of Europe — but also confronted them with eroticized black characters who challenged social and sexual taboos. Furthermore, the United States could vicariously sample the pleasures of colonization and imperialist exploitation that, as a nation, it had essentially been denied. On the other hand, such films as *White Zombie* and *I Walked with a Zombie* must also be seen fundamentally as manifestations of the complex relationships between masters and slaves and the tensions that exist between both races and genders. In effect, the Caribbean, like other colonial regions, represents a dialectical, liminal space, and zombies literalize the tensions that remain from such imperialist histories because they represent enslavement at its most basic levels. Zombies, in other words, are the ideal "New World" terror because of their essential ties to imperialist hegemony and oppression.

Edna Aizenberg approaches the zombie as "an example of the trope of hybridity through which we can enjoy postcolonialism's pleasures, explore its perils, and create a more precise, newer, critical model."[8] She recognizes how, in addition to the featured monster's originality, the popularity and success of the voodoo zombie movie can largely be linked to its implicit dangers and exoticism. Western people, particularly at the turn of the century, were becoming more acquainted with and fascinated by primitive cultures. Brett A. Berliner pursues the reasons behind this interest in the exotic in his 2002 book *Ambivalent Desire*. Although he focuses his study on the French obsession with Africa in the 1920s, his understanding of *exoticism* clearly applies to Americans' perception of the Caribbean in the 1930s. Berliner links exoticism with escapism, defining the *exotic* as being "constructed as a distant, picturesque other that evokes feelings, emotions, and ideals in the self that have been considered lost in the civilizing process."[9] He also emphasizes how travel literature, a fundamentally exotic genre, established the mythology of the "noble savage" in the minds of Western readers[10]; how the French of the 1920s began to see the black natives of Africa as mysterious, unusual, and entertaining; and how "some metropolitans traveled in search of ethno-erotic adventure, and many discovered beauty in the black body."[11] On a basic level, then, intellectual Westerners wanted an escape from their own hectic, "modern" lives and looked to native cultures to recapture the (perceived) simplicities of the past.

This obsession with the exotic and markedly different Other also carries with it a fascination with sexual difference, especially in regards to black (male) virility and white (female) vulnerability. Miscegenation was an established social taboo during the 1930s and '40s, and Aizenberg emphasizes how the Caribbean became a channel through which sexually curious North Americans could "project their fantasies and insecurities, the id forces of the libidinous, irrational, violent, dangerous, and, yes, miscegenated, intermingled, or hybrid."[12] In fact, most early ethnographic accounts of Caribbean voodoo and zombiism focus on the enslavement of a woman, from Seabrook's to Hurston's to Métraux's.[13] According to Lizabeth Paravisini-Gebert,

> The various versions of the story of Marie M's zombification [such as Hurston's] posit sexual desire — the erotic — as a fundamental component of the zombified woman's tale, hinting at, although never directly addressing, the urge to transcend or subvert race and class barriers as one of the repositories of the sorcerer's lust.... The underlying truth behind this tale is that victim and victimizer are separated by insurmountable race and class obstacles that would have precluded a legitimate union even if the victim had not been physically revolted by the victimizer, as she often is; her social inaccessibility lies at the heart of her heinous zombification.[14]

Zombification, therefore, addresses and challenges the sexual constraints imposed by social or cultural difference by violating the taboos of racial miscegenation as well.

Voodoo zombie movies not only exploit the exoticism of black natives,[15] both physically and sexually, but also take advantage of the popular tendency to romanticize ancient lands, imposing castles, and mysterious figures. The tone and style of most early zombie movies echo the Gothic stylization of films such as Browning's *Dracula* and Whale's *Frankenstein*—yet the tales told by *White Zombie* and *I Walked with a Zombie* take place a lot closer to home for North American audiences. Although all the action occurs in the Caribbean rather than on United States soil, these films are certainly more a part of the New World than those set in Romania, Eastern Europe, or even England. In a way, voodoo-themed horror movies represent the "West's East." That is, for many in the United States, Africa, India, and Asia were locations too remote to seem tangible; they represented the colonies of European empires and existed on the other side of the globe. Caribbean lands, however, were more local and "real," providing North Americans conceptually

Movies such as Jean Yarbrough's *King of the Zombies* capitalized on Caribbean exoticism and voodoo ritual, as in this scene featuring the ensorcelled Barbara (Joan Woodbury), Mac (Dick Purcell), and Admiral Wainwright (Guy Usher) (Monogram Pictures Corporation, 1941; Jerry Ohlinger).

accessible "primitive" countries and mysterious "native" peoples. Of course, zombie movies invariably function as horror-inducing narratives because of the presence of the zombies themselves. Unlike modern zombie movies such as those created by Romero, the fear incited by these early films comes from being turned into a zombie rather than being killed by one.[16] The central horrific feature is therefore the loss of autonomy and control—having one's will stripped to become a slave of a native (i.e., black), pagan authority.

Aizenberg emphasizes how "Hollywood's zombie is thoroughly enclosed within a colonialist discourse that usurps history and identity. Here, hybridity menaces, unmasking the fear of black and white intermingling, the terror of black (male) bodies dominating whites."[17] In other words, unlike most movie monsters of the 1930s and '40s, the zombie was sired directly by the imperialist system and was so effectively frightening to viewers because of its direct ties to the racial dichotomies of colonialism. As we have seen, creatures such as Dracula, Frankenstein's golem, and the werewolf were primarily European constructs, born of diverse Western mythologies and ethnic folklore. The zombie, on the other hand, was a new monster for a new world — it was discovered in the actual contemporary religious practices and daily folklife of colonized and postcolonial societies in Haiti and on other islands in the Caribbean. For the local populations of these "exotic" islands, zombies were more than just escapist entertainment and fantasy; they were a real part of life and an actual potentiality. Furthermore, the zombie was an ideological manifestation of the social and political superstructure in these newly liberated colonies, using fear to encourage hard work and subservience. When the Western cinematic versions of these folkloric creatures are examined, zombies may be recognized as a metaphorical manifestation of the Hegelian master/slave relationship and the negative dichotomous social structure of colonialism.

Dayan's discussion of Haitian zombie folklore makes it clear why voodoo in general and zombiism in particular must be examined through the theoretical lens of postcolonialism. Although the original term *zombi* was a Creole word for "spirit," in voodoo culture it ironically refers to someone *lacking* a soul.[18] Anthropologist Melville Herskovits claims how, in Dahomean legend, zombies were creatures without souls, beings "whose death was not real but resulted from the machinations of sorcerers who made them appear as dead, and then, when buried, removed them from their grave and sold them into servitude in some far-away land."[19] Dayan emphasizes how no supernatural fate could echo the realities of slavery more, for "the phantasm of the zombi — a soulless husk deprived of freedom — is the ultimate sign of loss and dispossession." Zombification results in the total capitulation of autonomy, making it the most feared threat to the Haitian folk; becoming a zombie (either by having a sorcerer steal one's spirit or by turning one into the "living dead") is the "most powerful emblem of apathy, anonymity, and loss." Dayan ultimately succeeds in tying the history of Haiti with the mythology of the zombie: "Born out of the experience of slavery, the sea passage from Africa to the New World, and revolution on the soil of Saint-Dominque, the zombi tells the story of colonization."[20]

By presenting the zombies as a marked "Other" vis-à-vis the human protagonists, movies such as *White Zombie* literally manifest G. F. W. Hegel's master/slave dialectic.[21] According to Hegel, the dialectical relationship between a master and his slaves is grounded in the need for recognition and self-consciousness — and this interaction must occur on both sides. Fanon makes the distinction between Hegel's dialectic and an actual master/slave relationship clear:

> At the foundation of Hegelian dialectic there is an absolute reciprocity which must be emphasized. It is in the degree to which I go beyond my own immediate being that I apprehend the existence of the other as a natural and more than natural reality. If I close the circuit, if I prevent the accomplishment of movement in two directions, I keep the other within himself.[22]

According to Fanon's critique, this reciprocity is missing in the real-life relationship between a master and a slave, for "the master laughs at the consciousness of the slave. What he wants from the slave is not recognition but work."[23] Because Fanon's Negro wants to become like the master, he is "less independent than the Hegelian slave. ... [turning] toward the master and abandon[ing] the object."[24] Even less recognition and interaction occur between a voodoo master and his zombie slaves. Because zombies lack self-consciousness, autonomy, and even the desire for liberation, an inflexible relationship exists between them and all humans. In the voodoo priest/zombie relationship, the interaction is fundamentally one sided: the zombie lacks the intellectual capacity to recognize the master at all, firmly closing Fanon's circuit. Zombies thus represent an exaggerated model of colonial class/race segregation, for there is no possible dialectical model in such an exaggerated and literal master/slave relationship.

This loss of agency and the reinstitution of a system of domination is a cultural manifestation of the colonial politics criticized by Césaire. According to his ruminations in *Discourse on Colonialism* (1950), the system of imperialism leads to the perception of other humans as animals, what Césaire calls the "boomerang effect of colonization."[25] By embracing an ideology of superiority, colonization encourages not human contact but rather the "relations of domination and submission"; in other words, colonization means "thingification"[26]; or, as René Depestre insists, "The history of colonization is the process of man's general zombification."[27] Such declarations clearly apply to the zombie mythology, wherein human individuals are reduced to beasts of burden, dumb animals incapable of any real human contact or discourse.[28] In fact, the zombie represents the ultimate imperialist dream — a slave laborer that is truly a thing, unthinking, un-aspiring, and non-threatening. Césaire continues with a more far-reaching critique of the West, for he sees all postcolonial barbarism as being tied to the bourgeois class.[29] The result is the exploitation of the proletariat worker, and the zombies in films such as *White Zombie* are the ultimate manifestation of the subservient working class.

The zombies are not only subservient due to their lack of will and autonomy; they also lack the power of speech. This characteristic leads one naturally to Spivak and her essay "Can the Subaltern Speak?" (1988). In her detailed analysis of the subordination of women in subaltern cultures, Spivak presents the colonial social hierarchy (specifically of India) as outlined originally by Ranajit Guha:

1. Dominant foreign groups
2. Dominant indigenous groups....
3. Dominant indigenous groups at the regional and local levels.
4. The ... "people" and "subaltern classes."[30]

In Spivak's critique, women and slaves constitute a social level beneath the lowest group, creating a fifth level that is doubly subordinated. This group is generally ignored and marginalized by not only the dominant foreign (i.e., white) class but also their own indigenous (i.e., native) populace. Spivak's primary interest lies in issues of (re)presentation, and the purpose of her investigation is to find ways of recognizing how members of the subalternized classes communicate. Although the subaltern are "silent" in terms of official politics and culture, they do have the ability to talk with each other, which can potentially result in organization and revolution. The subaltern thus constitutes a potential threat to the imperialist powers, not merely a marginalized group worthy of intellectual study.

Spivak's critique of the colonial class system can be related to the social system of the zombie narrative as well. When the same hierarchy is applied to movies such as *White Zombie* and *I Walked with a Zombie*, the essentially mindless creatures are seen to constitute a sixth level — what I call the "sub-subaltern" class — below that of indigenous women and (living) slaves. They are subordinated for two reasons: (1) the master has no responsibilities towards a group of automatons that requires little food, no pay, and no time off, and (2) the zombies have no voice, no opinions, no consciousness, and (most importantly) no ability to organize (although they do appear threatening when they mass together, as they often do). Spivak's subalternized women *can* find a voice once they have an audience that is willing to listen; ethnographers can interview them, document their opinions and ideas, and re-present them to the Western world. Zombies, however, have no such audience and no such ability; in fact, they have no opinions, ideas, or even voices with which to speak. Instead, such unnatural slaves are completely and thoroughly dominated by those who create and command them — they are almost literally tools of labor with no conscious mind or autonomy. Thus, the sub-subaltern differs from Spivak's conception in kind and not just degree. They are truly "other" both because of their fundamental lack of "humanity" and because their physical appearance, their "stain" of the human, makes them decidedly uncanny.[31]

Hegel's dialectic does become useful, however, when examining the voodoo and imperialist origins of the zombie mythology. In his interview with Bing, Métraux defined *voodoo* as "a syncretic religion that has blended together not only different African cults but also certain beliefs from European folklore."[32] Thus the invention of the zombie is a direct consequence of imperialism and cultural synthesis — the natives of French West Africa and emancipated slaves from the United States were relocated to the West Indies (and Haiti in particular) where their tribal beliefs were "integrated" with Western Christian ideology. In other words, a literal manifestation of Hegel's dialectic resulted from the merging of the slaves' pagan heritage with the Christian religion of their masters. The synthesized outcome is a hybridized form of Western voodoo mysticism, where natives offer food and wine to statues of the Virgin Mary, pray to their dead family members for guidance and protection, and hire priests and witch doctors to carve voodoo dolls of their enemies, and, most importantly, where supernatural creatures such as the zombie metaphorically represent (and literally recreate) the colonial experience. The only real dialectic at work in the Caribbean, therefore, is in the union of pagan with Christian beliefs — the ancient theological and ritual practices of Africa provided voodoo sorcerers the ability to turn people into zombies; the Christian belief system made the loss of agency and self-control all that more horrific.

Essentially, then, the creation and (mis)use of zombies is the perfect realization of the imperialist hegemonic model: those in power (or rather, those who *have* power, such as a voodoo priest) can enslave and conquer others; those "others" literally lose their language as well as their autonomy and become the ultimate iteration of a slave. Whereas colonial peoples were subjected to the control of their *imperialist* masters, the zombies must similarly do all commanded them by their *voodoo* masters. Therefore, on one level, the zombie provides the oppressed the opportunity to oppress, and Western civilization is thus threatened. Furthermore, making a zombie is a process of "uncivilization"; the creature, now othered in more than one sense, becomes subservient and marginalized — and unlike the educational and missionary efforts in most European colonies, there is no attempt made to civilize the zombies and improve their place in society. The horrors of imperialism thus made their way into North American popular culture via the voodoo zombie films of the 1930s and '40s. *White Zombie* demonstrates the cultural atrocities of the subaltern while illuminating the fear of imperialist whites vis-à-vis the native black (and erstwhile slave) population. *I Walked with a Zombie*, on the other hand, illustrates how the attempted usurpation of native culture by the imperialist whites leads to the subjugation of that improperly perceived superior culture by the (post)colonial one.

The Sub-Subaltern Monster and the Perpetuation of Imperialist Hegemony

Although the early texts about voodooism and Haiti (as discussed in Chapter 1) eventually led to a variety of voodoo-based zombie movies, Rhodes limits his critical investigation to *White Zombie*, written by Garnett Weston and directed by Victor Halperin. As the author of one of the first short stories about the walking dead, "Salt Is Not for Slaves" (1931), Weston was well equipped to adapt Seabrook's sensational accounts to the screen, creating a "carefully packaged piece of sensationalism, sex and the living dead."[33] In addition, the general structure of Halperin's film comes from fairy tales and Browning's *Dracula*; Rhodes presents a detailed comparison of the plot of *White Zombie* with that of *Dracula* to show how "its use of travel to a foreign land, its treatment of the hero and heroine, [and] its inclusion of a wise elder" parallel the earlier film precisely.[34] However, Rhodes also points out that the primary literary antecedents for *White Zombie* are Goethe's *Faust* (1808), George Du Maurier's *Trilby* (1894), and, of course, Seabrook's *The Magic Island*.[35] *White Zombie* features the virtually unknown zombie creature from Seabrook's accounts, but since the mystical details of the creature's construction were unknown (or at least undocumented) at the time, Weston and the Halperin brothers drew on the concept of hypnotism and mesmerism featured in Du Maurier's novel.[36] Through a method of synthesis, therefore, the filmmakers were able to invent a cinematic monster as yet unseen by Western audiences.[37]

The story of *White Zombie* is relatively straightforward, and its production style is essentially melodramatic and histrionic.[38] Although the actual time period of the film is unclear, dress and hairstyles imply the contemporary 1930s,[39] which would have been concurrent with the ending of the American

The scheming "Murder" Legendre (Bela Lugosi) uses a zombie (Frederick Peters) to threaten the butler Silver (Brandon Hurst) in Halperin's *White Zombie* (Edward Halperin Productions, 1932; Jerry Ohlinger).

occupation of Haiti. Close financial and social ties to the United States clearly continue to exist, for *White Zombie*'s protagonists are both Americans: a beautiful young woman named Madeleine Short (Madge Bellamy) has traveled to the island of Haiti to marry her fiancé Neil Parker (John Harron), who works at a bank in Port-au-Prince. While on the ship bringing her from the United States, Madeleine had met a wealthy French banker named Charles Beaumont (Robert Frazer), who had magnanimously offered not only his plantation mansion as the site of Madeleine's wedding, but also a job for Neil at the New York offices of Beaumont's bank. Madeleine was naturally overcome with gratitude, never suspecting Beaumont's designs to be anything more than they initially appear.

All of this backstory is revealed gradually through later dialogue; the film itself opens with Neil and Madeleine traveling the dark roads of rural Haiti in a horse-drawn carriage. On their way to the Beaumont estate, they must drive through a crowd of locals performing a mysterious funeral ritual; according to their coachman (Clarence Muse), the natives bury their dead in the middle of roads to prevent grave robbers from exhuming the corpses. Before the bewildered Americans can ask why, a number of shambling figures, harshly backlit and nondescript, are seen on the horizon, and the coachman drives the horses like a lunatic until they reach the safety of Beaumont's mansion. When confronted by an angry Neil, the coachman explains how it would have been better to die in a traffic accident than to be caught by the mysterious figures. He explains further, "They are not men ... they are dead bodies! ... Zombies! The living dead. Corpses taken from their graves who are made to work in the sugar mills in the fields at night."

Of course, the "enlightened" Westerners believe nothing of the local superstition; they are more interested in their impending nuptials — and in each other. They meet Dr. Bruner (Joseph Cawthorn), the local missionary contracted to perform their wedding, and Neil finally has the chance to meet Beaumont. Unlike Madeleine, Neil is suspicious of Beaumont, and he has good reason. The affluent Frenchman soon leaves his home to rendezvous with a mysterious figure named Murder Legendre, a native sugar cane plantation owner and witch doctor played by Béla Lugosi. Beaumont pleads with Legendre for a way to steal Madeleine away from Neil and make her his own, but the only solution the voodoo priest offers is a powder that will turn the hapless maiden into a zombie. Beaumont is initially horrified, but in his later desperation, he gives Madeleine a rose laced with the powder at her own wedding ceremony. At the following dinner celebration, Madeleine appears to die suddenly and is quickly entombed.

The rest of the plot unfolds quite rapidly. Neil, naturally, is distraught and goes on a drinking binge; Beaumont, on the other hand, has a change of heart, finding no comfort in the reanimated Madeleine's beauty when there are no sparks of a soul in her eyes. He begs Legendre to restore her to life, but the sinister voodoo master double crosses the Frenchman, administering him a dose of zombie powder so Legendre can have the "white zombie" all to himself. Meanwhile, Neil has discovered the disappearance of Madeleine's body and approaches Dr. Bruner for solace. The missionary explains that Neil's wife may not be dead at all — although the local natives believe the zombies to be reanimated corpses, the good doctor suspects they are merely the victims of coma-inducing poison.[40] Together they storm Legendre's fortress, defeating the evil witch doctor and restoring Madeleine to her former self.

Taken simply as an exploitative horror film designed to thrill the North American populace during the trials of the Great Depression, *White Zombie* lends itself to a relatively straightforward historical interpretation. Many moviegoers in the 1930s were likely suffering at sporadic, menial jobs or facing unemployment, and Halperin's stark depiction of mindless slave labor must have resonated with the beleaguered crowds. In other words, the zombie arrived in the United States at the most opportune of times, for, as Russell emphasizes, "a dead worker resurrected as a slave into a hellish afterlife of endless toil ... was the perfect monster for the age."[41] Legendre's soulless zombies shuffle sluggishly across the screen, trudging through the fields and performing required tasks in the sugar mill with mechanical repetition. These images, along with the horrific transformation of Madeleine herself, surely connected with viewers, as "everyone faced the awful possibility of joining the shuffling, blank-faced, down-and-outs waiting in line for bread and soup" in 1932.[42] Although initially unfamiliar to most North American viewers, the zombie would nonetheless have constituted a recognizable trope, as those watching White Zombie would have seen the horrific realities of their own economic situations mirrored in the monstrous screen metaphors.

However, the complex — if overly reductive — social system depicted in White Zombie does more sophisticated cultural work as well, closely resembling the postcolonial nationalism that Said warns of in Culture and Imperialism (1993). Said points out that "the national bourgeoisies and their specialized elites, of which Fanon speaks so ominously, in effect tended to replace the colonial force with a new class-based and ultimately exploitative one, which replicated the old colonial structures in new terms."[43] This scenario precisely describes Legendre's role in White Zombie: although the imperialist French and occupying Americans have left Haiti to its own rule and independence, a powerful voodoo priest has come to prominence and continues the same system of colonial domination towards others. The imperialist master has been reborn, although this time in the guise of a native — one who uses black magic and voodoo ritual to exceed the degree of control once practiced by the French or the Americans. Although Legendre has no official political power, the people fear him; he exercises authority over friend and foe alike by turning those around him into wholly subservient zombies.

The depicted social system of the film is, of course, economic as well as political, for the small cast of White Zombie each portray specific and exaggerated types of economically classed individuals. Beaumont, the French bank owner, is the representative of the wealthy, aristocratic class; furthermore, he is the symbol of former French colonial power. Neil is an American working for the financial system of Haiti; he typifies the bourgeois middle class. Legendre, on the other hand, owns a sugar mill and plantation; he represents a hybridized form of capitalism. Although Legendre stands in for the latent feudal system of the agrarian Haitian economy, a lord who oversees slave labor, he is also the factory owner, the new capitalist who is poised to achieve financial success. Either way, the zombies represent the lowest level of the economic system: they are the ultimate slaves, or in industrial terms, the downtrodden, unrepresented proletariat labor force, what Marx calls the *Lumpenproletariat*.[44] Because they have no will or mind of their own, the zombies are not only unrepresented but also *unrepresentable*. No political power, labor union, or social activist exists to plead their case, for they themselves lack the cognitive ability to even articulate that plight.

Applying Spivak's hierarchical structure to the world of *White Zombie* produces the following model:

1. Dominant foreign groups — Beaumont (economic), Neil (social), and Dr. Bruner (religious)
2. Dominant indigenous groups (macro) — the conspicuously absent Haitian government and police system
3. Dominant indigenous groups (micro) — Legendre (who embodies the economic, the social, and the religious apparatuses)
4. The male working class — the nameless coach driver and Beaumont's servant
5. The female working class — the maids
6. The zombies (the sub-subaltern)

The white, Western men are portrayed as superior to all the Haitians on multiple levels. Beaumont's wealth and authority are almost overemphasized through the excesses of his mansion, clothing, and servants, and Dr. Bruner provides both the religious and scientific enlightenment to see the truth behind the native's "foolish superstitions." (Madeleine, although technically a member of the highest order, is purposely absent from my diagram; her place in the hierarchy is the most capricious, as will be discussed later.) Legendre presents a distortion-mirror version of the Western elites; he tries to set himself up as a Western "captain of industry" with his own spacious palace, his careful Western dress, and his command of a vast workforce of slaves and servants.[45]

Understanding the imperialist — at times almost fascist — role of Legendre requires a closer look at those individuals who make up his zombie work force. Like most despots, Legendre focuses his initial attacks on those close to him and those in positions of political and military power. The audience learns the former identities of Legendre's closest zombie servants as he brags about his prowess to a frightened Beaumont: an elderly zombie was once the voodoo master who taught Legendre how to make zombies in the first place (a marked representation of the political coup), and another zombie was once the Haitian minister of the interior, another the captain of the Port-au-Prince police force, and yet another the head executioner (who had once tried to kill Legendre). Such a cadre of conquests emphasizes a Machiavellian rise to power that transcends that of the simple imperialist — or capitalist, for that matter.

His machinations go beyond the enslavement of a workforce; they expose political aspirations as well, elevating the voodoo master to the level of an unrelenting despot. In terms of Spivak's hierarchy, then, Legendre is moving from the third position to the second; and because of his attack on Madeleine, the power-hungry native is challenging those at the top position as well.

Yet at the most fundamental level, Legendre *is* an aspiring capitalist, and the zombies are the definitive exploited proletariats. Although involved in the primarily agrarian trade of sugar cane production, the witch doctor has created a massive factory for the refining of that cane, and the majority of his zombies are not servants or bodyguards but "laborers in a capitalist regime."[46] Deep in the bowels of his seaside fortress, an army of zombies operates the machines of production, cranking a massive grinder by hand and transporting a seemingly endless supply of sugar cane to the mouth of the mill. This scene in *White Zombie* emulates a similarly pejorative depiction of the factory as in Fritz Lang's *Metropolis* (1927), where seemingly mindless workers run the relentless machines with no apparent thought for their own lives and safety. In fact, one of Legendre's zombies falls into the mill to be crushed into a pulp, and none of the other workers even pauses to notice. Legendre's factory is an appalling hyperbole of the furthest limits of a capitalist system: he owns not only the means of production but the labor force as well. Since the zombies earn no wages, require little sustenance, and work ceaselessly around the clock, Legendre enjoys the ultimate profit margin.

At this point in my analysis, though, I must part ways with Rhodes' otherwise excellent interpretation. Although he performs a limited psychoanalytic reading of the text,[47] Rhodes openly denies the presence of any racism in *White Zombie*.[48] He does acknowledge the "unfortunate" Hollywood practice of casting white actors in black roles (and the appalling use of black face), but he claims that "for a film set in a predominantly black country and built around superstitions and religious beliefs stemming from that ethnic group, *White Zombie* certainly does not pursue a racist argument."[49] Perhaps Halperin and Weston were personally unaware of any racist subtext in their project, but the stark reference to race in the film's title is the very least of the several indicators that cannot be ignored. Like Fanon's *Black Skin, White Masks* (1952), Halperin's title indicates a contradiction and duplicity, establishing a racial dichotomy from the very beginning. Furthermore, in *White Zombie*, the protagonist couple are clearly white Americans; the sagacious Dr. Bruner is a white, Christian missionary; and even the treacherous Beaumont is shown to be superior to the natives in his dress, accommodations, and ultimate redemption. The villains of the plot, in contrast, are the implicitly black Legendre and his cadre of black zombies.

Legendre is ethnically a part of Haiti, and it appears socially acceptable

Legendre and his bevy of zombies welcome the "white zombie" (Madge Bellamy) into their ranks (Edward Halperin Productions, 1932; Photofest Digital).

for a native voodoo priest to create and possess native zombies. Dr. Bruner tells Neil how he has been trying for years to challenge Legendre's abominable practices (what he calls a sin of which even the devil would be ashamed), but it takes the zombification of a white woman to spur him to action. By attacking Madeleine (and to a lesser extent, Beaumont), Legendre appears to cross a crucial moral line. As in the ethnographic zombie legends considered by Paravisini-Gebert, Legendre violates the boundaries established not only between woman and man, white and black, but also between upper-class and working-class, imperialist and native. Thus, the white, Western, Christian characters shift from tolerating the grisly practice of zombification among the natives to being incensed to "righteous" action. This sudden motivation parallels Césaire's discourse on Hitler and his critique of France's reaction to the rise of fascism. The West accepts barbarism committed against the so-called savages but reacts violently against barbarism committed against themselves.[50]

Ultimately, the real horror of films such as *White Zombie* for its American and European audiences is the violation of the white heroine, the imposition of a native-centric hegemony on an enlightened Westerner. In Spivak's hierarchy of the subaltern, colonial society, Madeleine is dragged from the top level down to the bottom — a level even below that of the subaltern people and of their women. This injustice is a form of cultural rape and emphasizes the prevailing racism of *White Zombie*. The Western need to preserve cultural and ethnic "purity" leads to Neil's undisguised horror and disgust when Dr. Bruner speculates that Madeleine might indeed still be alive. "You don't think she's alive — in the hands of natives?" Neil exclaims, "Better dead than that!" To the Westerner, an untimely death in a foreign land is a better alternative to being made prisoner and slave to a primitive, "oriental" culture. This scenario represents the greatest fear of the colonizers — that the natives will rise up and become the dominating force. For a contemporary, 1930s audience, living in the midst of a still imperialist period, such a reaction to the suggestion of a white woman being made subservient emotionally, intellectually, and physically to a native "other" arouses a tangible and marked paranoia deep in the Western *Zeitgeist*.

Luckily, for Madeleine, the zombification process is reversible (albeit in a Hollywood *deus ex machina* incompatible with the ethnographic realities of the zombie ritual),[51] and the noble white hero and the righteous white missionary have the chance to restore balance to the cultural and social systems. Unlike the colonial revolutionaries encouraged by Fanon and Said, the zombies by themselves cannot reverse the binary construction of their domination; they have no will of their own and must therefore be liberated by an outside force. The Haitian zombies are doubly inferior and marginalized (as both blacks and slaves), and they can only be "rescued" by the white men of the West. Although the creatures are voiceless and lack autonomous minds and souls, they are still capable of representation by the white characters. Neil sees the zombification of Madeleine as the ultimate affront and recognizes her inherent purity in spite of her tragic state, and Dr. Bruner perceives the zombies as tragic and pitiful creatures, abused through Legendre's black arts to defy the natural order of God. Thus, in a very one-sided and imperialistically-minded way, the sub-subaltern zombies *are* finally heard, but they speak with their very existence rather than their voices. The white heroes are the only ones capable of giving them a voice, and that recognition of their condition comes at a price.

Although Neil and Dr. Bruner ultimately save Madeleine and the other enslaved zombies, they accomplish this redemption in two markedly different (and telling) ways. In *White Zombie*'s resolution, Madeleine somehow resists Legendre's controlling powers and refuses to stab Neil; Madeleine's purity and inherent "moral superiority" seem to give her some power over the pagan magic. A climactic scene on the ramparts of the fortress follows, wherein the missionary Bruner knocks Legendre unconscious long enough for his mindless servants to plunge helplessly off the cliff, heralding the triumph of God over the pagan. Immediately thereafter, a partially zombified Beaumont throws Legendre into the sea before following him to his death, symbolizing both an assumed French superiority and their abandonment of the Haitian colony. In the end, the stereotypes of imperialism are proven to be the saving grace of the day: the white, God-fearing Westerners triumph over the native pagan. The white zombie has been redeemed and returned to the loving arms of her capitalist husband, and the native zombies have been "put down" and destroyed by the cleansing power of God's chosen servant.

As one of the first major American horror films of the sound era, and the first feature-length treatment of the zombie monster, *White Zombie* is undoubtedly a culturally significant and important film.[52] Yet when read critically through the lens of colonial and postcolonial theory, a number of alarming themes and sub-textual messages become apparent. For one, instead of enlightening Western audiences about the cultural realities of Haiti, *White Zombie* merely exploits rumors about voodoo practices and paganism. Racial dichotomies are only enforced by portraying whites as universally righteous and casting blacks as potentially wicked. Although the United States had failed to colonize Haiti directly, it can be argued that they have ended up doing it after the fact by producing troubling texts such as *White Zombie*. Ultimately, the film mirrors colonial stereotypes and imperialist hegemony, establishing another link in the long chain of perceived Western superiority in terms of economics, politics, religion, and race. It would take ten years before Hollywood was ready to address the ethnographic realities of the Caribbean with a less sensationalist film, *I Walked with a Zombie*.

An Inversion of Jane Eyre and the Unavoidable Legacy of Slavery

Despite the financial success enjoyed by *White Zombie*, other major studios seemed reluctant to produce similar films featuring the living dead.[53] Nevertheless, a handful of zombie-related movies did appear during the 1930s, such as Terwilliger's reductively racist *Ouanga*, also set in Haiti,[54] and the Boris Karloff vehicles *The Ghoul* (1933), *The Walking Dead* (1936), and *The Man They Could Not Hang* (1939). These uninspiring films from Karloff, however, completely divorce the risen dead from their Caribbean heritage; in fact, even the Halperins elected to take the mythology in a new direction with their follow up to *White Zombie, Revolt of the Zombies*. Not until the 1940s would voodoo return as a major theme in zombie movies, beginning with the Bob

Hope comedy *The Ghost Breakers* (1940) and continuing through such Monogram titles as *King of the Zombies* and its sequel, *Revenge of the Zombies* (1943). Unfortunately, these low-budget films are fundamentally racist and play their horror with a mixture of sight gags and comedy[55]; it would take the proven production talents of Lewton at RKO Pictures to resurrect the zombie to the ranks of respectable cinematic horror.

After the financial and critical success of Lewton's first production, *Cat People* (1942), he attempted to apply "the same blend of psychological horror, hysteria and eerie atmosphere" to the zombie narrative,[56] and thus, together with his team of director Tourneur and screenwriters Curt Siodmak and Ardel Wray, Lewton produced *I Walked with a Zombie*. The film took its title from an *American Weekly* article written by Inez Wallace, "a non-fiction meditation on the existence of zombies."[57] Wallace's quasi-ethnographic account is hardly a narrative in the traditional sense but rather a collection of first-hand accounts of the Haitian zombie, not unlike those related by Seabrook. For example, Wallace begins with the story of George MacDonough, a white man living in Haiti who had pursued a relationship with a native girl named Gramercie before marrying a white woman. Shortly after their nuptials, MacDonough's wife Dorothy grew ill and died, but reports of the woman's appearance began to crop up six months later. Fueled by his fears of the rumors, MacDonough opened the grave of his wife to find it empty, and when he impulsively confronted Gramercie in her cane fields, he saw Dorothy's corpse working alongside the other slaves. Recognizing the horror of the situation, MacDonough took the "living-dead body" of his wife home, fed her salt, and reburied her now "truly dead" corpse.[58] Unfortunately, Wallace's collection adds up to "little more than a blatantly sensational piece of pulp anthropology"; nevertheless, it remains a significant text because it brought some ethnographic realities of voodoo back to the zombie narrative tradition.[59]

Wallace clearly provided Lewton, Tourneur, and their writers much-needed inspiration and an anthropological focus, but for the key narrative elements of their film, the team turned to the established Gothic tradition of Brontë's *Jane Eyre*. In *I Walked with a Zombie*, Brontë's Edward Rochester becomes Paul Holland (Tom Conway), the doting governess Jane becomes Betsy Connell (Frances Dee), Bertha Mason becomes Jessica Holland (Christine Gordon), and Bertha's angry brother Richard becomes Holland's angry brother, Wesley Rand (James Ellison). Furthermore, Betsy quickly overcomes her employer's gruff and surly exterior and finds herself in love, willing to sacrifice almost anything to be with Holland and to make him happy. Yet rather than attempt an adaptation based on point-by-point fidelity, Lewton and his team perform something of a reversal of Brontë's tale: most obviously, they transplant Thornfield Manor to the West Indies, and they change the "mad woman in the attic" from a raving Creole to the pale and ethereal zombie Jessica. In addition, Lewton and Tourneur's tale features a powerful mother-figure in Mrs. Rand (Edith Barrett), a character who attempts to bridge the gulf separating the different races and classes on the Caribbean island. Such inversions turn the world of *Jane Eyre* upside down, exposing the colonial tensions only implied in Brontë's story to be central and disturbing manifestations of racial, cultural, and class difference.[60]

In a very direct parallel to not only *Jane Eyre* but also Hitchcock's film *Rebecca* (1940), *I Walked with a Zombie* begins with the first-person narration of a female protagonist. In voiceover, Betsy explains how she had once "walked with a zombie," despite the foolishness of such a claim, and she begins to reveal the specifics of her fantastic adventure. In the opening scene, which also clearly evokes Brontë's novel, Betsy interviews for a position as caregiver for a wealthy, if mysterious, man named Holland. However, Betsy is a nurse, not a governess, and the job requires her to move to the remote

The curious nurse Betsy (Frances Dee) finds herself menaced by the exotic sights and sounds of Saint Sebastian in Tourneur's *I Walked with a Zombie* (RKO Radio Pictures, 1943; Jerry Ohlinger).

island of Saint Sebastian (fictional, yet clearly an analogue for Haiti) to tend to Holland's as-yet-unseen ailing wife. Betsy travels to the West Indies by boat, accompanied by the pessimistic and distant Holland, and she soon finds herself surrounded by exotic sights and sounds. The voiceover narration returns, introducing the audience to Fort Holland, a rather opulent plantation mansion that includes a tropical garden and a mysterious tower. Betsy soon settles in, but she doesn't meet her mysterious charge until later in the film; in fact, her chief character trait is curiosity, an additional plot parallel to both *Jane Eyre* and *Rebecca* that moves the story forward.

Betsy meets a number of interesting characters, most of whom function to emphasize polarities in race, culture, and class. In addition to the black servants — who offer a marked visual contrast to the white protagonists — Betsy is introduced to Holland's half-brother. Rand is immediately established as bitter and prone to drink; as the younger brother, Rand resents Holland, both because he must work for his elder at the sugar plant and because of their rivalrous love for the mysterious Jessica. Betsy eventually meets her invalid charge as well, a woman who looks healthy except for her inability to speak or act of her own accord. Jessica appears as a tall, graceful, and beautiful woman, her pale skin made all the more stark because of her white sleeping gown. This "white zombie" of *I Walked with a Zombie* contrasts not only with the dark-clad and brunette Betsy, but also with the character of Bertha from *Jane Eyre*. In Brontë's novel, Jane describes Rochester's terrifying wife as "fearful and ghastly" with a "discoloured face," "red eyes," swollen lips, and "black eyebrows,"[61] racial labels that designate Bertha an animal, a "thing" in Césaire's sense of the word. Jessica is white, yet she is no less terrifying because of her unnatural deportment and behavior; she experiences "thingification" because of her lack of autonomy and free will, traits that become even more alarming in their absence precisely because she is white.

After recovering from her initial shock about her patient's unusual condition, Betsy dedicates herself to her new situation and her new charge. She learns that Rand is tragically in love with Jessica and that Holland cares for the woman mostly out of a sense of marital duty. Furthermore, as in *Jane Eyre*, the young, starry-eyed employee soon falls in love with the gruff master of the house, and she recognizes how Holland is tied down to his life of misery because of his ailing wife. However, Betsy doesn't flee her Thornfield; instead, she dedicates herself to Jessica's health and recovery, selflessly hoping to bestow happiness on Holland by curing his wife. Betsy consults with Dr. Maxwell (James Bell) and tries to reject the local rumors about Jessica's condition. Considering voodoo and zombiism things of pagan mythology, the two submit Jessica to experimental shock treatments. Their efforts fail, however, and Betsy is forced to look elsewhere for a remedy.

Showing far more initiative than Jane Eyre, Betsy sneaks Jessica out of Fort Holland one night and, with the help of the native maid Alma (Theresa Harris), takes her to the nearby *hounfour*, or voodoo house of healing, to visit with the local *houngan* priest. Once there, Betsy is surprised to find Mrs. Rand involved in the proceedings; the older woman is not only present but also operating in a position of authority akin to that of the native *houngan*. The matriarch tires to warn Betsy about the ultimately false hope of voodoo ritual, but, unbeknownst to the two white women, the *houngan* (Martin Wilkins) stabs the catatonic Jessica through the arm with a sword and confirms her to be a true zombie. After Betsy and Jessica return to the safety of the plantation house, the natives begin to stir up trouble, playing their drums incessantly and attempting to summon Jessica to join them in their rituals at the *hounfour*. When the local authorities finally do get involved, Mrs. Rand confesses how she is the one truly responsible for Jessica's condition; she had asked the *houngan* to turn her daughter-in-law into a zombie because Rand had threatened to run away with her, an act that would have torn the family apart. Tensions between the whites and blacks, the Christians and the voodoo practitioners, remain unresolved until Rand finally leads Jessica out of Fort Holland, kills her on the beach, and takes her body into the surf where he drowns.

Even a cursory viewing of *I Walked with a Zombie* reveals its stark differences in both style and content from *White Zombie* and the other voodoo-themed films that appeared between them. For one thing, Tourneur's direction and cinematography are far more stylized than is Halperin's clumsy imitation of Browning; Tourneur uses real locations, more convincing acting, and eerie chiaroscuro lighting and shadows. Furthermore, Lewton had been adamant about making a realistic film during preproduction, telling his staff to gather and study as much about voodoo as possible.[62] This attention to factual detail shows from the moment Betsy arrives on Saint Sebastian: she travels through seemingly authentic villages, observes working locals — played by black actors, not people in blackface — and hears both French dialect and ritual drum music. Her journey to Fort Holland stands in stark contrast with the one endured by Neil and Madeleine in *White Zombie*, for Betsy travels during the day, the roads are pleasant and safe, and her coach driver (Clinton Rosemond) chats with her amicably about the history of the island. Later, when Alma explains the local customs and traditions of Saint Sebastian, she uses such accurate voodoo terms as *hounfour*, *loa*, and *houngan*. Because of these efforts, "Tourneur and Lewton present an unsensationalist analysis of Voudon as a religion, rather than mere superstition."[63] In other words, taking their cues from Wallace's article, the producers of *I Walked with a Zombie* want to thrill viewers with ethnographic mystery, not merely Hollywood fantasy.

Partly as a result, Young can note how "*I Walked with a Zombie* can be read as a text which, on some levels, challenges the dominant representation of blacks and black discourse in American cinema and society."[64] Although the social hierarchy separating administrative whites from laboring blacks remains in Lewton and Tourneur's film, the black characters are given active roles and serious dialogue, Alma in particular. In Halperin's film, most of the Haitian characters are relegated to the background or featured merely as voiceless zombies; in fact, the coachman is the only black actor in *White Zombie* who has any lines. In addition, Lugosi's take on voodoo ritual essentially boils down to weird hand contortions and exaggeratedly wide eyes. By contrast, the voodoo rites and rituals in *I Walked with a Zombie* are treated with both seriousness and gravity. At the *hounfour*, for example, the black characters sing in French and perform intricate and exotic native dances, and although the white characters initially scoff at the power of voodoo, they never seem to dismiss the local culture. In fact, much of the mystery and intrigue of *I Walked with a Zombie* comes not from the fear of a racial and cultural other, but rather from the white characters' inability to understand what is really going on around them. As Russell states, "Whereas earlier zombie films had explicitly used the living dead to suggest the primitive Otherness of the Caribbean and its black populace, *I Walked with a Zombie* turns the focus back on the white world itself. The zombies in Lewton's film are terrifying not because they're symbols of some primitive culture, but because their existence can't be explained."[65]

Finally, the female characters are substantially more independent in Lewton and Tourneur's film than they are in *White Zombie*. To begin with, there are simply more women in the movie, and the plot doesn't devolve into merely an opportunity for the white men to rescue a helpless and imperiled white woman. Betsy remains the heroic protagonist throughout, an educated nurse who isn't afraid to disobey Holland to do what she thinks is right. Furthermore, Betsy shows little fear in confronting both the rituals of voodoo and the zombies produced by those rites. Alma, the film's most prominent black character, is an autonomous woman as well, a fully-formed character who aids Betsy in secret, disobeying her employer and violating the codes of race, class, and culture. Mrs. Rand is the most powerful figure in the film; the widow of a missionary and the person perhaps most responsible for Jessica condition, she is a blend of Halperin's Dr. Bruner and Murder Legendre in one — yet she is both white and a woman. The only completely passive female character is Jessica. Nevertheless, although she has been turned into a zombie before the film even begins, her relationship with Rand implies that she was once a strong, free-willed figure like Betsy and even Mrs. Rand. She clearly wasn't timid about leaving her husband for his brother, if local rumor is to be believed. Of course, her status as the sub-subaltern monster of the narrative places her more on par with the helpless Madeleine, but I will discuss that complex aspect of her character later.

One thing *White Zombie* and *I Walked with a Zombie* do have in common is their exploitation of exotic differences to evoke feelings of mystery, unease, and terror in their viewers. Despite the attempt of liberal films of the 1940s and '50s "to integrate blacks into mainstream society, the fact remained that black culture in American society *was* radically different and *apart* from white culture. Films that touched upon the issue of difference usually represented this difference as threatening or exotic."[66] In the midst of the Second World War, most North Americans fostered a deep suspicion of those who looked and acted differently from the mainstream public, and this paranoia, which would only increase during the Cold War 1950s, often fixed upon racial, national, and cultural disparities. Lewton and Tourneur emphasize these fundamental differences overtly in a variety of ways, from the variations in spoken language to the decidedly unfamiliar voodoo rituals to the simple use of drums to signal shift changes at the sugar mill — and, of course, by showing that black characters work for and serve the white ones. Furthermore, in addition to the harsh black-and-white contrasts of Tourneur's cinematography, the most striking symbol of racial difference comes via Holland's statue of Saint Sebastian.

The ancient figurehead that stands in the courtyard of Holland's mansion has a recurring and poignant visual presence in *I Walked with a Zombie*. As Betsy travels by coach to Fort Holland, her amiable driver tells her, "The Hollands was the most old family, Miss. They brought the colored folks to the island ... the colored folks and Ti-Misery." Betsy is understandably confused by this reference, so the driver explains that Ti-Misery is "an old man who lives in the garden at Fort Holland. With arrows stuck in him and a sorrowful weeping look on his black face." Betsy quickly realizes the driver means the figurehead from a ship; in fact, the Ti-Misery statue came from the very slave ship that originally brought the locals' ancestors to the island from Africa, thus giving the colony the name of Saint Sebastian. Later, as Holland gives the nurse a tour of the grounds, he ruminates on the tragic history of the strange relic: "That's where our people came from. From the misery and pain of slavery. For generation they found life a burden. That's why they still weep when a child is born and make merry at the burial." The blackened statue, now a fountain with tear-like water dripping down its face, clearly evokes the colonial heritage of the island, emphasizing both the suffering of the slaves and their difference from the white imperialists. By making it an adornment of his garden, Holland is perhaps trying to remind himself of the shame of that heritage, but for viewers of the film, Ti-Misery stands as a reminder of the inexorable and lasting link between zombie and slave narratives.[67]

One of the most visceral sequences of *I Walked with a Zombie* emphasizes the exotic, and somewhat frightening, contrasts between the white Christians and the black practitioners of voodoo. Because her Western science has failed to restore Jessica to health, Betsy secretly takes her charge to see the *houngan* priest at the *hounfour* for help. As they leave the implied safety of Holland's gated mansion, Betsy covers her white nurse's uniform with a black cloak, a sign that although she is trying to live in both worlds, she cannot help but keep the two clearly separate. Jessica, in marked contrast, wears a gray gown that symbolizes her liminal state: she is neither alive nor dead, Christian or pagan, even white or black — instead, she has become something of both, linked to local heritage because her zombiism makes her more of a slave than the blacks ever were. This difference between the two becomes more prominent when Alma adorns the white women with "voodoo patches" to allow them to pass by the zombie who guards the crossroads to the *hounfour*. Betsy's scrap of cloth is a white square, but Jessica's is a black one. After an understandably eerie journey past skulls, a dead goat, and the glassy-eyed zombie Carrefour (Darby Jones), who silently allows the women to pass, the two arrive at the *hounfour*, where all the locals are wearing black voodoo patches like Jessica's. The "white zombie" is clearly seen to be one of them — or, at the very least, Alma has implied that Jessica *belongs to* them.

Paravisini-Gebert emphasizes the importance of the voodoo ceremony that follows: "The scene, the longest and most haunting of the film, implicitly links slavery to the state of living death embodied by Jessica, while erotizing Jessica through its accumulation of sexually charged motifs."[68] Throughout the journey to the *hounfour*, Jessica must be lead and directed: Alma had adorned her as one of the voodoo clan, and Betsey has directed her steps through the fields. In other words, Jessica has had no choice, no autonomy in this undertaking, just as she had had no say in her failed shock treatment. Once again, she has been "thingified," turned into a slave who must obey the wills of those around her. Once at the *hounfour*, Jessica stands listlessly in the background, and Betsy seems to forget her charge entirely, treating Jessica more like a dumb object than a person and leaving her unprotected. The participants in the voodoo ritual, however, take a decided interest in the white woman, gathering around her as she stands alone in her gossamer sleeping gown. The *houngan*, dressed in rather austere black, takes up a saber and moves towards Jessica menacingly, with the drums beating faster and faster. His approach, along with the frenzy of the drums, reaches a climax when he drives the blade through her arm. On the most basic symbolic level, Jessica has been raped by the *houngan*, and she is thereby confirmed to be a zombie and, thus, the property of the voodooists.

Jessica's subversion by the *houngan* and his voodoo rituals, through both her zombification and stabbing, indicates only one way the blacks in *I Walked with a Zombie* have risen up against their erstwhile oppressors. As Young points out, "What makes *I Walked with a Zombie* a radical film for its time is its exploration of the idea of *resistance*.... The blacks may be socially inferior (most of them are maids/servants) but in no way are they portrayed as morally or intellectually inferior."[69] As has already been discussed, the locals of Saint Sebastian constitute fully formed, independent characters, capable of speaking and acting on their own. Furthermore, they openly reject white authority, whether it be Alma's aiding of Betsy, the *houngan*'s violation of Jessica, or their eventual rebellion against Holland. In a folkloric example of the kind of insurgence white imperialists had always feared most, a black calypso singer (Sir Lancelot) at the local bar disseminates resistance through a subversive ballad:

> The Holland man,
> he kept in a tower
> a wife as pretty
> as a big white flower.
> She saw the brother
> and she stole his heart,
> and that's how the badness
> and the trouble start.
> Ah-woe! Ah-me!
> Shame and sorrow for the family.

Disregarding Rand's obvious annoyance at such a song, the singer performs for Betsy, letting her know the truth of what has happened at Fort Holland, openly mocking the decidedly un-fraternal behavior of the two men, and revealing the real reasons behind Jessica's zombification.[70] The native man has thus usurped both Holland's assumed right to privacy and Mrs. Rand's privilege to reveal the story on her own.

These complex social, cultural, racial, and gendered relationships and conflicts illustrate a complication of Spivak's colonial hierarchy. Although the white men appear to be in charge — their meeting with the local constable, for instance, occurs away from both Betsy and Alma — the black population is clearly not cowed into total obedient subservience. As in *White Zombie*, the natives of Saint Sebastian are shown to have an autonomous will that potentially threatens the stability of the white status quo on the island. Furthermore, Betsy repeatedly disobeys Holland and Mrs. Rand, and she actively seeks help and guidance from blacks such as Alma and the *houngan*. Jessica, however, remains at the lowest level of the ranking: as Dr. Maxwell explains, "Mrs. Holland had a tropical fever, very severe. We might say that portions of the spinal cord were burned out by this fever. The result is what you see:

a woman without any willpower. Unable to speak or even act by herself, although she will obey simple commands." Even though the white men scoff at the idea of zombiism, they nonetheless see her as a thing — an Other — void of free will or agency. Of course, if Jessica truly is a zombie, a victim of voodoo magic and ritual as the conclusion of the film implies, then she is subservient to the native population as well. As in Halperin's film, the blacks of *I Walked with a Zombie* have indeed challenged white authority and reenacted a form of counter-imperialism that, in this case, relegates a white woman to the position of the sub-subaltern.

In addition to allegedly causing Jessica's unnatural transformation, the (black) practitioners of voodoo on Saint Sebastian actively exert their will on the (white) zombified woman, claiming her as their own and thus replicating the transgressions of racial, social, and class lines addressed by Paravisini-Gebert in her analysis of the female zombie narrative[71] and as depicted by Halperin in *White Zombie*. After Betsy's nocturnal visit to the *hounfour*, the *houngan* attempts to summon Jessica by creating a voodoo doll, and his fol-

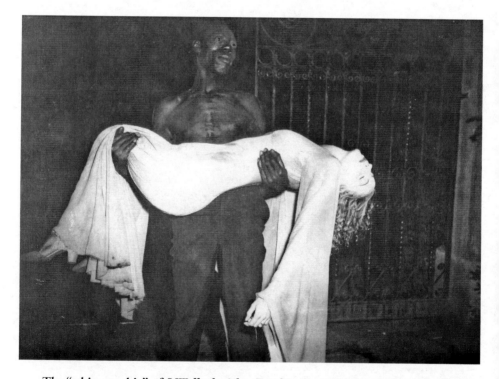

The "white zombie" of *I Walked with a Zombie*, Jessica Holland (Christine Gordon), is abducted as the property of the natives by the zombie Carrefour (Darby Jones) (RKO Radio Pictures, 1943; Jerry Ohlinger).

lowers cause a disruption by incessantly playing their drums and defying local authority. In addition, the *houngan* uses Carrefour as a tool — a native example of the sub-subaltern — to physically collect the "white zombie" from Fort Holland. Carrefour enters the gate, as the black "slave" "invading" the locus of white authority, and he menaces Holland and Betsy in his search for Jessica. The zombie is deterred, however, when Mrs. Rand appears and calls him off. In a strange inversion of an otherwise established hierarchy between race, class, and gender, Mrs. Rand establishes herself as a liminal power. Not only is her power unusual because she is a woman, Mrs. Rand also represents dual forms of authority: both that of the West in general, and the Holland family in particular, and locally because of her position of power over the natives and her established presence at the *hounfour*.

Earlier in the film, when Betsy had been shocked to find Mrs. Rand presiding over the *hounfour*, the older woman explained how she had risen to such an unexpected position of influence:

> When my husband died, I was helpless, they disobeyed me, and accidentally I discovered the secret of how to deal with them. There was a woman with a baby. Again and again I begged her to boil the drinking water; she wouldn't. Then I told her the god *Shango* would kill the evil spirits in the water if she boiled it. From then on, she boiled the water.... It seemed so simple to let the gods speak through me.

In a stroke of cultural manipulation reminiscent of the imperialist model of colonization, Mrs. Rand had found a way to "deal with" the black denizens of Saint Sebastian: she had usurped their mythology and folklore — the "ideological State apparatuses"[72] of voodoo — and turned them into the tools of control and oppression. When Dr. Maxwell warns everyone at Fort Holland that the local commissioner is launching a formal investigation into Jessica's condition, Mrs. Rand confesses how she is responsible for Jessica's zombification: "I entered into their ceremonies. I pretended I was possessed by their gods. But what I did to Jessica was when she wanted to go away with Wesley. That night I went to the *hounfour*.... I told him the woman at Fort Holland was evil and asked him to make her a zombie." Mrs. Rand, appearing to enjoy a place of power atop the hierarchies of both white and black cultural systems, has appropriated voodoo ritual both to control the disobedient natives and to enact punishment upon her transgressive daughter-in-law.

However, Mrs. Rand's position of authority is ultimately just an illusion; the true source of power on the island remains in the hands of the black, male *houngan*. At the *hounfour*, the voodoo priest tries once again to claim Jessica by pulling her voodoo doll towards him with a string. The zombie Jessica, helpless to resist the influence of the pagan magic, does indeed try to

leave the grounds of Fort Holland, but Rand and Betsy apprehend her. Rand
bemoans Jessica's condition and the way the natives have such power over her,
and the next shot cuts to reveal the "weeping" Saint Sebastian figurehead,
emphasizing how Jessica is the true slave on the island, slave to the one-time
colonial slaves and thus the inheritor — and now another victim — of the imperialist tradition. The *houngan* resumes his efforts later that night, and Rand,
now alone, opens the gate to let Jessica pass. He removes an arrow from the
Saint Sebastian statue and follows her. The film cuts to the *houngan*, who
suddenly stabs Jessica's voodoo doll with a long needle, and the next scene
shows Rand bent over Jessica's body on the beach: he has just stabbed her
with the arrow. The editing complicates a clear reading: was Rand acting on
his own, saving Jessica from living death and enslavement via euthanasia, or
was he merely another tool in the hands of the powerful *houngan*? Who truly
controls the will and destiny of the whites on Saint Sebastian?

At the same time, despite Lewton and Tourneur's stylistic trappings and
even-handed representation of Caribbean culture, *I Walked with a Zombie* taps
back into the same Western anxieties that made *White Zombie* and its ilk so
terrifying to a white audience in a high-imperialist world. As predicted by
Césaire's "boomerang effect of colonization,"[73] the descendents of slaves on
Saint Sebastian, who have learned all too well the power systems of control
and domination, have risen up to enslave the symbols of white, Western
authority on their island. Young emphasizes the true power dynamic at play
in *I Walked with a Zombie* and reveals the ultimate power of the zombie as a
symbol of imperialism:

> Effectively, the black "inferiors" have reduced their white masters to dolls, tak-
> ing life from them as they please. Even though Mrs Rand may have thought she
> was in control, using the natives' religion to exact her revenge, she clearly has
> sacrificed her autonomy when she entered the voodoo rituals. ... her unconscious
> anger against Jessica is turned, by the *houngan*, into a weapon of destruction
> against the family. Effectively Mrs Rand has been turned into a doll, just like
> Jessica.[74]

If the ultimate fear for those who believe in voodoo is to become a zombie,
then the analogous fear of the imperialist is to become a slave. Lewton and
Tourneur's film, like Halperin's before it, is therefore less about the authenticity of zombies and more about the intrinsic fears of those living under the
shameful shadow of imperialist injustice. The legacy of the colonial system,
according to Young, "has turned everyone into a kind of zombie,"[75] and the
films make a point of imposing this victim role upon white women.

Although the various voodoo-based zombie films of the 1930s, '40s, and
'50s each attempts to reinvent the fledgling genre in different ways, they all
remain inexorably tied to the racist ideologies of imperialism and slavery. By

and large, the zombies remain little more that exotic set dressing, frightening in their lumbering movements and dull stares, but never really constituting a mortal threat to the films' protagonists. As in Caribbean folklife, the true terror of such films comes from the one *making* the zombies, as subjugation and loss of self-awareness remain the most horrific aspects of the zombie legend. Even John Gilling's *The Plague of the Zombies*, a Hammer Film production from the late 1960s, fails to divorce the zombie from such Caribbean histories, roots in superstition, and racist undertones. Although this innovative film transplants the action to England, the zombies remain little more than slave laborers, victims of voodoo magic who terrify viewers not because they are dangerous but because they represent potential enslavement. In many ways, the voodoo zombie appears to have played itself out by the 1960s — that is, until an enterprising film student named George A. Romero became determined to reinvent the horror genre at its very foundations.

Chapter 3

THE RISE OF THE
NEW PARADIGM
Night of the Living Dead *and*
the Zombie Invasion Narrative

"They're coming to get you, Barbra!"—Johnny, *Night of the Living Dead*

By the late 1960s, zombie movies had virtually no remaining ties to voodoo or folklore, and, almost single-handedly, Romero reinvented the subgenre, enhancing the monsters and their stories with elements drawn from classical Gothic literature, vampire tales, and science-fiction invasion narratives. Romero's efforts at multi-source adaptation have proved so successful, in fact, that almost all zombie films to follow his *Night of the Living Dead* have been fundamentally influenced by this new "zombie invasion narrative." Because no short fiction, novels, or films featuring hordes of flesh-eating zombies predate 1968, Romero appears to have authored a wholly original text. However, upon closer investigation, the film proves instead to be an assemblage of multiple sources; primarily, voodoo zombie movies set in the Caribbean; Gothic tales of reanimated golems, insatiable vampires, fractured personalities, and haunted houses; and science fiction stories of alien invasion and the resulting paranoia. *Night of the Living Dead* is thus a synthesis — and transcendence — of these preexisting subgenres; by combining the most exciting and innovative elements from a variety of established texts and traditions, Romero created a new and vibrant narrative from what had become stale and predictable predecessors. Furthermore, the monsters of *Night of the Living Dead* differ from the zombies found in earlier films, and more closely resemble vampires and invading aliens, in four key respects: (1) they have no connection to voodoo magic, (2) they far outnumber the human protagonists, (3) they eat human flesh, and (4) their condition is contagious.

The invasion and horror narratives of the 1950s and '60s certainly upped the ante on the preexisting monster stories. For starters, by putting the human protagonists in the minority, the horror becomes literally overwhelming. In addition, monsters such as vampires, alien "pod people," and zombies look primarily like ordinary humans; this seemingly innocuous resemblance manifests visually what Freud calls the *Unheimlich*—an uncanny similarity between the familiar and the unfamiliar that makes such monsters even more disturbing and frightening. Furthermore, because these creatures infect and transform their prey into monsters such as themselves, once-trusted friends and loved ones prove the greatest threat to the few surviving protagonists, and that threat is often not apparent until it's too late. Yet the behavior of the besieged humans in *Night of the Living Dead* becomes even more monstrous and threatening than that of the zombies, making the film a cunning allegorical criticism of 1960s American society. Inspired largely by Matheson's *I Am Legend*, as well as its adaptation *Last Man on Earth* by Ragona and Salkow, the protagonists of Romero's film are systematically marginalized and "othered" by the overwhelming numbers of the monsters. Put in such a precarious position, they quickly devolve into a more selfish, barbaric state. Survival, not society, becomes the top priority, and that paradigmatic shift has terrible consequences.

As a metaphor for the modern age, Romero's *Night of the Living Dead* presents audiences with the true monster threatening civilization: humanity itself. Whereas the screen zombies of the 1930s and '40s function primarily as allegories for racial inequality and imperial injustice, the "new" zombies of the late 1960s and beyond work as uncanny manifestations of other repressed societal fears and insecurities, such as the dominance of the white patriarchy, the misogynistic treatment of women, the collapse of the nuclear family, and the unchecked violence of the Vietnam War. Additionally, Romero's narrative builds strongly on the established Gothic literary tradition, particularly the use of "antiquated space," locations where the beleaguered protagonists must hide and defend themselves from a monstrous threat from without — and from within. In Romero's complex parable, then, the *Unheimlich* appearance of the walking dead forces characters and viewers alike to confront their own fallibility and mortality, and the similarly *Unheimlich* location — the cozy farmhouse that has been turned into a besieged fortress — reveals deep-seated tensions about social structures and human relationships. Finally, Romero establishes audience connection and subjectivity not only with the human characters of *Night of the Living Dead*, but also with the abhorrent zombies that mirror them, thus breaking down the barriers that separate "us" from "them." As this chapter will show, *Night of the Living Dead* not only represents an important and largely original development in both the zombie and the Gothic horror traditions, but the innovative film also establishes the zombie as a powerful psychological symbol for social and cultural anxieties and tensions.

Assembling Night of the Living Dead
from the Existing Monster Tradition

Night of the Living Dead, which has now become the standard zombie narrative model, became a cult classic because of its visual shock, excessive violence, and perceived originality. Yet Romero didn't invent the film from nothing; he was working in an established generic tradition and drawing from a variety of inspirations and antecedents. The essential motifs and tropes of *Night of the Living Dead* have many thematic and stylistic roots in Haitian travel narratives and the zombie films of the 1930s and '40s, but they also developed out of Cold War horror and science-fiction short stories, novels, and cinema of the 1950s and '60s, particularly their end-of-the-world scenarios. Performing what Jauss calls the "reappropriation of past works" by art of the present,[1] Romero used his own imagination and invention to unite the tried-and-true zombie legend with these newer stories of the primal struggle for survival, creating a terrifying tale of the walking dead and cannibalism the likes of which no one had yet seen. Although movies such as *White Zombie* were first, Dendle points out that "Romero liberated the zombie from the shackles of a master, and invested his zombies not with a function ... but rather a drive."[2] With the creation of *Night of the Living Dead*, then, Romero decisively established the structure of the now classic zombie invasion movie, and many directors have since followed his lead and conformed to the criteria of the new subgenre.

The key feature of most horror narratives is the presence of a foreign or unfamiliar Other, and this fear both *of* the Other and the forcible domination *by* the Other are two themes that appear in a variety of nineteenth-century Gothic and science-fiction narratives. Perhaps the most famous monstrous Other from literature is the creature in Shelley's *Frankenstein*. Literally stitched together from different human corpses, the pitiful golem is rejected by both his creator, Victor Frankenstein, and the rest of humanity. Because he is already treated as a monster, the creature resorts to acting like one, embracing his otherness because no other option is offered to him. Stoker's *Dracula*, another pillar of the Gothic monster pantheon, exemplifies the paranoia of *becoming* an Other. Stoker presents the mysterious Count as a foreign invader who infiltrates England and attempts to convert the innocent to his own dastardly condition. Through his powers of mind control, hypnosis, and hemophilic infection, Dracula robs Lucy Westenra of her autonomy, controlling her from a distance and forcing her to act against her noble (i.e., British) nature. Finally, Robert Louis Stevenson's *Strange Case of Dr Jekyll and Mr Hyde* (1886) explores the duplicitous nature of the monstrous Other. In his efforts to purge himself of his own evil tendencies, Henry Jekyll creates the hideous

Edward Hyde, a monster, as Judith Halberstam points out, that has been lurking in the master all along.[3] Not only is Stevenson's monster always already hiding inside every one of us, his Other becomes far more insidious that either Shelley's hulking creature or the pale-faced Dracula because Hyde is a master of disguise who readily passes as human.[4]

Shelley, Stoker, and Stevenson each illustrate how fear of being or becoming the Other ultimately means fear of disenfranchisement from society and the risk of becoming a literal monster. These very real fears can be found in decidedly non-fantastic stories as well. Stephen Crane's short story "The Monster" of 1899, what Nick LoLordo describes as a Gothic tale "at war with a realist social critique,"[5] chronicles the tragic story of an African-American man named Henry Johnson. Although his race makes him something of an Other in society already, most members of the Whilomville community treat him with kindness and show him respect — especially his employer, Dr. Trescott. One day, an unexplained fire rages through the doctor's home and laboratory, imperiling his young son Jimmie, and Johnson is the first on the scene, ready to risk his life to save the boy. He almost succeeds unscathed, but Johnson is ultimately overwhelmed by the conflagration of the lab, where the "red snake" of a chemical fire horribly scars his face and head.[6] An overwhelming sense of gratitude impels Dr. Trescott to save the wounded man's life, over the protestations of Judge Hagenthorpe, who thinks the "poor fellow ought to die."[7] As a result, and in a clear parallel with the creature from Shelley's macabre tale, Johnson is transformed into a literal, physical monster by the unpredictable dangers of scientific hubris.[8]

Despite his former good standing in society, and his heroic efforts to save Jimmie's life, Johnson is loathed and feared by the community because of his disfigurement; he is both human and inhuman at the same time. Alek Williams, the man paid to board and care for Johnson, demands an exorbitant amount of money because he claims his children cannot force themselves to eat in Johnson's presence, and because members of the community begin to call the poor man a devil.[9] Things get even worse when Johnson spends an evening roaming the town unaccompanied and memorably interrupts a birthday party for Theresa Page. After being frightened by Johnson's face at the window, the children are all in a panicked state of disarray; the young Theresa cannot describe the sight to her father as anything other than "a thing, a dreadful thing."[10] The physical disfigurement turns Johnson into an object — a thing — and were it not for the humane intervention of Dr. Trescott, the community would likely have dealt with Johnson as a thing. They want the monster institutionalized.

By preventing him from dying from his injuries, Dr. Trescott has acted as Victor Frankenstein; as Judge Hagenthorpe so simply puts it to Dr. Trescott,

"He will be your creation, you understand. He is purely your creation. Nature has very evidently given him up. He is dead. You are restoring him to life. You are making him, and he will be a monster, and with no mind."[11] As a man merely othered by his race, Johnson still had the ability to work hard, make a name and place for himself in the community, and pursue a promising relationship with a girl such as Bella Farragut. His physical disfigurement, however, changes everything. Everything Johnson had before the accident is lost to him — he can no longer roam freely through the city streets, he cannot labor for his room and board, and any chance of pursuing a romantic or even social life is beyond him. Perhaps things would have been better for the doomed hero had Dr. Trescott simply let him die, but this Frankenstein sees his duty towards his son's savior, and the good doctor takes the monster under his own roof in spite of the town's indignation and social punishments.

Of course, the naturalist critique offered by Crane in his macabre parable also draws attention to the social and cultural monstrosities that had been collectively repressed before Johnson's disfigurement. Despite the successes Johnson had enjoyed as a free man in the community prior to the accident, he had remained, nevertheless and unavoidably, a black man in a largely white township. In other words, according to LoLordo, "Henry is a monster before his face is melted: the black man (or more specifically, the black man in unsegregated social life) is inherently monstrous."[12] Johnson is therefore a monster on two levels — physically and racially — and his facial disfigurement only manages to expose the repressed racist fears the town continues to harbor for a black man who has intruded into a white boy's bedroom. That is, even though Dr. Trescott willingly recognizes Johnson's heroic actions towards his son, the rest of the community cannot help but see "the monster" as a black man who has abducted a white boy from his home. Johnson thus functions in Crane's story as an uncanny figure, a concept I will explore in more detail shortly, because his transformation into a monster causes the failure of Whilomville's collective repression.[13] That is, Johnson's melted face reminds the white people not only of his essential, inherent difference, but also of their own racial history of discrimination, oppression, and even lynchings.

In a much different vein, Henry James' "The Jolly Corner" (1908), clearly influenced by Stevenson's tale of monstrous duality, provides another example of this fear of becoming the Other. After a long period of living abroad, Spencer Brydon returns to New York, where he spends an agonizingly long night of paranoia and self-reflection alone in his ancestral home. In the early hours of dawn, he is confronted by a terrifying specter — "rigid and conscious, spectral yet human, a man of his own substance and stature"[14] — a representation of the man he might have become had he stayed in New York. As Brydon gets closer, the dark figure drops its hands to reveal to Brydon his own changed face: "The presence before him was a presence, the horror within him a horror, but the waste of his nights had been only grotesque and the success of his adventure an irony. Such an identity fitted his at *no* point, made its alternative monstrous. A thousand times yes, as it came upon him nearer now — the face was the face of a stranger."[15] Brydon had been seeking himself, a manifestation of his own potential, but the spirit he locates ends up being unrecognizable. Although Brydon is not physically or literally othered by the ghostly presence, the vision of such a transformation — especially the unexplained loss of two of his fingers — strikes terror in his soul.

Appearing to be someone other than oneself or something other than "normal" lies at the heart of paranoia about and fear of the Other. Most people long for acceptance, and any physical or social variations (either real or merely perceived) stand at odds against that status quo — especially variations of race, gender, religion, class, or even physical deformity. Many popular and literary works of the modern era explore these themes, investigating the problems with disenfranchisement, alienation, and marginalization. Although the two tales discussed above, "The Monster" and "The Jolly Corner," don't feature literal monsters or alien creatures, they both present the kind of fears rampant in the early twentieth-century *Zeitgeist* and pave the way for the genre fiction that followed. Horror and science fiction narratives are fundamentally well suited to explore cultural concerns of alienation and marginalization because of their ability to quite frankly and literally represent the Other as strange or alien — and the zombie narrative tradition is a quintessential example of such fiction.

As we have seen, the American zombie movies of the 1930s and '40s remain relatively grounded in the folkloric traditions of the monster; the films usually take place in Haiti or another postcolonial country and feature the (mis)use of voodoo magic. Romero, however, transcends these early, developmental narratives, drawing from other sources to reinvent the cinematic zombie. One of his primary antecedental sources is Campbell's science-fiction story "Who Goes There?" This serialized tale features a group of scientists trapped in an Antarctic research station with a malevolent alien creature. The monster has the ability to invade a host body at the cellular level, converting those cells into alien tissue and accomplishing an othering on the most fundamental and literal level. Furthermore, the creature usurps its host's thoughts and memories, allowing the resulting doppelganger to pass among the humans without detection. The central theme of Campbell's story is one of paranoia; in a parallel to *Dr Jekyll and Mr Hyde*, it becomes virtually impossible to tell who is human and who is an alien Other (a trope that will also appear later in Finney's *Invasion of the Body Snatchers*). Furthermore, by putting the protagonists in an inescapable location — even when confronted by the threat of death *inside*, the harsh conditions *outside* keep them trapped — Campbell creates a claustrophobic environment with little hope for a favorable resolution. Both the themes of the doppelganger and environmental entrapment surface in other influential texts as well, and they become essential protocols in *Night of the Living Dead*.

In the wake of the global atrocities of World War II, the 1940s and '50s saw a dramatic upswing in other horror media as well, most notably the publication of *Tales from the Crypt* by EC Comics in 1950. According to columnist and comic aficionado Digby Diehl, "Horror comics of the 1950s appealed to teens and young adults who were trying to cope with the aftermath of even greater terrors — Nazi death camps and the explosion of the atomic bombs at Hiroshima and Nagasaki."[16] Terror had become a tangible part of daily life, and these early graphic novels brazenly presented images of rotting corpses, stumbling zombies, and gory violence. Film scholar Paul Wells claims the young Romero would have been directly influenced by such comics,[17] for a predominately visual narrative format can be seen in his zombie movies, where the action is presented through a series of carefully framed and largely silent images. Romero confirms this connection himself in a documentary by Roy Frumke, referring to the filming of his *Dawn of the Dead* as "making a comic book."[18]

Zombie films continued to be produced into the 1950s, as we have noted, featuring not only voodoo zombies but also corpses reanimated by scientific or technological means. Such films as Cahn's *Invisible Invaders* and Fisher's *The Earth Dies Screaming* depict hoards of reanimated human corpses used as armies by alien forces to invade and subjugate the human race, and they represent obvious sources of visual inspiration for Romero.[19] Furthermore, even though Gilling's *The Plague of Zombies* returns to the voodoo roots of the monsters, this film firmly establishes the now-familiar decaying appearance of zombies.[20] Yet while all of these movies clearly influenced the look and feel of *Night of the Living Dead*, the pre–1968 zombie films almost always feature the animated dead as servants or soldiers, usually controlled by a master (a voodoo priest, a mad scientist, or alien invaders). One of the few exceptions is Cahn's *Zombies of Mora-Tau*, which features a hoard of zombies that have outlasted their creator. In this noteworthy film, the creatures act out of instinct alone, following the orders of no one individual.[21] *Night of the Living Dead* builds further on this idea, presenting the zombies as seemingly autonomous monsters, fueled by the basest, but also most unknown, of motives and desires.

Romero was likely influenced by other popular science fiction and horror films of the 1950s as well, especially those featuring apocalyptic scenarios. According to Frumke, Romero's earliest film influence was Christian

Nyby's *The Thing from Another World* (1951).[22] Based on "Who Goes There?" this Howard Hawks–produced movie transfers the action of Campbell's story to the North Pole, thus justifying the strong American military presence at the outpost, and also changes the fundamental nature of the monster: rather than taking the form of humans, the extraterrestrial "Thing" is some kind of giant plant monster — although it basically looks and acts like Karloff's turn as Frankenstein's monster. Paranoia and the threat of a hostile Other continue to be the main source of terror, however, as would be expected of a Hawks film during the early years of the Cold War. Another major science-fiction film from 1951 is Robert Wise's influential *The Day the Earth Stood Still*. This movie is less about invasion and more about paranoia, and the alien creature proves to be benevolent. The primary importance of these films for the development of *Night of the Living Dead* is the strong presence of the media and the negative portrayal of the military. After all, in both movies the soldiers' first reaction upon encountering life from another planet is to shoot first and ask questions later.

All of these preexisting texts feature important developments in both the zombie narrative and the larger invasion tradition, but in *Night of the Living Dead*, Romero takes things to the utmost level: that of the apocalypse. Perhaps the most influential "end of the world" narrative from the mid–twentieth century is Daphne du Maurier's "The Birds" (1952), which Gregory A. Waller claims to be behind not only *Night of the Living Dead*, but also the inspirational source for all post–1950s apocalypse narratives,[23] including, of course, Hitchcock's adaptation *The Birds*. Du Maurier's short tale focuses on a hapless family, boarded up in their own home to escape an unexplained attack by flocks and flocks of enraged birds. Rather than dealing with one monster, as in "Who Goes There?," "The Birds" features an external hoard and overwhelming odds. Dillard considers Hitchcock's adaptation to be the primary artistic predecessor to Romero's *Night of the Living Dead*, pointing out how "in both films, a group of people are besieged by an apparently harmless and ordinary world gone berserk, struggle to defend themselves against the danger, and struggle to maintain their rationality and their values at the same time."[24] Romero certainly recreates this situation with *Night of the Living Dead*'s fortified farmhouse and its aggressive army of ghouls.

Film scholar Robin Wood offers another primary source of inspiration of *Night of the Living Dead*, claiming the most obvious antecedent to Romero's zombies to be the pod-people in Siegel's *Invasion of the Body Snatchers*, based on Finney's novel.[25] This unsettling story posits another view of the apocalypse, where one's best friends and family members become threatening monsters. As in "Who Goes There?" the body-snatching aliens pass for human, infiltrating the race by secretly replacing people one by one. Yet Finney's novel is surprisingly optimistic; faced with the resilience of humanity, the invading pod-people decide to abandon their plans and move on. The film's ending, however, departs drastically from the novel, implying an eventual victory for the aliens and thus illustrating the paranoia rampant in Cold-War America. King writes how critics usually read Siegel's film as an allegory about "the witch-hunt atmosphere that accompanied the McCarthy hearings," although Siegel always claimed it was really about the "Red Menace" itself.[26] Either way, fear of the Other is clearly present in both versions of the text.

Melanie (Tippi Hedren) is attacked by overwhelming odds in Hitchcock's *The Birds* (Universal Pictures, 1963; Jerry Ohlinger).

This elaborate genealogy of disparate texts addresses various issues and concerns of the Other, alienation, marginalization, enslavement, and invasion in different ways. They all, however, illustrate pervasive, widespread fears about modernity, some focusing quite deliberately on the paranoia surrounding threats such as Communism and (potential) global annihilation. Each of the novels, short stories, and films discussed above certainly influenced the content, look, and feel of those narratives that followed, even to the point of influencing each other. They consequently establish a progressive chain of texts and adaptations that reflect attitudes about the changing modern world, particularly attitudes about violence, inequality, and the shifting social dynamics of gender, race, patriarchal authority, and the traditional family unit. With these antecedental narratives in mind, Romero's genius and synthetic process become easier to understand. Yet while the different themes, motifs, and tones presented by each of these discussed narratives all influence Romero's ultimate vision for *Night of the Living Dead*, his story is inspired primarily by Matheson's novella *I Am Legend* and the cinematic adaptation of it, Ragona and Salkow's *Last Man on Earth*.

Inverting the Monster Narrative — *The Monsters* En Masse

With the help of writer John Russo, Romero established and codified the zombie invasion narrative. According to Perry Martin's documentary *The Dead Will Walk* (2004), the screenplay for *Night of the Living Dead* was adapted from an original if rough short story of Romero's called "Night of Anubis," a tale of isolation and supernatural peril that borrowed heavily from *I Am Legend*.[27] Matheson's chilling Gothic novella builds on the genealogical tradition discussed above and features hordes of vampires who rampantly infect and replace the world's human population. Richard Neville, the story's narrator and protagonist, literally becomes the last man on earth,[28] and he must garrison himself inside his home each night to avoid the hungry fangs of the vampiric infestation. During his struggle to survive, Neville acts with typical American pragmatism, fortifying his house, scavenging for and carefully storing food and supplies, and systematically killing the monsters his friends and family have become. These fundamental plot elements mark a dramatic change in the traditional vampire narrative, and each have now become firm protocols with the zombie invasion subgenre as well.

Stoker established the mysterious, aristocratic, and archetypical vampire with Count Dracula. Based on European folk legends and the real-life sensationalism surrounding Vlad Tepes, Prince of Wallachia ("Vlad the Impaler"), and building on earlier tales such as Polidori's *The Vampyre* and Joseph Sheridan Le Fanu's *Carmilla* (1872), Stoker's vampire possesses certain memorable traits and follows a number of intricate rules: Dracula is technically a dead creature, he continues to exist by feeding on the blood of the living, he infects others with his bite and can thus create additional vampires, and he has the power to seduce and hypnotize mortal humans. In *I Am Legend*, Matheson works within this tradition by featuring vampires that drink blood, hide during the day, and may be killed with a stake in the heart. Yet Matheson alters the vampire by making his nocturnal fiends more than just selectively procreative; *I Am Legend* turns the supernatural condition into a plague, resulting in a world dominated by an unstoppable vampiric horde. The vampires in Matheson's tale thus more accurately resemble the invasions of "The Birds" and *Invasion of the Body Snatchers*: creatures that attack in massive numbers and strive (and sometimes even manage) to replace the human race.

By inverting the structure of conflict — instead of a group of humans combating one vampire, an army of vampires assaults one human — Matheson reinvents the established "undead narrative." Neville becomes the central

Robert (Vincent Price) plays host to the vampire Ruth (Franca Bettoia) in his fortified home in a scene from Ragona and Salkow's film version of *I Am Legend*, *Last Man on Earth* (Associated Producers, 1964; Jerry Ohlinger).

figure of the tale, and the story focuses on his attempts to survive in spite of overwhelming odds. The action of the novella begins months after some unspecified global conflict (presumably an atomic one) has changed the climate of the planet, causing massive dust storms and the rampant spread of a variety of diseases. A plague soon follows, and the government begins ordering mandatory cremation for all corpses. Eventually the truth of the disease becomes public: those who die from the disease rise again as literal vampires, nocturnal creatures that feast on the blood of the living. Because the vampire condition is spread like a contagious disease, it takes just a few months for the entire human race to be infected — except for Neville, who is immune thanks to a bite he suffered from a vampire bat when he was younger. With the virtual destruction of humanity, the vampires set their sights on the last mortal survivor, and Neville goes to extreme measures to stay alive.

As in "The Birds," Neville turns his home into a fortress stronghold, but he does a much more effective job than the bewildered protagonists of du Maurier's story do because he has months to "dig in" instead of just an afternoon. The resourceful Neville installs a generator in his garage, stockpiles frozen and canned goods, boards up his windows, and even burns down the houses on either side of his to establish a defensible perimeter. He builds a similarly fortified greenhouse, grows copious amounts of garlic, and covers the outside of his house with garlic wreaths and mirrors. In spite of his supernatural situation, Neville approaches things with rational pragmatism. Having determined his foes to be vampires, he systematically employs the defenses required by the myths and legends of the Undead; in fact, his copy of *Dracula* becomes a kind of survivalist handbook. At night, when the fiends are abroad, Neville locks himself in, listens to classical music, and tries to read — as much as he can, the lone man attempts to live a "normal" life. Yet during the day, Neville burns any vampire corpses he finds and roams from house to house with a bag of sharpened wooden stakes. Rather than just hiding and waiting — like the protagonists in "The Birds"— Neville takes an active role and tries to reclaim a civilization that is essentially already lost.[29]

Eric Savoy claims the Gothic manifests gaps or rifts in history, chasms that are both nostalgic and openings to alternate horrors or possibilities,[30] and *I Am Legend* certainly falls under this classification because Matheson juxtaposes his horror with bittersweet nostalgia. This tragic longing for Neville's lost (and ultimately repressed) past is personalized through the second most important character in *I Am Legend*, the house itself. Not only does the dwelling offer Neville a refuge and a source of comfort and familiarity, the converted home unfortunately ties him down to one place and requires considerable attention and upkeep. Rather than roaming across the country in

search of other survivors, Neville must stay close to home; furthermore, he
cannot let go of the lost past that the house represents. This almost debilitating sense of nostalgia can also be seen in Willa Cather's 1925 novel *The
Professor's House*. Although certainly not a horror story in the traditional sense,
Cather's book can be read as a kind of ghost story, where the specters of God-
frey St. Peter's past haunt him and stifle his personal and professional progression. Even though he has a markedly modern new home to move
into — Cather emphasizes the house's electronic accoutrements and labor-
saving devices — St. Peter refuses to give up his office in the old house. There,
surrounded by the dressmaker forms that represent his daughters as children
and the old Mexican blanket that reminds him of the deceased Tom Out-
land, St. Peter suffers under the weight of melancholy and nostalgia, unable
to let the specters of his past go.

Nostalgia and loss are two major themes found in Cather's novel; in fact,
St. Peter's obstinate connection to the past becomes not only incapacitating
but also literally life-threatening. He fetishizes the contents of his old office,
even refusing to allow the maid Augusta to remove the dress forms to the new
house — "You shan't take away my ladies," St. Peter decrees[31] — because he so
desperately needs physical reminders of his past around him. He clings tight
to the old Mexican blanket because it's all he really has left of Tom, the man
he so wanted to become his son-in-law, who was killed fighting in World War
I. Throughout the course of the novel, the Professor becomes more and more
detached from his family and the present, choosing instead to edit Tom's journals and dwell on the past. This obsession culminates with St. Peter sleeping
alone in the old study with a dangerously faulty gas stove; when the pilot
light blows out, the Professor is nearly asphyxiated. His fixation on the past
leads him to the brink of suicide, but Augusta saves him at the last minute,
perhaps giving the man a new perspective on his life.

A similar irrational obsession with the irrevocably lost past also drives
much of the action of Matheson's story. In *I Am Legend*, Neville needs his
house not only as a place of safety but also as a reminder of his wife and daughter; yet the memories are more bitter than sweet. Even though he has his
choice of any location and dwelling in the essentially abandoned world, Neville
insists on seeing his *house* as still his *home*; unfortunately, the structure also
harbors the specters of his tragic past. Neville's inescapable haunting is first
manifested when he considers the need to ration his cigarettes:

> What will I do if I ever run out of coffin nails? he wondered, looking at the cig-
> arette's blue trailing smoke. Well, there wasn't much chance of that. He had
> about a thousand cartons in the closet of Kathy's —
>   He clenched his teeth together. In the closet of the *larder*, the *larder*, the *larder*.
> Kathy's room.[32]

Neville's need to rename his environment illustrates his attempt to forget his more painful ties to his past. His daughter was one of the first killed by the mysterious plague, and, like a dutiful citizen, he allowed her body to be incinerated by the military. That loss, and his perceived betrayal of his daughter's body and memory, cloud Neville's judgment while also tying him to his location.

Nevertheless, Neville isn't completely crippled by the past; although he won't leave the comforts of his home, he *is* trying to make something of his life and salvage the future stretching out before him. Emulating the rational mind of his father, Neville begins to approach the vampire problem scientifically. Recognizing the infestation as a kind of infection, Neville educates himself (slowly, but he has the time) in biology and pathology, procuring a microscope and performing systematic experiments on his own blood, on samples of infected blood, and on the vampires themselves. Having initially been convinced of the supernatural nature of the vampires, Neville pragmatically turns to science and reason for a possible solution. A marked shift in the vampire mythos from Stoker's archetype is Matheson's division of vampires into two distinct species: the infected, yet living, and the dead, yet reanimated. Those humans who have merely been infected by the vampire bacteria may possess all the essential characteristics of the dead variety, but they continue to live and breathe. Upon death, however, those thus infected rise again as a different kind of vampire, the more traditional "undead" variety. Recognizing the implications of this discovery — i.e., the mere infection of those still human — Neville resolves to find a cure for the virus, thus saving the "living dead" from the abhorrent fate of "undeath."

Therefore, Neville's story becomes more about humanity's attempted triumph over nature and less about survival against supernatural odds. Unfortunately, however, Neville's DIY biology proves fruitless; he cannot find a cure for the disease, so he once again resorts to killing every and all vampires he finds, regardless of the specifics of their condition. His rationale is that it's better for the living vampires to die at his hands than to die eventually from the disease and return as undead monsters. The twist in Matheson's narration, though, is that humanity has *already* triumphed and moved on — only without Neville. The diseased portion of the population has long discovered that which Neville so painstakingly unearthed; they have already come up with a treatment to control their infection, and they are beginning to rebuild society. Neville, the only non-infected (and, because of his immunity, non-*infectable*), suddenly becomes the marginalized Other of the story — his singularity literally alienates him. Because he must remain human, he cannot join the ranks of the new society, and his efforts to cleanse the earth for his own kind have turned him, albeit subjectively, into the monster. The "civilized" vampires see *him* as the monster of legend, an avenging angel who descends upon the helpless during the day, killing them in their sleep.[33]

I Am Legend therefore presents a new version of the vampire mythos and paves the way for future invasion narratives. Essentially, Matheson has taken the traditional vampire narrative, specifically the one pioneered by Stoker, and inverted it on two levels. First, he has put the human element in the minority and made the vampires the social norm. Second, rather than othering the monster in the traditional sense, he has challenged notions of subjectivity and turned the human into the Other — literally, not just metaphorically. This revolutionary twist in the nature of the supernatural monster would be further developed by the new zombie mythology of Romero. In *Night of the Living Dead*, Romero's masses of ghouls fuse the traditions of the vampire with those of the cinematic voodoo zombie, the house takes on the role of a nostalgic refuge, and the rational, decidedly pragmatic nature of humanity is unabashedly challenged. Yet to understand fully what Matheson and Romero have both accomplished in their re-imaginings of traditional monsters, particularly their explorations into human psychology, we must first consider Freud's notion of the uncanny and the return of the repressed.

The Invasion of the Home by the Unheimlich

Vampires and zombies — the key antagonists in *I Am Legend* and *Night of the Living Dead,* respectively — are not simply unimaginable monster or supernatural terrors; they are unimaginable monsters and supernatural terrors that look decidedly and eerily human. In the case of vampires, this resemblance can vary from gaunt, white faces with sunken eyes, long fangs, and animal-like claws, as in Murnau's *Nosferatu*, to the height of style and seductive beauty, as in most other cinematic depictions of Dracula. Zombies are generally less idealized or romanticized, being typically pale and sluggish, as in *White Zombie*, and/or violently injured and decomposing, as in *The Plague of the Zombies*. Regardless of such visual variations, however, both kinds of creatures have clear ties to the human. In fact, such foes are generally labeled as either "undead" or "living dead," that is, otherwise natural corpses that have been reanimated via magical or other supernatural means. Yet while they might look like "us," their unnatural state makes them a poignant representation of mortality itself, an uncanny *memento mori* that threatens the hapless living with either death or transformation to undeath. Furthermore, such creatures accomplish what Freud calls the return of the repressed and force us to face our deepest, our most primal fears.[34]

Freud defines the abstract concept of the *Unheimlich*, which is generally translated as the "uncanny," as "that species of the frightening that goes back to what was once well known and had long been familiar."[35] The true manifestation of this fear occurs, therefore, when something or someone familiar (such as a friend, spouse, or other loved one) returns in a disturbing, physical way (such as a corpse, ghost, or doppelganger); in other words, the familiar (*Heimlich*) becomes the unfamiliar or uncanny (*Unheimlich*).[36] Furthermore, the psychological effect of the uncanny becomes decidedly terrifying when the *Unheimlich* represents a manifestation of death. Dillard points out that "the idea of the dead's return to a kind of life is no new idea; it is present in all the ancient tales of vampires and ghouls and zombies, and it has been no stranger to films.... All of these tales and films spring from that ancient fear of the dead."[37] Dead bodies are not only a breeding ground for disease or a symbol of defilement; they are also a reminder to the living of their own mortality. For such reasons, creatures that have apparently overcome the debilitating effects of the grave are treated with revulsion and fear — especially when said creatures are hostile, violent, and ambulatory.

It is no surprise that those supernatural creatures able to defy the powers of death are usually at the heart of horror narratives and stories, for Freud claims that "to many people the acme of the uncanny is represented by anything to do with death, dead bodies, revenants, spirits and ghosts."[38] Perhaps the oldest campfire tale is the ghost story, for what is more uncanny than someone returning from the grave to wreak havoc on the living? Ghosts have a firmly established tradition, both orally and literarily, from Homer to Dante to Shakespeare to Dickens. However, ghosts are merely spirits, and although they may take on corporeal form and even interact with their environment, they are essentially consciousnesses that lack a biological body. Zombies, on the other hand, belong to a much more specific phylum: corporeal monsters that look uncannily like human beings. Such aberrant terrors include golems (unnatural creatures reassembled and brought back to life through the means of mysticism or science), vampires (demonic creatures that continue to cheat death by preying on the living), and zombies (in Romero's case, mindless automatons fueled by purely animalistic passions).[39]

The essentially *human* behavior of these supernatural creatures best explains the success of such fiends in nineteenth-century literature. Golems, such as Frankenstein's monster, are perhaps the most sympathetic Gothic creations — but, of course, Shelley's pathetic reanimated corpse is hardly "undead" in the traditional sense. He lives and breathes as a mortal human man brought back to life by Victor Frankenstein's (mis)application of science and technology. The vampire, on the other hand, is truly supernatural and certainly the most prolific of these monstrous foes. Yet although he is unequivocally undead, Stoker's archetypal Count behaves as though still alive, using his immorality to pursue primarily carnal desires. Dracula is mysterious, cunning, and seductive, and his piercing stare and eloquent tongue easily beguile young women and readers alike. He appears both attractive and familiar by wearing the guise of youth and vitality, but Dracula is fundamentally an uncanny symbol of mortality. Not only is he decidedly inhuman — he lacks a reflection, which is regarded as a manifestation of the soul[40] — he also represents the reality of death itself with his drinking of innocent blood, his propensity to murder women and small children, and his habit of sleeping in a coffin.

Zombies, in marked contrast, have lost all connection with their human behavior beyond the most superficial. They look human, they walk upright, and they can even use the simplest of tools, yet their motivating drive never transcends the animalistic; in Romero's version of the mythology, they exist only to feed. In other words, Romero's zombies have become pure id, governed by sheer animal drive — what Freud calls "the passions" — but without any "reason or common sense."[41] Furthermore, because these creatures are well and truly dead, they have no developed brain functions; that is, they cannot process information, learn from their mistakes, act in their own self-interest, or even speak.[42] Instead, zombies act on instinct and drive alone, mindlessly pursuing the basest of needs in a veritable orgy of unchecked indulgence. These qualities make Romero's zombies unavoidably flat characters, which could explain their virtual absence from novels and other written stories (at least prior to 1968); their essentially physical qualities, however, make zombies ideal cinematic monstrosities. By presenting zombies as literal walking corpses (the "living dead" rather than "undead"), zombie films horrify protagonists and audiences alike with the uncanny fusion of the familiar with the unfamiliar.

All cinematic monsters that essentially resemble humans must be considered uncanny on some level, but those that are fundamentally "dead" take the idea of the *Unheimlich* to a powerful extreme. Vampires, for instance, can talk and even pass as living humans; however, these qualities make them more familiar than unfamiliar and weaken the force of their uncanny appearance. Zombies, on the other hand, clearly look dead — pale skin, vacant stares, hideous wounds, and decaying flesh — and have lost the power of speech, which makes them even less human and all the more terrifying. According to Masahiro Mori's "Uncanny Valley," a corpse represents the lowest point of the graph between the human and the nonhuman for a nonmoving body (see "Masahiro Mori's Uncanny Valley").[43] However, because a zombie can move, it is even less familiar than a corpse, which, for all its repulsion, is nonetheless a natural thing. The more disturbing and unexpected the appearance of the zombie — the extent of its corporeal decomposition, for instance — the lower the valley will dip on Mori's scale, making the creature all the more unfamiliar or *Unheimlich*. Yet the more familiar the corpse is — by being a former friend or loved one — the closer the valley is to human likeness, enhancing the *Heimlich* familiarity. If the "*Heimlich Unheimlich*" represents the most terrifying combination (the monster that is both extremely familiar in its human-like appearance yet extremely unfamiliar in every other way), then the zombie represents an ideal manifestation of Freud's configuration.

The uncanny is not only physically frightening but also constitutes a return of psychologically repressed trauma.[44] As Freud points out, "This uncanny element is actually nothing new or strange, but something ... estranged from [the psyche] only through being repressed"[45]; in other words, the uncanny presents an element of that which may be familiar but isn't necessarily desired. For Freud, this repressed anxiety is the very concept of death itself, for, unfortunately, "*the aim of all life is death.*"[46] In *I Am Legend*, however, this same repression and return occurs on a very literal level. Neville is traumatized by the death of his wife, but he refuses to repeat the mistake made with his daughter and confine her body to the flames of the town incinerator. Instead, he secretly buries the body of his wife in a vacant lot across the street from his house. Not long thereafter, she rises from her shallow grave and returns to her home, rattling the door handle and calling her husband's name: "Rob ... ert."[47] Neville's repression — the burning of his daughter's body, the untimely death of his wife, and his guilt for staying alive and

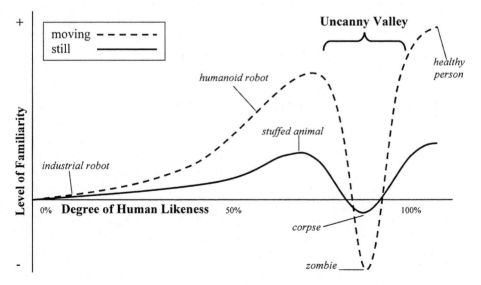

Masahiro Mori's Uncanny Valley (adapted by the author from Karl F. MacDorman's figure and used by permission according to the GNU Free Documentation License, Version 1.2).

healthy — *literally* returns and comes home.[48] This scene is substantially more powerful in the Ragona and Salkow's *Last Man on Earth*, in which audiences are confronted with much more detail than that offered by Matheson: a physical representation of Virginia (Emma Danieli), dressed in her ratty nightgown, stumbling through the front door, arms reaching for Vincent Price's Robert, her raspy voice repeatedly calling his name.

We can now see that Romero's zombies, although largely new creations, operate within the realm of the *Unheimlich* and build upon the themes and images presented in Stoker's *Dracula*, Matheson's *I Am Legend*, and other, perhaps less likely, literary texts. Yet as shall be examined in the next section, Romero took from a variety of additional sources to create a monster that is uncanny on an extra-textual level. Although it looks familiar, like the monsters audiences had become accustomed to in other horror films, the zombie is decided *un*familiar in specific ways. The audience thus experiences a sense of the *Unheimlich* similar to that experienced by the characters in the movie. They think they know what they are getting — zombies, vampires, pod-people, etc. — but in fact they are confronted by a disturbingly, uncannily new foe, one that closely resembles the familiar movie monsters of the past, but one that behaves according to a whole new set of generic rules and protocols. Furthermore, this new terror, the contagious, cannibalistic, "walking dead" ghoul, has since proven powerful and popular enough to continue as the feature attraction in a variety of other zombie films over the past forty years.

Reading the Zombie Invasion Narrative

Romero was not just making another tired zombie movie when he began the *Night of the Living Dead* project, but neither was he simply recycling the narrative structure and cinematic appearance of Ragona and Salkow's vampire invasion movie. Instead, he was inventing a new subgenre of horror — the zombie invasion narrative — by combining the two antecedents to create a film that Russell describes as having "pushed the envelope of modern horror in a manner that perhaps no other movie since *Psycho* had done."[49] This now classic zombie story has a number of specific characteristics that distinguish it from other tales of the supernatural. Drawing from the apocalypse tradition, zombie invasion narratives are almost always set at the apparent end of the world, where devastating events have rendered the human race all but helpless. Yet the primary details in Romero's series of zombie films are in essence bland and ordinary, implying that such extraordinary events could happen to anyone, anywhere, at any time. Perhaps most importantly, Romero has changed the nature of the central creature, presenting a synthesis of the voodoo zombie, the alien invader, and the vampire. This new threat effectively overwhelms the few human protagonists, othering *them* and raising probing questions about what it really means to be a monster. A detailed look at the prototypical zombie invasion film —*Night of the Living Dead*— illustrates these defining cinematic features and establishes why Romero's project so essentially changed the course of the horror film genre.

Night of the Living Dead is presented on a very pessimistic stage: that of the apocalypse.[50] A strange phenomenon suddenly and inexplicably overcomes society, resulting in a literal hell on earth where the dead walk and no one is safe. A space probe has returned from Venus, bearing some kind of unknown radiation, and this extraterrestrial fallout appears to cause all recently dead humans on Earth to rise and attack the living. There are pointedly no voodoo rituals here, as Romero taps into the plot tropes of the atomic-monster and alien-invasion films of the 1950s. Furthermore, unlike Murder Legendre's servants in *White Zombie*, the malevolent aliens in *Invisible Invaders*, or even the army of the dead in Ed Wood's *Plan 9 from Outer Space*, Romero's zombies have no master and act on sheer drive and instinct alone.

Romero brings on the dead in *Night of the Living Dead* (Image Ten, 1968; Jerry Ohlinger).

This plot inversion thus alters the master/slave dialectic present in the voodoo zombie films: the monsters are no longer simply slaves acting on the orders of others; if anything, they symbolize a slave or even proletarian revolution. Unfettered from death, the ghouls turn on those who could be seen as their one-time oppressors; after all, the living humans get to enjoy life while the dead have no access to such physical pleasures. Yet the zombies constitute more than just a rebellion; in Romero's world, they are also the new social order. Having no singular master, other than the basest of drives, these creatures quickly prove a real threat for the living; in fact, the zombies of *Night of the Living Dead* function as a type of master themselves, converting and enslaving others to their grisly force of sheer numbers.

Like vampires, Romero's flesh-eating villains communicate their condition to others. In *Night of the Living Dead*, it's unclear whether zombiism is viral, born in the blood, or merely a prevailing effect of extraterrestrial radiation; in a reversal of *I Am Legend*, hard science plays little role in Romero's movie at all. What is clear is that those attacked by zombies eventually and inevitably die from their wounds, and they soon rise from the dead as cannibalistic ghouls themselves. Regardless of the rational explanation, Romero's zombies themselves act like a virus, for direct contact with the living unavoidably results in conversion to the dead. The ghouls feed on human flesh — in a horrific and blatant disregard of society's cannibalism taboo — and those thus killed are soon resurrected and become the walking dead, assuming there is enough flesh and bone remaining for their corpse to become mobile. The logistical problems are obvious: the dead rise as zombies, those attacked by zombies become zombies, and even humans killed by other humans become zombies. As a matter of simple statistics, it doesn't take long for the dead to far outnumber the living, and the apocalypse of *Night of the Living Dead* appears to be in full swing within mere hours. The dead become mechanical juggernauts, and those left struggling to survive are forced to adopt a much more primordial stance. The order of the day becomes kill or be killed, and average folks are quickly transformed into desperate vigilantes.

As in other end-of-the-world narratives, such as Ray Milland's *Panic in Year Zero!* (1962), *Night of the Living Dead* depicts the almost immediate breakdown of society's infrastructure, especially those systems associated with the government and technology. Russell points out the timeliness of these apocalyptic images, for Romero's debut film hit theaters "at the height of the [Vietnam] war, as race riots, peace demonstrations and the angry outbursts of a youthful counterculture raged through America," and the movie "pulled no punches in its representation of a nation falling apart on every level."[51] *Night of the Living Dead* portrays law enforcement as incompetent and backwater — the local country sheriff is a stereotyped yokel with a "shoot first" attitude — so the beleaguered population must fend for itself instead. The media does what it can, broadcasting tidbits of helpful information and advice by way of radio and television, such as the revelation that marauding ghouls can, in fact, be killed (or rather, re-killed?). Their motor functions must still be managed by the brain, because destruction of the head keeps a zombie from rising again.[52] Yet the overall outlook presented by police and journalists is fundamentally grim: hide if you can, fight if you have to. In the end, the once orderly structure of society proves little help; human survivors are left to their own devices with no real hope of rescue or support. One of the defining features of Romero's zombie films is how motley groups of humans are forced into hiding, holing up in "safe houses" of some kind where they barricade themselves in and wait in vain for the trouble to pass. This claustrophobic situation invariably reiterates societal problems and tensions, particularly those of the patriarchy, gender, and race, which I will discuss later.

Of course, such a bleak scenario is not necessarily limited to zombie invasion movies; "slasher" films and alien-invasion movies often rely on similar plot devices. However, whereas those movies usually feature an unrealistic cast of vivacious eye candy, computer-savvy geniuses, or stylized superheroes, zombie cinema pursues the struggles of bland, ordinary (i.e., *Heimlich*) citizens.[53] As *Night of the Living Dead* opens, a rather plain, average young woman and her equally pedestrian brother are traveling to visit the grave of their father in rural Pennsylvania. While they are paying their respects at the gravesite, an innocuous gentleman (Bill Heinzman) can be seen shuffling across the background of the frame. Johnny (Russell Streiner) begins to tease his sister Barbra (Judith O'Dea) about her childish fear of cemeteries, and he uses the passing stranger to feed the fire: "They're coming to get you, Barbra!" he taunts, forcing his sister's disgusted retreat. As Barbra embarrassingly approaches the strange man to apologize, the unthinkable happens — he *is* out to get her! Although the zombie looks like a normal human being (albeit a bit pasty), he attacks Barbra with wanton savagery and kills her ill-fated brother when Johnny tries to intervene. Although this shocking development does match the cinematic tradition of a male monster menacing a woman, and a white one at that, Russell points out how "by exercising both the supernatural and the magical connotations for the zombie's voodoo origins, *Night of the Living Dead* foregrounds its horror in the real world as it is transformed from safe to horrific by an inexplicable shift in the natural order."[54] Romero presents his world as the "normal" one of everyday life, but normality has now suddenly been altered into something terrifying.

The threatened Barbra does her best to cope with such an unexpected change in "the natural order," and, in the grand tradition of most horror films, she runs away, stumbling and tripping, to her car. The zombie begins a methodical, if rather slow, pursuit, its every movement highlighted by lightning flashes and dramatic camera angles. Echoes of the voodoo zombie are evident in both the look and mannerisms of the zombie and the stark, black-and-white cinematography. The gaunt, albeit clearly white, man shuffles and gropes his way after his harried prey, and, although Barbra makes it to her car, she is thwarted in her escape: the keys are still in Johnny's pocket. Another dramatically measured footrace ensues, and Barbra makes it to an isolated farmhouse. On the verge of hysteria, she calls for help and frantically searches the rooms, but she is horrified to discover the former occupants are already dead and partially decayed or eaten. Barbra — and the audience with her — is mystified, confused, and understandably traumatized, but at least the creature from the cemetery is safely locked outside. Almost immediately, Barbra is joined by a young black man named Ben, another survivor of the mysterious onslaught, who has come to the farmhouse in search of refuge and, he hopes, some gasoline for his truck. The two quickly realize it isn't safe to venture out of doors, especially not after dark, so at this point Romero's zombie film establishes one of the most defining characteristics of the subgenre: hiding out.

As I will explore in more detail later, the literally *Heimlich* nature of the house (since *Heimlich* translates literally as "homey") quickly becomes something far more *Unheimlich* as the film progresses. The farmhouse itself symbolizes the comforting idea that one's home is a place of security, but this eerily empty place does not belong to either Barbra or Ben. Unlike the family homes that play such central roles in "The Birds" and *I Am Legend*, the house of *Night of the Living Dead* constitutes a decidedly foreign, unfamiliar environment; Ben and Barbra are indeed strangers in a strange land. Unfortunately, the house is quickly established as neither empty nor safe: soon after Barbra finds the masticated corpses of the presumed owners, Ben must defend her from more creatures like the one from the cemetery that have somehow broken in. Out of desperate necessity, Ben immediately begins a radical home renovation to convert the farmhouse quickly into a makeshift fortress. Visual ties to *The Birds* and *Last Man on Earth* are obvious; Ben uses rough tools to attack and incapacitate the zombies, he systematically tosses the bodies outside, and he starts dismantling furniture to board up the doors and windows. In fact, Ben becomes a heroic icon of American pragmatism, hardly slowing down to let the gravity of his horrific situation sink in. Barbra, on the other hand, can apparently do little more than sit and stare, bemoaning the loss of her brother in a borderline catatonic state. Although the home comes to regain its physical sense of security (the *Heimlich*), it clearly has no power to provide any psychological comfort (it has become *Unheimlich* despite all efforts to the contrary).

That the seemingly harmless and ordinary can prove to be so life-threatening is one of the fundamental precepts of the zombie invasion formula. In addition to the slow-moving ghouls and the common farmhouse, the film's protagonists never become anything unusually heroic. The female characters of *Night of the Living Dead* have advanced little since *White Zombie*— Barbra remains a passive victim, traumatized into inaction by the brutal slaying of her brother. Ben, although a young, dynamic black man, appears as little more than a workaday "everyman"; he focuses on the essentials of survival and does not even stop to ask many questions. The cast of the film does expand when additional survivors are found hiding in the basement, but Tom (Keith Wayne) and Judy (Judith Ridley) are merely a stereotyped young dating couple, and Harry (Karl Hardman) and Helen (Marilyn Eastman) Cooper are little more than a generic married pair with an injured daughter named Karen (Kyra Schon). These links to normalcy are emphasized by Dillard, who describes the essentially mundane nature of *Night of the Living Dead* as "the story of everyday people in an ordinary landscape, played by everyday people who are, for the most part, from that ordinary locale."[55] In his afterword to the graphic novel *Miles Behind Us*, Pegg points out that the protagonists of zombie invasion movies are not superheroes or professional monster slayers like Van Helsing — they are common, average folk forced to "step up" and defend themselves.[56] The ordinary and familiar once again functions to emphasize the horror created by the *un*familiar, *Unheimlich* scenario.

The relevance of Freud's uncanny reaches its zenith, however, in the physical form of the zombies themselves, as their outward appearance constitutes their most striking and frightening aspect: the creatures were once — quite recently — living people. Russell points out how the human body consistently functions as "the inevitable focus of any zombie movie,"[57] whether the body is that of the racially-charged victims of voodoo magic in the early films or that of the animated corpses of Romero. Zombies are not dramatically supernatural in behavior or appearance: no fangs, no wings, no translucence, no monstrous features — just pale skin, gaping wounds, and noticeable decay. Furthermore, in *Night of the Living Dead*, the menacing creatures are not merely the harbingers of death; they are iconic representations of Death itself. Russell emphasizes the importance of what Romero has done in reinventing the voodoo zombie as a decaying cannibal: "By forcing audiences to sit up and recognise the zombie for what it really was — a cadaver — Romero challenged our understandings of the monstrous and our long-held beliefs about the finality of death."[58] With the country embroiled in the violence of Vietnam, American moviegoers were being saturated daily by horrific images of death and dismemberment on the evening news. For a generation that hadn't lived through the dark days of World War II, the grim reality of death was finally being driven home, and *Night of the Living Dead* both forces viewers to confront that shocking reality and gives them an avenue to deal with such trauma via a dramatic catharsis.

Moreover, Romero's conception of the zombie amplifies the mere physical horrors of death by marrying mortality with the loss of autonomy. Those killed by the zombies of *Night of the Living Dead* are not allowed to "rest in peace"; instead, they become unwilling recruits in the army of the walking dead. In other words, the one-time *pro*tagonists of the film become its eventual *an*tagonists. Because those who die come back as aggressive and violent zombies, the characters cannot fully trust each other. As Dillard points out, "The living people are dangerous to each other ... because they are potentially living dead should they die."[59] *Night of the Living Dead* may introduce its audience to a number of diverse characters, but these so-called heroes, when infected, rapidly become the most savage and threatening of villains. This potential for violence lies within everyone, of course, but we choose to repress this knowledge, especially considering the danger loved ones or young children really pose. Romero's zombies thus reveal these repressed fears, and this stark manifestation of the uncanny is chillingly illustrated when poor Johnny returns near the end of the picture as a zombie, "still wearing his driving gloves and clutching for his sister with the idiotic, implacable single-mindedness of the hungry dead."[60] Like Virginia's return in *Last Man on Earth*, Johnny represents the literal "return of the repressed" for Barbra. His deceptive yet essential familiarity is what ultimately leads Barbra to her doom. While trying to defend the farmhouse's fortifications, she hesitates at the sight of her brother, failing to recognize the dangers of his zombification until it's too late.

This terrifying prospect — the metamorphosis of one's friends and family members to intractable monsters — is shown even more graphically when the young girl Karen murders and feasts upon her own parents. As the climactic battle with the swarming zombies rages upstairs, Karen finally dies from her wounds and succumbs to the effects of the mysterious radiation. In a terrifying literalization of Bruhm's claim that "Gothic children threaten the role of the parent by consuming or incorporating that parent's power,"[61] the girl rather quickly revives as one of the living dead and immediately falls upon her dying father, gnawing hungrily on Harry's arm. Helen rushes down to the perceived safety of the basement but is horrified by the shocking act of incestuous cannibalism she finds there, and the zombie Karen brutally attacks her mother with a trowel.[62] Helen does little more than allow herself to be butchered; shock at seeing her daughter turned into a zombie and a binding sense of love and compassion combine to render her impotent. Like many of the characters in "Who Goes There?" and *Invasion of the Body Snatchers*, Helen cannot accept that her daughter has become a monster, and that inability to comprehend the *Unheimlich* leads to her death. When Ben eventually retreats to the perceived safety of the cellar himself, he is forced — yet willing — to kill the zombies the Cooper family have become. Such visceral shocks obviously work well in a cinematic medium because the audience also instantly recognizes the former protagonists in their zombified forms and can intimately relate to the horrified reactions of the survivors. The "familiar unfamiliarity" of the one-time heroes elicits a disturbing psychological reaction from the film's characters and the viewers alike.

The uncanny effect of Romero's zombie monsters makes them fundamentally terrifying because in them one sees one's self. Pegg discusses this essential function of the zombie: "Metaphorically, this classic creature embodies a number of our greatest fears. Most obviously, it is our own death, personified. The physical manifestation of that thing we fear the most. More subtly, the zombie represents a number of our deeper insecurities. The fear that deep down, we may be little more than animals, concerned only with appetite."[63] In a very real sense, then, *Night of the Living Dead* is the story of humanity's struggle to retain its sense of humanity. Ben and the others try to fight the zombies together just to stay alive, but they also argue and clash with each other. Their ultimate failure to "cooperate and put aside their petty differences" invites the chaos of the film and results in the tragic death of all the human protagonists.[64] Although he manages to remain uninfected by the zombie plague, Ben's civility suffers and crumbles under the stress of the siege; because he has been effectively othered by the monstrosities threatening from without, he becomes something of a monster himself. He strikes Barbra for being hysterical, physically assaults Harry for disagreeing with his plans, and eventually shoots Harry in the stomach with a rifle. In fact, Ben is almost as violent and irrational as the zombies themselves, although he is the closest thing the movie has to a real hero.

Of special significance, of course, is Ben's race. As the only African American in the cast — and in a black-and-white film as well — Ben appears visually different from the other human protagonists, not to mention the pasty-faced zombies. And although he is just trying to resist white patriarchy's "othering" of his autonomy and authority, Ben's determination to take charge of the situation early on and to bark orders with an almost arrogant impunity at the film's white characters recalls the threat of the Other as depicted in the voodoo-zombie films. When he bosses around the glassy-eyed and inert Barbra, even daring to slap her across the face, the parallels between Ben and the menacing black voodoo priests of *White Zombie* and *I Walked with a Zombie* become abundantly clear. In the midst of the social upheavals of the Civil Right's Movement, Ben manifests the greatest fear of many white Americans:

that black men would become socially impertinent and come to threaten the safety of white women. Furthermore, the escalating tension between Ben and Harry mirrors the racial conflicts raging in America at the time, and contemporary violence between whites and blacks reappears symbolically in *Night of the Living Dead* through the physical altercations between humans and zombies. Of course, coming on the heels of Martin Luther King Jr.'s assassination, and in light of abundant lynchings and racially motivated murders, Ben's eventual death at the hands of a white posse becomes a scathing condemnation of unchecked violence and social injustice in 1968 America.

Romero's Redeployment of the Gothic Tradition

Despite its likely classification in either the horror or science fiction camps, Romero's *Night of the Living Dead* is fundamentally a part of the Gothic literary tradition as well, particularly in the way it adopts and adapts its "antiquated space" to reflect the key cultural concerns and anxieties at play in the contemporary environment that produced it. The Gothic tradition has a well-proven ability to adjust and change over the years, and the central trope of the "haunted house" has changed as well, from the castles of *The Castle of Otranto* (1764) and *The Mysteries of Udolpho* (1794), to the crypts of *The Monk* (1796), to the dark caverns of *Edgar Huntly* (1799), to the mansions of *The Turn of the Screw* (1898) and *Rebecca* (1938), to the plantation houses of *Uncle Tom's Cabin* (1853), *Light in August* (1932), and *Absalom, Absalom!* (1936). *Night of the Living Dead* places its besieged protagonists in a traditional farmhouse, and Romero's successive films shift the location of the action to tellingly singular settings: a shopping mall, an underground military bunker, and a dystopian, post-apocalyptic apartment building. All of these settings prove essential to understanding the cultural resonance of their respective films; in fact, the locations are perhaps more important in interpreting the complex messages of the movies than the zombie monsters themselves. Approaching these cinematic texts through the critical lens of the Gothic tradition will both establish the underlying, unresolved cultural foundations of such popular films and facilitate new readings of their implicit social critiques.

Although undeniably part of the American horror film tradition, Romero's movies are not regularly viewed as part of the *Gothic* tradition. Nonetheless, Romero's zombie narratives actually fit more comfortably within the generic structure of the Gothic mode than in the categories of invasion horror or science fiction. According to Hogle's matrix, the defining characteristics of the Gothic include (1) an antiquated space, (2) a hidden secret from the past, (3) a physical or psychological haunting, and (4) an oscillation between earthly reality and the possibility of the supernatural.[65] To be sure, while the spaces and settings used by Romero are fundamental to the narratives themselves — as the protagonists must invariably hide in and defend besieged locations to survive — they are not obviously antiquated, and their haunting secrets are not necessarily apparent to the casual viewer, nor are they exclusively from the past. Yet the locations of Romero's zombie movies *are* clearly haunted, in one way or another, and the supernatural plays an obviously central role as well. Hogle argues further that these four distinctive characteristics make the Gothic especially suitable to both a psychological and a social/Marxist critical approach, which helps to explain how "the longevity and power of Gothic fiction unquestionably stem from the way it helps us address and disguise some of the most important desires, quandaries, and sources of anxiety ... throughout the history of western culture."[66] The Gothic features of *Night of the Living Dead* reveal how the film uses its central location to comment on contemporary anxieties, particularly the state of the family during the 1960s.

In fact, *Night of the Living Dead* proves to be the most traditionally Gothic of Romero's zombie movies. By setting the action in a typical house, Romero is addressing cultural anxieties connected to the American family of the 1960s, emphasizing in particular the breakdown of the nuclear family, the rising independence of women, the racial struggles of the Civil Rights Movement, and the horrors of the Vietnam War. David Punter emphasizes how the film follows a diverse group of survivors holed up in the farmhouse, "a 'representative' group of Americans": the quarreling siblings, the take-charge black man, the young romantic couple, and the dysfunctional married couple with an injured daughter. The behavior of all of these characters illustrates the erosion of conservative social and family structures through Romero's "investigation into what happens to people under the dual stress of external danger and internal claustrophobia."[67] By the end of the movie, the brother has killed his antagonistic yet prayerful sister, the independent and aggressive black man has been lynched by the local (white) militia, the young couple has died in an explosion, and the young girl has murdered her quarreling parents. Romero's film clearly manifests both Bruhm's vision of the contemporary Gothic as one that "registers the (Freudian) impossibility of familial harmony" and Anne Williams' view that "the nightmarish haunted house as Gothic setting puts into play the anxieties, tensions, and imbalances inherent in family structures."[68] Romero literalizes these observations by staging *Night of the Living Dead* in the symbolic confines of what was once a traditional family home, which has become something of an "antiquated space," one could say, in 1968.

The farmhouse can be read as a Gothic space because of this implied antiquation, the secrets it conceals, and the role it plays as a location of safety that "hides" the besieged human protagonists. Most of the action of *Night of the Living Dead* takes place in the old house on the isolated country farm, a symbol for both a traditional social organization and a rather antiquated agrarian lifestyle. The farmhouse appears to be in good condition from the outside, and Barbra's initial investigation of its rooms reveals all the trappings of a dwelling that is still being used by its owners. Yet those owners are initially nowhere to be found; in fact, the house takes on an antiquated cast because it looks to be, albeit recently, abandoned. In addition, the taxidermied animal heads on the walls of the living room give the space the feel of an old hunting lodge or even a European castle, and they underscore the location's implicit association with death and decay. Later in the film, Tom reveals how he and Judy, who are from the area, have long known about the "old house" and thus considered it to be a logical place for them to hide once they heard reports of the zombie crises on the radio. This quality of the house thus establishes it as a place of safety; however, Williams emphasizes how "the walls of the house both defend it from the outside world ('A man's home is his castle') and hide the secrets is thereby creates."[69] The farmhouse therefore quickly becomes both a location to be defended and a place where the vulnerable protagonists have hidden themselves, along with all of their dysfunctional qualities.

Yet even though the farmhouse begins the film as a familiar and comfortable location, a symbol for stability and protection, the supernatural events of *Night of the Living Dead* soon transform it into something else entirely. In his review of Daniel Sanders' *Wörterbuch der Deutschen Sprache*, Freud emphasizes definitions of *Heimlich* that include both "belonging to the house, not strange, familiar, tame, dear and intimate, homely" and "concealed, kept hidden, so that others do not get to know of it of about it and it is hidden from them."[70] *Unheimlich* is clearly the antonym of the first definition — being that which is unfamiliar, eerie, not of the house — but it can also be used in opposition to the second definition in Freud's sense: revealing the hidden or repressed, "everything that was intended to remain secret, hidden away, and has come into the open."[71] Freud uses these definitions to emphasize how the most frightening thing is the "*Heimlich Unheimlich*," the unfamiliar familiar, or the revealing of that which was hidden (i.e., repressed) in the most commonplace levels of existence. The farmhouse can be seen as a setting both familiar and comforting, which explains why the survivors of Romero's film are drawn to it in the first place, but it becomes disturbingly unfamiliar and even threatening because of both the actions of the surviving humans hiding inside and the increasingly formidable assault from the zombies on the outside.

Ben (Duane Jones) fights to defend his house-cum-fortress in *Night of the Living Dead* (Image Ten, 1968; Jerry Ohlinger).

In fact, the very appearance of the house changes as the film progresses, with Ben literally tearing the house apart in his efforts to convert the expected comforts of the middle-class home into the fortifications and defenses needed in his desperate situation. When Barbra (and the audience) first sees the house, it appears as a white structure in the distance; more importantly, it appears as a symbol for civilization and community, a place where Barbra hopes to find help and safety. Luckily, the back door stands open, and Barbra immediately enters and fastens the catch behind her, emphasizing the role the house will play in the plot as a refuge and beginning its systematic transformation into a fortress. However, the home quickly changes to a dark and sinister space on the inside, with harsh shadows and dark corners that give the location a decidedly Gothic feel. In fact, Waller calls the farmhouse of *Night of the Living Dead* a "haunted house — dark, full of shadows and frightening sights, potentially a trap."[72] When Ben arrives at the house, he recognizes it might be better to keep running, since the very presence of Ben and Barbra makes the house an appealing destination for the zombies as well. Nevertheless, Ben lingers, and although he tries to make the house more familiar and comforting by turning on all the lights, he immediately transforms things with his efforts to add structural fortifications. He uses all the spare wood and lumber he can find to board up the doors and windows, giving the interior a decidedly unfamiliar cast. The house is no longer a home but a rag-tag fortress. In other words, Ben must tear the house apart to build it up as something new, different, and un-homey (*Unheimlich*).

The farmhouse thus epitomizes Freud's conception of the uncanny because it continues to vacillate between states of familiarity and unfamiliarity. On the one hand, it represents a place of at least limited safety: despite their numbers, the loitering zombies show little capacity to organize or to use tools to break through Ben's rather weak defenses. In addition, the radio broadcast emphasizes how people should stay inside if possible, particularly in their homes, as simple locked doors prove to be a good defense against the clumsy zombies. By preserving this aspect of the location's familiarity, *Night of the Living Dead* constructs a traditionally Gothic space: the dwelling becomes both a place of comfort and safety *and* a structure of imposition and menace. For example, when the electricity goes out near the climax of the movie, the house is filled with increased darkness, chiaroscuro lighting, and even deeper shadows. At the same time, the zombies launch their final assault on Ben's fortifications, and the monsters begin to break windows and displace boards, ultimately forcing their way in through the front door and driving Ben down into the basement. The upper rooms of the house become their most uncanny and disturbing when filled with the milling zombies, giving the space the look and feel of some kind of macabre dinner party for the dead. By morning, the house has almost regained its familiar appearance, looking calm and peaceful once more, but rather than being a place of safety for Ben, it proves to be the location of his death, as he is gunned down by one of the militia who sees him through a window.

The house of *Night of the Living Dead* fulfills another requirement of Freud's uncanny too in that it functions as a site that hides the repressed traumas and anxieties of society, and it provides a location for the return of these repressed cultural quandaries. Savoy argues that rather than simply replicating formulaic plots and European situations, the American Gothic manifests the anxieties associated with historical crimes and taboo desire through innovative figures and tropes, especially *prosopopoeia*, which is the personification of abstract ideas, usually as a ghost. The specter thus achieves the effects of the haunted, the uncanny, and the return of the repressed within the life and psyche of America.[73] As mentioned above, the house in *Night of the Living Dead* establishes the family as the central feature of contemporary life being explored by Romero's narrative, and because a host of human fears are projected onto and focused by the farmhouse itself, Romero gives the structure a certain degree of animation. Therefore, the Gothic use of prosopopoeia and the uncanny indicate that this "house" is a whitewashed façade that conceals repressed anxieties and secrets about the American family. After all, America was changing during the 1960s: people were beginning to challenge both the traditional, middle-class, nuclear family and the concept of the all-powerful patriarchal authority. Not all families were happy, as they were generally depicted on television, and father did not always "know best."

Like all great Gothic narratives, then, *Night of the Living Dead* uses allegory to present audiences with these contemporary cultural anxieties and concerns, and Romero focuses primarily on the symbol of the house to accomplish his didactic purpose. Anne Williams stresses how the house (mansion, castle, cave, abbey, etc.) is such a vital part of the Gothic as to be seen as a character by itself[74]; for that reason, the location of the action proves essential to understanding the allegorical function of any given Gothic narrative. According to Savoy, allegory is the "strangest house of fiction," and it is therefore "not surprising that the house is the most persistent site, object, structural analogue, and trope of American gothic's allegorical turn."[75] Many American Gothic stories focus on the house as a symbol for familial genealogy, racial purity, and hidden secrets, such as the ancestral home of Nathaniel Hawthorne's *The House of the Seven Gables* (1851) or the plantation mansions of William Faulkner's novels, but Savoy claims that "the psychic 'house' turns towards the gothic only when it is 'haunted' by the return of the repressed, a return that impels spectacular figures. More specifically, prosopopoeia may be conceptualized as the master trope of gothic's allegorical turn, because prosopopoeia ... disturbs logocentric order, the common reality of things."[76] Savoy discusses how Edgar Allan Poe used the corpse, the face of the dead, to enact this allegorical prosopopoeia,[77] which has obvious implications to zombie narratives, but the "face" functions in other ways as well.

As if the zombies themselves were not enough of a reminder about the film's obsession with death and decay, *Night of the Living Dead* features an additional rotting corpse as the allegorical "face of the tenant," revealing one fundamental secret repressed by the farmhouse to be mortality itself. When Barbra investigates the upstairs rooms of the seemingly abandoned house, she rather shockingly discovers the literal face of the house's tenant — a decayed and partially eaten skull. The head is lying on its side, but one remaining eye glares accusingly at the intruding young woman, establishing both Barbra's identity as a trespasser and her mortally tenuous situation. The shock is so powerful that Barbra drops the kitchen knife she has been holding and actually rushes out of the house, unmindful of the zombie presence that drove her into the building in the first place. She luckily meets Ben, who pushes her back inside, but even he is visibly shaken by the specter of the corpse at the top of the stairs. The audience should experience a similarly abject revulsion upon seeing the rotting face, and its dead-eye gaze directly into the camera can perhaps be read as an accusation linked to the grisly deaths occurring in Vietnam.[78] However, after Ben has finished most of his fortifications, in effect taking over the house as his own, he ventures back upstairs and moves the body from its location as a kind of guardian at the top of the stairs. In other words, Ben usurps the place of the tenant, hiding the face from the past and replacing it with his own. Nevertheless, the profusion of dead bodies — from the corpses, to the zombies, and even to the stuffed animal heads on the walls — all work to underscore the true secret of the film: everyone in the house — and by extension, the audience — is going to die.

Of course, the house functions allegorically on another level as well: if the rotting face of the tenant rises up from the repression associated with mortality and the atrocities of Vietnam, Barbra's initial invasion of the house recalls the Bluebeard myth and manifests cultural anxieties concerning the liberated status of women during the 1960s. Anne Williams illustrates how Bluebeard's story "suggests how a 'central term' of Gothic, the 'haunted castle,' may be read as a complex metaphor for the structures of cultural power (whether private or public, sexual, political, or religious) and for the gender arrangements such institutions both found and mirror."[79] She also emphasizes how the female Gothic story presents "a world in which men have money and hence power" and that "Bluebeard's secret is the foundation upon which patriarchal culture rests: control of the subversively curious 'female,' personified in his wives."[80] When Barbra first approaches the farmhouse, she finds the front door locked, and her entrance through the back constitutes a kind of transgression, for she unlawfully enters a private space in a manner analogous to the wife in the Bluebeard legend. Once inside the home, Barbra's independence and subjectivity begin to break down almost immediately. Whereas she had been fiercely opinionated and strong willed during her banter with her brother, the imprisoned Barbra is cowed, silent, and almost catatonic. As Ben breaks up the contents of the house in his efforts to add to the building's fortifications, Barbra seems more interested in perpetuating female stereotypes: she plays with a music box and quite needlessly folds a tablecloth.[81]

Another key dynamic that figures into all of Romero's zombie films is the relationship and even conflict between upstairs and downstairs. According to Leslie A. Fiedler, "The upper and the lower levels of the ruined castle or abbey represent the contradictory fears at the heart of gothic terror: the dread of the super-ego, whose splendid battlements have been battered but not quite cast down — and of the id, whose buried darkness abounds in dark visions no stormer of the castle had even touched."[82] This careful description of classic Gothic literature could not be more apt for *Night of the Living Dead*.

Throughout the film, the main floor of the house represents the realm of the male authority figure, the albeit conflicting voices of Law that attempt to maintain the increasingly insufficient defenses of the house, and one of the key secrets of the house, one that goes unnoticed by Ben for the first half hour of the film, is the presence of a cellar. While Ben boards up all the windows on the ground floor of the house with Barbra, the other five protagonists of the film are hiding downstairs. Only when Ben goes upstairs do Tom and Harry emerge from their subterranean hiding place, the cellar that Harry declares to be "the safest place." Harry and Ben immediately begin to argue because Harry had been focused on preserving his life below and Ben had expected the other men to come upstairs to help; in other words, the selfish id stands in contrast to the social superego. Thus the dichotomy between the upstairs and downstairs, the superego and the id, becomes personified in the divergent characters of Ben and Harry, and the result is, of course, Harry's death and Ben's eventual retreat to the safety of the cellar later in the film.

Finally, because anyone can (and will) ultimately become a zombie, this potentiality helps zombie invasion narratives such as *Night of the Living Dead* to deal unabashedly with human taboos, murder, and cannibalism, a defining focus of the plots that Dillard proposes has much to do with the genre's success.[83] Additionally, the dead are not allowed to rest in peace: Barbra's attempt to honor the resting place of one relative turns into a nightmare where she vainly combats the remains of another dead relative. Ben, in contrast, becomes a kind of avenging angel, bashing, chopping, and shooting people with wild abandon. He is not only forced to disrespect the sanctity of the dead, but he in fact becomes a type of mass murderer. The other familial relationships symbolized by the farmhouse also prove too closely tied to death to survive the film, as Tom and Judy suffer a senseless death and the Cooper family literal destroys itself. Approaching Romero's first film from a psychoanalytic and culturally critical viewpoint, along with an understanding of the narratological tradition of the Gothic, reveals the movie to be a devastating criticism of 1960s culture. In quite simple terms, when confronted with the grim and frightening realities of mortality, the human characters of *Night of the Living Dead* prove themselves incapable of coping, just as America in 1968 was suffering under a similar inability to cope with both climatic social changes and the stark realities of death.

Although once considered an example of "low art" or B-movie making, *Night of the Living Dead* exemplifies the ability of the best genre fiction to address the issues explored by literary fiction. Romero was reacting to the social problems and cultural environment of the 1960s, using his low-budget film to comment on the widespread conflict arising from feelings associated with the Civil Rights Movement and the ongoing war in Vietnam. In addi-

tion, *Night of the Living Dead* must be considered an important cultural artifact for two key reasons: (1) the movie represents a major shift in the stylistic and thematic "rules" of the cinematic zombie narrative and (2) it illustrates
a particularly pessimistic turn in the invasion narrative tradition, one in which
the human — not the monster — is the disenfranchised Other. Romero's deft
application of the *Unheimlich* establishes his film in the grand tradition of
both supernatural and family-centered terror. Ultimately, too, the film is
important because of its timeless ability to induce fear and reflection in moviegoers. The horror of this and other zombie movies comes from recognizing
the human in the monster, and the terror of such films comes from knowing
there is little to do about it but destroy what is left.

Chapter 4

THE DEAD WALK THE EARTH
The Triumph of the Zombie Social Metaphor in Dawn of the Dead

My granddad was a priest in Trinidad. He used to tell us, "When there's no more room in hell, the dead will walk the earth." — Peter, *Dawn of the Dead*

Roughly half an hour into the bloody rampage of Romero's *Dawn of the Dead*, the four human protagonists who have been fleeing the chaos of Philadelphia by helicopter come across an abandoned shopping mall. A handheld camera, shooting from inside the cockpit of the helicopter, replicates the point of view of the beleaguered humans and reveals a decidedly eerie and uncanny landscape. Parallel yellow lines establish a vast asphalt parking lot, populated by only a few cars and a scattering of slow-moving zombies. The unease of the audience is further heightened by Romero's canted and oblique camera angles, a montage of shots that take the towering lampposts, the chain link fences, and the friendly welcome signs out of expected context. Furthermore, when filmed from above, the large structure of the mall appears strangely isolated from the rest of civilization, surrounded by the buffer of the parking lot and clearly void of human life. Yet because they need a place to stop, eat, and rest, the four protagonists tentatively land their helicopter on the roof of the imposing structure. Once they feel secure in their lofty position, the four cautiously investigate the condition of the building, assessing its level of safety and the potential spoils there for the taking. Looking down through the skylights, a perspective once again replicated as a subjective point-of-view shot, they see a modern-day shopping palace, complete with fully stocked stores and ample electrical power, and the few zombies roaming the concourses seem to be of little threat. Fran (Gaylen Ross), the only woman in the group, looks on the ghouls and asks, "What are they doing? Why do they come here?" Her boyfriend Stephen (David Emge), impassive behind his "tough guy" sunglasses, answers, "Some kind of instinct ... memory ... of what they used to do. This was an important place in their lives."

Most scholarship concerning *Dawn of the Dead* rightly focuses on the film's rather overt criticism of contemporary consumer culture. By setting the bulk of the action in a shopping mall, Romero consciously draws the audience's attention towards the inherent relationship between zombies and consumerism. In Romero's allegory, the insatiable need to purchase, own, and consume has become so deeply ingrained in twentieth-century Americans that their reanimated corpses are relentlessly driven by the same instincts and needs. The metaphor is simple: Americans in the 1970s are the true zombies, slaves to the master of consumerism, mindlessly migrating to stores and shopping malls for the almost instinctual consumption of goods. In fact, by reducing the zombies to such a heavily symbolic role, the monsters become little more than supporting characters; of greater critical interest are both the shopping structure itself and the four surviving humans who come to isolate themselves on the mall's upper levels. Having been essentially brainwashed by American capitalist ideology, the human protagonists of *Dawn of the Dead* find it impossible to see the shattered world around them in any terms other than those of possession and consumption — and this misplaced drive ultimately proves strong enough to put all their lives in jeopardy.

In other words, I argue that Romero's zombies are not merely a metaphor; they also act as the catalyst that reveals the true problem infecting humanity. That is, after the zombies effectively destroy human society, the few survivors attempt to rebuild that society according to one single paradigm: pervasive consumerism. The presence of the zombies reveals the four surviving humans to be essentially and inescapably consumers, and because the shopping mall provides them with all the supplies they could want, they no longer have the need — and perhaps even more importantly, the ability — to produce any goods themselves. Thus in the new social and economic paradigm of *Dawn of the Dead*, the few remaining humans lose what Marx would call their identity as "species beings" and are reduced to the level of "life-activity" alone. Any labor they do expend is for sheer survival instead of productivity — establishing barricades for safety, pilfering the stores for food and clothing, and seeking empty recreation to pass the time. According to Hegel, labor is necessary to achieve consciousness and self-awareness,[1] and by losing their productive labor, the feckless individuals living in Romero's mall ultimately lose that which makes them essentially "human," causing them to regress to a more primitive state. In a manner far more deliberate than in his *Night of the Living Dead*, then, Romero shows little difference between the zombies and the surviving humans — they are all monstrous — and therein lies his criticism of his contemporary society.

In the decade that passed between *Night of the Living Dead* and *Dawn of the Dead*, the zombie subgenre exploded in both production and popularity, and Romero's imitators became increasingly bold in their use of violent and graphic imagery and adept in their application of the zombie as cultural metaphor. Romero's sequel becomes part of this trajectory, and his stunning abjection of the human body further blurs the lines between subjective humanity and the objective "thingness" of slavery. Zombies, both by being fundamentally dead bodies and by reducing their human prey to mere meat and sustenance, challenge the viewer's conception of humanity and independence. Furthermore, the elaborate set piece of the shopping mall in *Dawn of the Dead* functions as another character in the morality play, one that might best be read through the critical perspective of theories about the Gothic. The mindless zombies and the sterile shopping center work together to offer a scathing critique of the pervasive role consumerism plays in the lives of Americans, and Romero suggests a harshly grim outlook for humanity, a future that will fail to realize the utopian "end of History" predicted by such theorists as Alexandre Kojève and Francis Fukuyama. According to Romero, the progressive dialectic of society will ultimately stall and fail because humans only consume — they cannot do anything else. When given the chance to transcend the framework of a late-capitalist society in an environment that provides them with all their needs, the surviving humans of *Dawn of the Dead* only seem able to attempt a recreation of the lost structures of society, and they ultimately become fatally overwhelmed by the perceived need to *own* rather than *produce*.

An Increase in Abjection, from Night until the Dawn

As I have demonstrated in Chapter 2, the zombies featured in voodoo-themed films from the 1930s and '40s act primarily as cultural metaphors for enslavement. The victims of voodoo sorcery (and in later movies, extraterrestrial science) blatantly lose their independence and autonomy, becoming instead the puppets of diabolical masters. In other words, the most terrifying aspect of the zombie, as established by its folkloristic characteristics, becomes the depiction of a human subject as nothing more than an object, a dumb tool to be used and abused by others. This object-ness — a disturbingly inhuman condition that literalizes Césaire's "thingification"[2] — is further heightened by the overtly dead appearance of the zombie creatures, a look that becomes more grotesque as this cycle of films progresses into the 1960s. Ultimately, the zombie becomes a graphic *memento mori* that does little beyond eating, bleeding, oozing, and decaying. In her foundational *Powers of Horror* (1982), Julia Kristeva explains how the base physical realities of life and death challenge the subject's understanding of self by disturbing "identity, system,

[and] order."[3] According to Kristeva, the *abject* describes the blurred condition between life and death and many other antinomies that all human subjects strive to ignore or to put off—to ab-ject—in an attempt to defy their own object-ness. This unavoidable state of abjection can be visually represented by base and mortal bodily fluids, such as blood and pus, or by betwixt-and-between conditions, such as the zombies' unnatural state between animation and decay.

With *Night of the Living Dead*, Romero not only challenges and transforms the zombie subgenre into something far more violent and sinister, but he also increases the allegorical nature of the creatures to become an even more dramatic affront to human subjectivity. By depicting his zombies as creatures that are not only dead but also openly and activity decomposing on the screen, Romero forces viewers to confront their own repressed sense of mortality, their own essential and abject identity as little more than imperfect "things." In his analysis of *Night of the Living Dead*, Russell emphasizes how "Romero never lets us forget that this is a film about the body. Or, to be more accurate, the horror of the body."[4] Throughout his films, in fact, Romero demonstrates how frail the human body really is, and he bombards viewers with abject imagery that emphasizes the body's nature as sheer object. For example, in the opening sequence of *Night of the Living Dead*, Johnny dies a painfully simple death, his neck snapping effortlessly against a headstone after a frankly realistic struggle with a zombie. Additionally, when Barbra seeks shelter in the empty farmhouse, she comes face to face with that rotting and exposed human skull—a thing with no human life or value that Ben quite unceremoniously tosses aside. And, of course, the zombies assault the beleaguered humans with blank stares, stiff limbs, and blind purpose—they have neither the will nor the independence reserved for thinking human subjects. In all these ways, Romero shows the body to be little more than a shell and subjectivity to be fleeting at best.

More than any of the zombie films that precede it, *Night of the Living Dead* takes full advantage of the cinematic medium—and the recent lifting of content restrictions once imposed by the Hays Code—to bombard audiences with base and graphic images. Of particular note and infamy is the highly abject scene that follows the tragic deaths of Tom and Judy. The young couple dies when their truck explodes in a gasoline fire, and the eagerly waiting zombies quickly descend upon the smoldering flesh and human body parts. For this so-called "Last Supper" scene, it turns out, Romero "shipped in real animal entrails from a Pittsburgh butcher" and "found extras who were willing to chomp greedily on pig hearts and sheep intestines."[5] The director shows no restraint in his relentless close-up shots of the walking dead as they smear blood on their faces, tear hungrily into tripe and other offal, and even gnaw on raw bones. Romero accomplishes the objectification of the human body by both depicting human flesh to be nothing more than meat, aligning human beings unapologetically with stockyard animals and game, and by having his zombies act according to the basest of natures — they feed because they are things desiring food, and they show none of the decorum or reservations a living human subject would most likely have. Furthermore, this one scene forever changes the course of the subgenre, introducing cannibalism as a stunning companion to decomposition, and these two new protocols of the cinematic zombie intensify the loss of autonomy and subjectivity that the living dead have symbolized since their inception.

Of course, the teenagers who flocked to theaters to see *Night of the Living Dead* were probably more interested in the film's ability to shock, disgust, and push the boundaries of propriety than they were concerned about any social and cultural work the movie was doing. Did the average filmgoer recognize Romero's scathing criticism of civil-rights era sexism and racism? Did his metaphor decrying the atrocities of Vietnam find a receptive audience? Although the allegorical nature of the zombie remained its primary value as a cultural artifact for directors such as Romero, young viewers were more likely just looking for new ways to be horrified and revolted, and the horde of copycat filmmakers to follow in Romero's footsteps were generally little different. Russell provides a thorough survey of many of these lackluster films, including Bob Clark's *Children Shouldn't Play with Dead Things* (1972), Freddie Francis' *Tales from the Crypt* (1972), Ken Wiederhorn's *Shock Waves* (1977), Jesus Franco's *L'Abîme des morts vivants* (1981), and Jean Rollin's *Le Lac des morts vivants* (1981).[6] While these films continue to employ the visual imagery of ambulatory corpses and the abjection of mortality, they mostly do so to shock, horrify, and titillate a receptive teenage audience. Indeed, most of the low-budget schlock that follows *Night of the Living Dead* focuses on campy sensationalism and undisguised sexual exploitation — such as zombified Nazi soldiers and naked female victims — instead of meaningful social criticism.

However, some zombie filmmaking from the 1970s manages to reflect a larger cultural revolution, for, according to Russell, "the films that followed in the wake of *Night of the Living Dead* took the disillusionment and rude awakening of the acid generation as their starting point."[7] The younger generation of the '70s was rebelling against the war in Vietnam, the status quo of their parents, and the general attempt of society to mandate social conformity. In fact, most zombie movies after *Night of the Living Dead* "are dominated by storylines in which our friends, neighbours and families reveal their threatening Otherness by becoming flesh-eating ghouls whose only aim is to make us become part of their horrific group."[8] Thus the trope of enslavement remains active throughout this period of zombie films, and it manifests itself through both impressed conformity and increased abjection. Clark's second film, *Dead of Night* (1972), represents one of the bolder examples of such reactionary filmmaking. A war-era version of W. W. Jacobs' "The Monkey's Paw" (1902), the film tells the tragic story of a young man who dies in Vietnam and returns home to America as a blood-drinking zombie. Although Andy Brooks (Richard Backus) is perhaps more vampire than zombie, "this Canadian production offers the most explicit tie-in between zombies and post-traumatic stress disorder."[9] Andy cannot find his place in civilian life not only because he is a corpse but also because his military training has reduced him to little more than a mindless killer, a castoff (abject) tool or object interested only in blood and death.

Clearly, some directors understood the power of the allegorical nature of the zombie, including Romero's abject imagery, and attempted to make their own culturally relevant films. For example, Spanish director Jorge Grau — the "true successor to Romero's crown"[10] — produced *Non si deve profanare il sonno dei morti* in 1974,[11] a B-level shocker that uses its zombies to present a didactic ecological parable. If *Plague of the Zombies* is the English equivalent to *White Zombie*, then Grau's film is an international version of *Night of the Living Dead*, at least in the beginning. The movie opens with an antagonistic young couple driving across the English countryside, but, unlike Johnny and Barbra, George (Ray Lovelock) and Edna (Christine Galbo) hardly know each other. The two have merely been thrown together after Edna backed into

A newly risen zombie (Vito Salier) suffers an ignominious death by fire in Grau's *Non si deve profanare il sonno dei morti* (Flaminia Produzioni Cinematografiche, 1974).

George's motorbike, and they are both simply trying to get to their respective relatives' houses before dark. After getting lost, however, George must leave Edna and the car to ask for directions, and he discovers a team of scientists experimenting with a kind of radiation that gets rid of bugs and insects by causing them to attack and kill each other. This high-tech pesticide is supposedly harmless to humans, the scientists assure George, because their nervous systems are too complex to be affected by the radiation. Nevertheless, after a pale-faced transient (Fernando Hilbeck) attacks Edna, it becomes clear that this assumption does not apply to human corpses. In fact, any recently dead body can be reanimated by the unnatural experiment.

The rise of the zombie infestation takes much longer in Grau's film that it does in *Night of the Living Dead*, but it does so with a dramatic increase in violence, gore, and abject imagery. Although George and Edna make it safely to the house of her sister Katie (Jeannine Mestre), they are unable to prevent the single roaming zombie from strangling and killing Katie's husband Martin (Jose Ruiz Lefante). In fact, the three become suspects in the grisly murder, as the local authorities are loath to believe the trio's stories of the walking dead, and George, Edna, and Katie spend the remainder of the film ineffectually trying to warn people. Unlike Romero's zombies, Grau's creature appears to have preternatural strength, crushing Martin's throat and ribcage effortlessly and later, assisted by a brace of newly risen comrades, ripping open the abdomen of a helpless police officer (Giorgio Trestini). The use of color film stock certainly enhances the blood and the gore, but Grau's movie also transcends Romero's violence by more thoroughly connecting its cannibalistic feasts with the suffering of the dying human victims. For example, Grau's zombies begin to devour the bright red intestines of the screaming Officer Craig before the man has even died, and one ghoul relentlessly plucks the man's bloodshot and staring eyes right out of his head. An even more disturbing scene occurs later, after the creatures have infested the local hospital, when a blood-splattered zombie reaches into the blouse of a nurse (Anita Colby) to perform a kind of "zombie mastectomy," tearing off her left breast as she screams helplessly.[12]

Such horrifying visual images — blood, blood, human flesh as meat, and more blood — compound Kristeva's conception of abjection and underscore Grau's larger theme that humans are little more than mindless insects. As the scientists on the farm continue in their misguided efforts to exercise dominion over the natural creatures hindering human efforts in the fields, more and more human bodies rise from the dead as uncontrollable and unnatural creatures. In fact, by the climax of *Non si deve profanare il sonno dei morti*, little difference remains between the humans and the insects, or between the humans and the zombies, for that matter. Edna tries to rescue her sister from the dangers of the hospital, but Katie is attacked by her zombified husband first. Then, too, the disturbing theme of "zombie incest," initiated by Romero when Karen murders her parents in *Night of the Living Dead,* continues in Grau's film, especially when Katie attacks, kills, and begins to eat her own sister. Arriving too late to help, George nonetheless storms into the abattoir of the hospital with a singular heroic purpose reminiscent of Romero's Ben, and, like his misguided forefather, George is senselessly shot and killed by human law enforcement officers when they mistake him for a zombie.[13] Thus, in the grand tradition of Romero — albeit after just the one film — the violent, uncontrollable, and abject nature of the zombies again challenges the superior subjectivity of humanity and underscores our place in the world as potentially little more than objects, things, or mindless beasts.

Variations on the living dead also develop during the 1970s, but almost every iteration of the zombie continues to focus on the abjection of the body. In 1971, for instance, the Spanish director Amando de Ossorio began a series of films about reanimated Knights Templar who prolong their unnatural existence by feasting on the blood of the living. The first film, *La noche del terror ciego* (a.k.a. *Tombs of the Blind Dead*), works as an allegory to condemn the loose morals of the generation that followed Franco's regime. The blood-sucking mummies repeatedly menace a preponderance of scantily clad women, punishing those who wantonly display the flesh of their bodies by symbolically raping and literally killing them. Yet de Ossorio's Templars behave more

A host of grisly Knights Templar zombies from de Ossorio's *La noche del terror ciego* (Interfilme, 1971).

like vampires than zombies (although they move with an almost painful lethargy, thanks to de Ossorio's excessive use of slow motion); they act with purpose, organize their efforts, and even ride horses and use swords. Nevertheless, the creatures wantonly assault the living and drink their blood, reducing the (female) human body to little more than an object used to maintain the Templars' existence.[14] Another noteworthy effort is Rollin's 1978 film *Les Raisins de la mort* (a.k.a. *The Grapes of Death*), which attempts to fuse the pacing of such Hollywood disaster films as *The Poseidon Adventure* (1972) with the inexpensive production requirements of horror films such as *Night of the Living Dead*.[15] The result is an unusual take on the cannibalistic zombie: homicidal maniacs who have been infected by a batch of wine that has been contaminated by pesticide. Although the infected are not technically dead, these "zombies" bear oozing sores and relentlessly pursue sexualized female protagonists with violent and disturbing results, such as the crucifixion and beheading of a topless blind girl (Patricia Cartier). The film also eroticizes the monsters, with porn star Brigitte Lahaie featured as a homicidal, and gratuitously naked, maniac who aids the diseased creatures.

After less commercially successful films like *The Crazies* (1973) and *Martin* (1977), Romero finally returned to the zombie scene in 1978, when he once again took the fledgling subgenre under his control by directing the most thematically and symbolically complex of the entire zombie canon, *Dawn of the Dead*. With a greatly increased budget, Romero was able to take the concept of the zombie in "unexpected directions," reviving the subgenre "with comic panache just as it was threatening to become moribund."[16] In addition to more money, a larger scope, and greater thematic depth, Romero had Savini's special effects genius at his disposal. Savini had been unable to work with Romero on *Night of the Living Dead* because the makeup artist had been serving a tour in Vietnam as a combat photographer. Skal explains how Savini drew unabashedly from his war experiences to bring a heightened level of realism to the look of the corpses in *Dawn of the Dead*, not to mention the results of their violent attacks. Notable examples such as a head being blown away by a shotgun blast, a zombie ripping flesh and sinews from his panic-stricken wife's shoulder, and the now infamous scalping of a zombie by a helicopter blade all prevented the film from receiving a distributor-friendly R-rating from the MPAA; instead, *Dawn of the Dead* was released with no rating at all. Such graphic verisimilitude represents what Skal rightly calls a cinematic version of posttraumatic stress syndrome, with "endlessly repeated images of nightmare assaults on the human body, especially its sudden and explosive destruction."[17] Filmmakers such as Grau had indeed increased the bodily abjection of zombie movies, but, continuing in his role as an innovator, Romero took things to an even greater extreme.

With *Dawn of the Dead*, Romero shows little reticence in tearing back the skin of humanity, as it were, to reveal us for whom we really are. In his narrative of the besieged shopping mall, Romero crafts an apocalyptic world in which the zombies have already won the war — the initial outbreak having already been documented in *Night of the Living Dead*— and in which humans have been reduced to little more than livestock whose only purpose is to support the needs of the ever-increasing zombie horde. The gross and decaying appearance of Romero's latest zombies, many bearing traumatic wounds and dripping blood, confront audiences with an abject version of themselves, for all humans are basically biological creatures and all of us will eventually die. In addition, Romero demonstrates the essential frailty of human flesh, repeatedly showing the violent capacities fingernails, teeth, knives, and bullets have to reduce living tissue to bleeding and inert flesh. By objectifying the human body in such a graphic manner, Romero relentlessly dissolves the boundaries between the living and the dead, the human and the zombie, and living beings and inanimate products. Furthermore, the zombies of *Dawn of the Dead* seek to "own" humans for unceasing consumption just as real-life humans seek to buy, own, and consume the relatively useless items for sale in shopping malls around the country. By casting humans as the products on display in shop windows, Romero enacts his most haunting cultural allegory: the post-apocalyptic "zombie economy."

The New "Zombie Economy" of the Apocalypse

With *Dawn of the Dead*, the zombie invasion narrative reaches a new level of terror by being depicted as a full-blown global apocalypse, one far more starkly and fully realized than the limited, microcosmic view provided by *Night of the Living Dead* or even *Non si deve profanare il sonno dei morti*. Furthermore, Romero appears less interested in offering only an implied social allegory; this time, the film overtly attacks Americans where they live, as it were, providing an unmistakable criticism of the Western World's capitalist economic systems of the late 1970s. This cultural and economic morality tale functions through three distinct if interrelated outlets: the insatiable zombies themselves, the sterile halls of the modern shopping mall, and the seemingly hopeless plight of the surviving humans. Because the creatures obviously represent the key defining feature of the zombie subgenre, I will consider their functional and allegorical role in *Dawn of the Dead* first. Although the existence of the zombie phenomenon goes largely unexplained in Romero's film,[18] they share certain unavoidable and defining characteristics with the earlier zombie films: they are animated corpses, they eat human flesh, and they appear to be driven by instinctual desires. This implacable drive makes zombies the perfect allegorical figures for consumerism, an economic ideology that has important parallels with enslavement.

In other words, the glassy-eyed zombies that relentlessly assault the shopping mall in *Dawn of the Dead* are slaves, although their "master" has changed significantly since the 1930s. With *Night of the Living Dead*, Romero had established two original, essential characteristics in the monsters' tradition — limited autonomy and insatiable cannibalism. That is, rather than being driven by the whims of a voodoo master, Romero's "post-modern" zombies[19] act largely of their own accord: they don't take orders from anyone or anything, except their own deeply ingrained desires. Yet whereas *Night of the Living Dead* somewhat inverts the master/slave dialectic present in the voodoo-based zombie movies, *Dawn of the Dead* reestablishes the old system, although, in this case, the master is animalistic instinct and subconscious drive, not vindictive and plotting voodoo priests. Furthermore — again, in stark contrast to the minions of *White Zombie*— Romero's ghouls don't do anything beyond simply attacking humans and eating their flesh. This singular purpose means the zombies of *Dawn of the Dead* represent consumers on the most fundamental and primitive level — all they do is take, and what they take is food. Therefore, while the voodoo-based zombies of the 1930s and '40s largely represent the slaves of a colonial society, *Dawn of the Dead*'s "mall zombies" function as an exaggeration of the late capitalist bourgeoisie: blind consumption without any productive contribution, the "colonization" of humanity by their own consumerism. Or, as Rob Latham describes mall culture, "Marx's gluttonous capitalist rat has been transformed into an army of consuming mallrats."[20]

Romero offers additional developments in the nature of his zombies, ones that work to enhance their allegorical role. For example, the zombies of *Dawn of the Dead* manage to retain some vestigial memory of their human lives, using tools in the most primitive manner and mimicking the actions of their former existence. Most significantly, the creatures are physically and inexorably attracted to the shopping mall. On the most obvious level, the ghouls desire access to the mega-complex so they can attack and eat the humans living inside. However, the zombies are already present in the mall when the four protagonists land their helicopter on the roof, long before the living humans take up residence there. As Stephen explains to Fran, the zombies must be drawn there by a subconscious memory; they somehow remember they were once happy in such a place. This instinctual "drive to shop," as it were, is repeatedly emphasized by Romero, who shows the mindless creatures pressed up against glass doors and windows, clamoring to get inside the shops, in a gross parody of early-morning-sale shoppers, to resume their earthly activities of gluttonous consumption — indeed, as Kim Paffenroth points out, their addiction for the place exists beyond death.[21] Of course, in the new zombie economy, the goods on display in the store windows are living, breathing humans, not merely clothes, jewelry, and modern gadgets.

On a purely metonymical level, then, the zombies represent the existing horrors of a society brainwashed by the capitalistic need to consume. According to Paffenroth, the zombies are "devoid of intellect and reduced just to appetite."[22] Although they have some primitive ties to their former lives, they don't organize or act according to any kind of plan; as in *Night of the Living Dead*, any autonomy the zombies manifest is merely a direct result of an instinctual drive to consume. In fact, according to Botting, the version of culture presented by *Dawn of the Dead* is "marked out as one utterly determined by consumption. The undead bodies, returning to the scene of so many purchases are virtually indistinguishable in habit and action from their former living selves."[23] Matthew Walker offers another insight into the mindless behavior of the zombies, describing the actions of Romero's ghouls in terms of Aristotle's *pleonexia*, which he defines as "the disposition to have more."[24] Because all biological functions have ceased to exist in the zombie's dead physiology, they don't eat for sustenance — instead, they eat simply for the sake of eating, for the desire to "have more." Philip Horne emphasizes how this insatiable appetite, an essential characteristic of Romero's zombies that has been religiously maintained by his imitators, ideally epitomizes the excesses of modern consumerism. Horne writes how "'consumer society' is literalized in the zombies' process of ingestion; they devour human beings as they couldn't a TV or a sofa."[25] In a disgusting parody of human capitalism, the ghouls eat and eat and eat, yet they always want more.

The zombies of *Dawn of the Dead* thus represent the problems with materialism and consumer consumption that exist for Romero's contemporary audience. Horne describes a society peopled by "dazed consumers, haunted by impossible yearnings, [who] shop for shopping's sake, freed from the causal chains of necessity but feeling endlessly incomplete, hungry for the diffused excitement of pursuit and purchase."[26] This description certainly applies not only to the zombies of Romero's movie, but also to the eager viewers sitting in the audience as well.[27] As the megalomaniacal governor from Kirkman's Walking Dead series callously observes about zombies, "The thing you have to realize is that they're just us — they're no different. They want what they want, they take what they want and after they get what they want — they're only content for the briefest span of time. Then they want more."[28] The comforts of a modern society, therefore, come with an unavoidable (and necessarily insatiable) desire and need to consume, and all share that instinctual drive. Thus for the civilization presented by Romero in *Dawn of the Dead*, as A. Loudermilk points out, the real apocalypse is the end of late capitalism: "Its consumer citizenry — figuratively zombified by commercial culture — is literally zombified by those who once were us, our *simulacral doubles* as cannibal consumers."[29] Of course, while humans may *act* like zombies when shopping and consuming, *real* zombies prove to be far more dangerous; the goods they consume are the very flesh and blood of humanity.

In *Dawn of the Dead*, "civilization" itself proves to be the first victim of the zombie onslaught; the establishing scenes of the movie show not only the mass chaos resulting from the supernatural invasion but also the collapse of all societal infrastructure and social organizations. The first sequences of the film depict the chaotic decay of two of the most powerful institutions in America: the media and law enforcement.[30] *Dawn of the Dead*'s first shot introduces Fran, a young and successful television news producer who awakens from a nightmare to find herself trapped in the midst of a much worse one.[31] Amid the frantic shouts of so-called experts, reporters, and panicking technicians, Fran proves to be a level head; she takes charge of the situation, asserts her logical decisions, and even challenges the irresponsible actions of those around her. Romero quickly establishes Fran as a professional with a purpose. She has a job to do, and that labor gives her and the others at the news studio a reason to come together. This scene also introduces Stephen, the pilot of the news channel's traffic helicopter. He has been observing the chaos erupting on the streets of Philadelphia from above, and he shares a plan for escape with Fran — thus Stephen also has a distinct purpose: flight and survival. Fran seems reluctant to leave her responsibilities behind, but when she learns the station will soon go off the air anyway (removing her reason to be at the studio), she agrees to join her boyfriend Stephen in his daring exodus.

The dialogue of *Dawn of the Dead* repeatedly emphasizes that zombies can only be destroyed by shooting them in the head, an assault on the reasoning centre of the body that Russell sees as being indicative of the film as a whole. With the rise of the zombie infestation, he observes, society experiences an "apocalypse of reason" that results in an irrational, "headless" world.[32] This lack of leadership and control is illustrated in the film's next major sequence, an extended and horrifically violent one, that shows both the police and civilians as militants gone berserk. The Philadelphia SWAT team has surrounded an apartment building housing both lawless renegades and those innocents who are harboring their zombified dead. Caucasians make up the bulk of the police force, while those inside the structure are African American, Hispanic, and Puerto Rican — an ethnic diversity emphasized by the racist epithets and complaints hurled by some members of the SWAT team. A heated gun battle ensues, with humans shooting other humans almost indiscriminately, with no initial signs of zombies at all, although the sequence is admittedly chaotic for the characters and audience members alike. The police soon storm the building supposedly to protect the innocent from the marauders and eradicate any menacing ghouls, but some of those once sworn to "protect and serve" attack the helpless civilians, and the police are forced to turn on their own. When zombies are finally discovered in some of the apartments, the humans struggle to unite against the more dangerous foes. Yet the resulting scenes depict humans murdering creatures that at least appear human; in fact, because members of the SWAT team are wearing gas masks, the zombies look more human than the police officers do. In this way, then, the uncanny nature of the zombies makes them a perfect metaphor for humanity's already existing inhumanity to itself, as if the racist and excessively violent police officers weren't enough proof already.[33]

Yet amid all the action-movie chaos, some order is maintained, at least for a little while. *Dawn of the Dead*'s third principal character, Roger (Scott Reiniger), is introduced as a man of reason and purpose. As a seasoned police officer, he attempts to direct the operation, taking a younger SWAT member under his wing and trying to curb the violence of his fellow officers. Like Fran and Stephen, Roger's role in society is largely predicated upon his produc-

Bewildered families have hidden their zombie kin in the basement in Romero's *Dawn of the Dead* (United Film Distribution Company, 1978; Jerry Ohlinger).

tive labor — his "use value," as it were. Roger soon meets up with Peter (Ken Foree),[34] another police officer, and the two of them begin the grisly task of dealing with a room full of zombies in the apartment building's basement. Confronted by dead friends and relatives that fail to "die" fully, the residents of the apartment complex have confined the zombies to the basement — treating them more as possessions or things than individuals — rather than see them "killed" or destroyed. Visibly shocked by the pitiful crowd of creatures cowering on the floor, Peter, almost nobly backlit by a single light bulb, opens fire with his pistol, and, during the grisly exterminations, tears stream down his face. Because of the essentially human appearance of the monsters, Peter finds his task odious and heartrending, but he and Roger exterminate them all anyway because it is their job; it's what they have been conditioned to do, and part of that job means maintaining order at all costs. The two men find purpose and identity, therefore, within the institutional apparatus of law enforcement, but this apparatus also makes them virtually as mindless as the zombies they destroy.

As in *Night of the Living Dead*, *Dawn of the Dead* graphically depicts the collapse of American society into anarchy and terror. Roger, who is revealed in the next scene to be a close friend of Stephen's, takes Peter with him to join the other two at the airport to prepare for their flight away from the chaos of the city. As Peter is introduced to the others, he asks Fran if Stephen is *her* man — this exchange, along with the group's refusal to share cigarettes with another group of fleeing police officers, begins to establish how they perceive everything in terms of ownership and commodification, a trope that will become even more important later in the film. The four survivors travel all night, only stopping in the morning to refuel at a rural airport. During their trip, they observe from the air the actions of scores of military and militia, men who have taken to the countryside to kill zombies as if hunting animals for sport in scenes clearly reminiscent of *Night of the Living Dead*. Whereas someone like Peter feels a lingering emotional connection to the human-like monsters, the masses combing the countryside below them appear to take great pleasure in their activities. In fact, Romero's extended montage of "rednecks" dressed in both hunter-orange and army-green shows the rabble voraciously drinking coffee and beer, laughing and joking with each other, mugging for snapshots, and taking shots at zombies as if in the world's largest shooting gallery. Martial law has clearly been imposed, and average civilians have become almost as dangerous as the zombies themselves, killing for recreation and showing no remorse. The bloodlust shown by the racist SWAT officer early on is intensified by the levity and insensitivity exhibited by the rural militia.

By the time the four heroes make it to the relative safety of the shopping mall, they have learned to fear both zombies and other humans alike, and as the film progresses, they slowly recognize that help will be long in coming — if it comes at all. Chaos and lawlessness have replaced the security of society's infrastructure. In fact, most social institutions have completely fallen apart: all media eventually goes off the air, the military and its most powerful weapons prove ineffectual, and the day-to-day activities of modern life — driving to work, doing a job, using a phone, watching television, going to the movies, spending money, etc.— come to a screeching halt.[35] The new "zombie economy" that results undermines all the existing social and economic models and theories. In a shocking example of overkill, a grotesque kind of revolution has come to fruition: the economic base of production has been, perhaps permanently, disrupted and destroyed, and the cultural superstructure has come crashing down in ruins. Yet the speed and severity of this "revolution" is such that humanity finds itself in shock. Hence, the survivors' only course of action is to go through the motions of "capitalist habit" and to attempt to rebuild the systems of that cultural society within the confines of their new home — the modern indoor shopping mall.

The Gothic Mall of Dawn of the Dead

Building upon the spatial premises of Romero's first zombie movie, *Dawn of the Dead* transfers the action from a rural farmhouse to a spacious shopping mall, which, as established above, opens the film to its most cultural and materialist interpretation. Fortunately, Loudermilk has provided us with a thorough discussion of the dual role the shopping mall enjoyed during the 1970s and '80s, social as well as commercial. People went (and still go) to the mall for recreation, meeting friends and dates, window shopping, and going to arcades and movie theaters. Everyone can enjoy the mall on the same level, coming together to revel in the relatively shallow pleasures of modern society. According to Loudermilk, "At the mall, we're supposed to feel legitimized in our commodity culture, each of us part of a seemingly democratic weave of capitalism and individualism."[36] Furthermore, *Dawn of the Dead* quickly establishes its primary location as part of the Gothic tradition, for the mall gradually shifts over the course of the film from a familiar, if strangely antiquated, space of consumer comfort and physical safety to a site of uncanny mystery, suspense, horror, and, ultimately, death. The balance of the film's narrative unfolds in this increasingly disturbing environment, and the four protagonists begin by attempting to transform the nature of the building in an effort to recreate something of a "civilized" way of life.

Contemporary viewers must remember that, in 1978, the shopping mall was still a relatively new cultural phenomenon; therefore, although it would have been received as something exotic or even foreign, the vast structure at the center of *Dawn of the Dead* can hardly be called an antiquated space. However, despite the efforts of the protagonists to reclaim the mall, efforts that gradually transform the essential nature of the structure as the film progresses, the virtually empty building becomes a rather marked symbol for the past. For example, when the four human survivors first enter and investigate the mysterious shopping mall, they find its hallways and shops in almost pristine condition. All the multifarious merchandise remains undisturbed on the shelves, the windows and linoleum are spotless, and the place looks ready to open for the day's business. In fact, a number of "customers" are already inside, wandering from storefront to storefront, although they are all zombies. Yet this total absence of human life, the eerie emptiness of most of the stores and rooms, and the harsh shadows created by Romero's chiaroscuro lighting all give the structure the feel of a haunted house, especially when Peter and Roger explore the dark and confined service corridors in search of the power and security controls. Furthermore, because only the dead inhabit the building, the shopping mall has become something of a tomb, a space representing the past rather than the present. This contrast between the old and the new manifests yet another level of the uncanny, in much the same way the contrast between the old house and the new hotel disturbs audiences of Hitchcock's *Psycho* (1960).

Therefore, and in contrast to the farmhouse of *Night of the Living Dead*, the mall of *Dawn of the Dead* begins as an essentially uncanny environment, and the four protagonists expend much time and effort in their attempt to reclaim this un-familiar space as a familiar, comforting, and safe location. After thoroughly exploring the zombie-infested building, Peter, Roger, and Stephen decide the place is exactly the kind of thing they are looking for — a "castle and keep" in which to hole up and ride things out.[37] Furthermore, because the men clearly see the world only in terms of commodities, the mall represents everything they could possibly desire: food, clothing, recreation, and — perhaps most importantly — weapons and ammunition. The supplies in the mall's many stores can satisfy all of their immediate and long-term needs, the place continues to enjoy electrical power (thanks to the wonders of nuclear energy), and the imposing structure itself constitutes a formidable and easily defended refuge. Even though Fran — who, as in the opening sequence of the film, proves to be the only level head in the group — pleads with the men to simply re-supply and keep flying north, they are blinded by the sights and sounds of the mall itself; their judgment has been irrevocably clouded by the need to possess and own "things." This need for familiarity coupled with their almost instinctive consumer drive leads the men to a dan-

gerous plan: they reason they can capture the mall for their own use if they
first block the outer entrances with semi-trucks and then exterminate the
zombies trapped inside.

In an extended, and admittedly exciting, sequence of action and carnage,
the movie unexpectedly reestablishes the zombies as pathetic metaphors for
colonial native peoples. Using aural and visual tropes reminiscent of early
zombie films such as *White Zombie, Dawn of the Dead* conjures up images of
colonial injustices and enslavement. In a disturbing parallel to invading imperialist forces seeking commercial gain from the lands they are colonizing, the
four surviving humans from the city arrive at the rural mall to invade and
plunder an existing, exotic location, "securing its borders" before wiping out
the "indigenous population" in a bloodbath of reckless violence. After lock-
ing down the mall's exits and the entrances to the various stores, Peter and
Stephen enter a gun shop to prepare for their "final solution." With explicitly tribal drum music playing diegetically in the background and taxidermied
animal heads hanging on the walls — cinematic elements that recall *I Walked
with a Zombie* and *Night of the Living Dead,* respectively — the two men fill
bandoliers with ammunition, strap on pistols, and load hunting rifles. They
then embark into the "jungle" of the shopping mall's main concourse, which
is choked with topiaries and dense foliage, to slaughter zombies at will. For
the humans, the zombies are nothing more than a nuisance to be exterminated. The remorse Peter showed at the beginning of the film is gone, and
Roger shoots zombie after zombie with almost orgiastic pleasure. Now that
these characters have been uprooted from the labor systems that once gave
them identity, securing the mall — and reestablishing their racial superiority — seems the only way to bring them together again as a social group with
a clear purpose.

With the zombie threat safely contained outside the building, then, the
four protagonists convert an upstairs storage room into living space, bringing up furniture and other décor to turn the rooms into a facsimile of an apartment. This deliberate alteration of the building into living quarters manifests
another consumer fantasy concerning the mall — the fusion of life with shopping; the site of purchase and the site of consumption become the same place.
Fully secure in their new abode, the four protagonists have time to relax and
enjoy the (perceived) pleasures for the taking around them. Because the essential needs of survival have been fulfilled, they have time and opportunity to
enjoy themselves — they eat whatever they want, wear whatever they want,
play on the indoor ice-skating rink, and pass time in the video arcade.[38] Loudermilk calls this rather idealized vision of the apocalypse the "*Mall Fanta-
sia*" in which each character indulges in a kind of consumer utopia[39] — a
fantasy of gluttony also seen in such other post-apocalyptic films as Boris

Robert Neville (Charlton Heston) steals himself a new car in Sagal's *The Omega Man* (Warner Bros. Pictures, 1971).

Sagal's *The Omega Man*. Two separate montages show things such as Roger eating food directly from the jar, Fran putting on makeup and posing with a pistol in front of the mirror, and everyone trying on expensive clothes. Wright describes Romero's mall as a playground: "[F]or all the bleakness and uncertainty, there are chances to play out long held fantasies, the knowledge that essentially you can do anything."[40] Peter and Stephen even mug for the security cameras as they rob the mall's bank branch.

Yet all of these efforts to restore a sense of familiarity to the shopping center ultimately underscore the uncanny nature of the environment. Although the upstairs apartment does have a decidedly homey feel, complete with a kitchen and television, it must be accessed via service corridors and ductwork, as the men have blocked off all the staircases for additional safety. The downstairs shops of the mall remain eerie and strange despite everyone's best efforts, not only because they are empty of human life, but also because access to their goods is so convenient and easy. There is no system of exchange in place anymore, and while that situation might facilitate fantastic consumption, it only underscores the loss of normal capitalist society and the complete absence of the traditional economic infrastructure. Botting claims that early Gothic fiction articulates a shift from a feudal economy to a capitalistic one,[41] and Romero is performing a similar shift, one that abandons a culture based on the production and exchange of goods in favor of one focused on consumption alone. Furthermore, whereas the first montage of gluttonous consumption is accompanied by a cheerful score and emphasizes how much fun the four are having, the second series of shots is emphatically more sobering, showing the remaining survivors to be lonely, isolated, and unsatisfied. With the end of capitalist culture, items have lost all exchange value, and the mall becomes a decisively antiquated space that manifests the ultimate foolishness of rampant consumerism. The world of capitalism has become a world of the past in the course of the film. In fact, the remaining humans find no joy or satisfaction from the mall's many pleasures; it has become a prison and the symbol of their now essentially meaningless lives. The uncanny in *Dawn of the Dead* works to manifest the repressed secret of consumerism: there's little true joy to be had from consumption alone.

In other words, the apparent comforts of the shopping mall in *Dawn of the Dead* are ultimately revealed to be little more than illusions, the ghostly remnants of a lost, albeit not yet forgotten, way of life. This stubborn affectation recalls the very origins of the Gothic mode, specifically the artificial trappings of Walpole's Gothic estate-house, Strawberry Hill, what Frederick S. Frank calls "a fantasy building whose sole function was to gratify the imagination of a medieval dilettante."[42] Starting in 1747, Walpole gradually transformed a modest country house into a representation of a Gothic castle, doubling it in size, adding ornate towers and battlements, and filling it with suits of armor, looming portraits, and other antiquated curios and works of art.[43] Yet by relocating these objects outside of and divorced from their original contexts, Walpole merely counterfeited the signs of the past, falsifying the "social and personal substances once associated with them in the Middle Ages."[44] Furthermore, like Strawberry Hill, Walpole's Gothic mode is "founded on a quasi-antiquarian use of symbols that are quite obviously signs only of older signs," references to the past that are distinctly "*hollowed-out.*"[45] In an obvious parallel between the Gothic Revival in late sixteenth-century architecture and Walpole's new mode of writing, the Gothic story is revealed to romanticize a past that has already lost all real significance and value. Hogle calls this essential trope of the Gothic "the ghost of the counterfeit"; that is, the use of signs that are "partially emptied-out remnants of their former status-attachments."[46] In *Dawn of the Dead*, the abundant goods housed in the shopping mall no longer have the cultural or economic significance they once had, making them ghostly signs of the lost past, but because those goods never had any real value to begin with, they were already counterfeited products. In other words, the mall doubles its artificiality: it falsely represents a comforting lifestyle that was never really comforting in the first place.

Romero's mall thus represents the United States' rather hollow obsession with commerce and consumption during the 1970s, an exaggeration of capitalism that reduces people to the status of mindless shoppers and automatons, a metonymic connection manifested by both the zombies and the mall's many mannequins. Savoy argues that the tradition of the American Gothic "can be conceptualized as the attempt to invoke 'the face of the tenant'— the specter of Otherness that haunts the house of national narrative — in a tropics that locates the traumatic return of the historical preterite in an allegorically preterited mode, a double talk that gazes in terror at what it is compelled to bring forward but cannot explain, that writes what it cannot read."[47] The eerie mannequins of *Dawn of the Dead* clearly fulfill this Gothic role, being not only ghostly remnants of the now-defunct consumerist machine, but also physical representations of what those hypnotized by such consumerism look like. In other words, these uncanny simulacra of the human society that has been virtually destroyed by the zombie outbreak stand as allegorical representations of mindless and blank-faced consumption: the mannequins may wear the latest fashions and enjoy the plushest surroundings, but they don't actually *do* anything. Furthermore, the mannequins become a foreshadowing trope that predicts the inevitable condition unbridled consumption will inflict upon the human protagonists: as repeated shots show them isolated from one another with blank, listless faces, Fran, Stephen, Peter, and Roger become unmotivated, bored, and emotionless. Although the zombies can obviously be read as metaphors for blind, hypnotized consumers, the glass-eyed mannequins provide a more striking symbol — the zombies are at least driven by some kind of purpose; the mannequins simply stand there.[48]

As we have seen, Fiedler's contention that the different levels of a Gothic structure represent the disparate realms of the id and super-ego clearly applies to Romero's zombie films, along with a marked division between conformist stereotypes regarding male and female spheres of influence. In *Night of the Living Dead*, for example, the basement of the farmhouse ends up as the locus of extreme family discord and even violence. Initially, Karen is simply sick, laid out on a stretcher, but her parents argue and fight across her inert body. Harry tries to assert himself as a traditional, powerful patriarch, but Helen questions his judgment and even mocks his decisions and reason. Helen almost spits, "That's important, isn't it? ... To be right and for everyone else to be wrong," and she overrides her husband's authority by going upstairs against his explicit orders. Helen's id, her own drive for survival that might be fulfilled through access to a television and the other survivors, causes her to defy the patriarchical authority of the superego. In addition, the cellar is established as the primary realm of the feminine: the dying Karen spends all of the film there, and she is alternatively watched over by either Helen or Judy. Harry, on the other hand, spends most of his time upstairs, and Ben will only go downstairs as a last resort. Both the id and the femininity of the cavern or dungeon space discuss by Fiedler become literalized through Karen's drive and hunger, and the repressed taboos of both cannibalism and incest are realized there in striking visual excess.

Fiedler's dynamic upstairs/downstairs dyad also remains quite prevalent in *Dawn of the Dead*, although the contrasts between superego/id and masculine/feminine are reversed from what they are in *Night of the Living Dead*. While the lower levels remain the realm of unchecked desire, the upper rooms of the mall become the site of female power and authority. The four survivors deliberately make their living quarters on the uppermost level of the mall; the shops on the ground floor are too dangerous, as they are initially threatened by zombies and later by both zombies and a marauding biker gang. In addition, the lower level of the mall is where the protagonists become their most violent, heartless, and careless, killing first zombies and eventually humans with unrestrained abandon, all in an attempt to preserve and protect the contents of the mall, the objects of their conscious and subconscious desires. The hidden upstairs apartment, on the other hand, is repeatedly shown to be a place where the four survivors bond, make plans, and take care of each other — all intellectual and social behaviors associated with the superego instead of the id. However, Fiedler's cavernous dungeon is relocated to the top of the mall and thus becomes part of the superego realm. At the same time, though, it remains the domain of the feminine, as Fran quickly takes responsibility for the apartment upon herself, largely giving over control of the lower levels of the mall to the men. In other words, the position of the female has, by 1978, become associated with the superego instead of the id; the shift in this perception of gender, from *Night of the Living Dead* to *Dawn of the Dead*, reflects a similar shift in the American cultural paradigm from the 1960s to the '70s. Fran holds the group together and remains the voice of reason and control throughout the film, as a reflection of the greater power and independence of the liberated woman of the 1970s.

Additionally, the allegory of the female Gothic also finds its way into *Dawn of the Dead*, again in a curious reversal of *Night of the Living Dead* and of the original Bluebeard myth itself. Rather than focusing on Fran, the movie demonstrates the three men to be insatiable in their curiosity, and they are ultimately punished for their rash transgressions. Their desire to explore and to exploit the mall leads them to linger at that location much longer than their original plans — and over the repeated objections of Fran. This curiosity quickly transforms into an obsession once the three men decide they can effectively defend the structure from both zombies and other humans alike, and this obsession soon becomes a matter of consumerist possession rather than safety. As Peter so tellingly points out near the beginning of *Dawn of the Dead*, these former members of the media and law enforcement have now become outlaws and criminals: they have unlawfully broken into the mall, they steal the contents of the many stores as they wish, and they assert a sense of ownership little different from that of squatters. The men rationalize this transgression of the old laws by establishing a new social order — one where possession alone equates lawful ownership. By ceasing to see themselves as curious trespassers, the four protagonists gradually invert their roles in the inherently Gothic structure of the mall; that is, instead of being haunted by the symbols of the past, they themselves will become the ghostly remnants that ultimately represent a lost, counterfeit way of life.

The Idle Proletariat: The Death of Species Being at the End of History

The supposed security of the shopping center's walls gradually makes the sequestered humans essentially as dead and numb as the zombies; the ghouls may be trapped *outside*, but the heroes are just as trapped *inside*.[49] The four survivors try to make their indefinite inhabitation as comfortable as possible by re-creating as much of "normal life" as they can: "playing" at normalcy, Fran, pregnant with Stephen's baby, sets up house, acting the role of the traditional housewife — despite her former career as an independent and successful newswoman — and the men use their worthless money to play high-stakes poker. Their ties to extinct social institutions are so strong that Stephen even weighs a bag of candy in the store to see how much it would cost. Like zombies, then, the humans resort to acting on instinctual memory. They simply consume the material goods and services provided by the mall because that's what they have been trained to believe will make them happy. Yet happiness is more than just living this way. In his analysis of *Dawn of the Dead*, Walker emphasizes Aristotle's argument that one must *flourish* and live *well* to be truly happy,[50] and the survivors living in the mall become increasingly isolated and despondent as the film progresses. Although the human protagonists enjoy an idealized capitalist life — unlimited consumption without the burden of labor or production — they face no challenges and have no goals, and this unsatisfying stasis leads to the eventual breakdown of their new society.

The lifestyle imposed upon the survivors by the artificial confines of the shopping mall, in fact, devolves into increasingly dissatisfying cycles of fantastic consumption and play. Yet that "play" operates on two levels, imitation as well as recreation. The human refugees are largely just going through the motions of their lost lives, exactly like the zombies clamoring outside at the sealed gates of the mall. The essential problem with this new paradigm is that the four humans have become fundamentally idle; having all their needs effortlessly taken care of, they don't have anything truly productive to do. Andrea Henderson emphasizes how, in Gothic literature, identity is valued more in terms of commodity — i.e., use and exchange value — instead of genealogical prestige.[51] This paradigm certainly holds true at the beginning of *Dawn of the Dead*, for it doesn't matter that Fran is a woman or that Peter is black; in fact, none of their back stories matter at all. Instead, the four protagonists are valuable members of the community because of the skills they possess and the work they do. However, once the zombie apocalypse is in full swing, the work they conducted in their former lives is no longer required — there is no news for Fran to report, no traffic for Stephen to observe, and no civil unrest for Roger and Peter to control. Furthermore, they cease to have any use value at all; since the consumable goods they require to survive exist in abundance, they have no reason to toil or labor to produce food, clothing, or even extravagances. According to Hegel's theory on subjective development, the dialectical progression of a human being from an ignorant slave to a self-aware individual hinges on this kind of labor. He emphasizes in *The Phenomenology of Mind* (1807) that the consciousness of the bondsman (i.e., the worker) only comes to itself through work; in short, labor "shapes and fashions the thing."[52] Thus the one-time blessings of the mall become a curse for the hapless survivors living there, since they have no real purpose (or *telos*) in their existence beyond simply existing.

Romero's *Dawn of the Dead* presents a view of what the end of history might look like, a world in which no forward progress can be made and in which everyone is completely satisfied in his or her needs.[53] According to Kojève, History — the formal and dialectical development of human society — has already ended with liberal democracy, because the "relationship of lordship and bondage" has been replaced with "universal and equal recognition."[54] Romero's film literally depicts this supreme society because the four humans inhabiting the mall come to share all things equally, have no visible conflicts between them, and enjoy safety from the physical threats contained outside. In effect, they have actualized what Friedrich Nietzsche describes as the "last man" of human development, an ideal being who only works by choice, has lost all ambition, seeks no advancement, and wants everyone to be the same.[55] However, Fukuyama argues that this superlative "last man" cannot be considered fully human because such a person no longer seeks recognition and because there is "a side of the human personality that deliberately seeks out struggle, danger, risk, and daring."[56] Paffenroth observes that, for the survivors hiding in the mall, "life is grindingly boring and pointless, the ultimate parody or degeneration of a domesticity that is useless without a purpose to fulfill or a goal to pursue. Human life requires challenges, and there are none in the mall where everything is free, and therefore worthless."[57] The only one with any *telos* at all is Fran, who worries about her unborn child and the uncertain future ahead of them.

In his conception of the end of History, Kojève theorizes an increase in art and aesthetic cultural production following the dissolution of profit-based consumer economics, where the members of Society replace the apparatus of the State.[58] Yet in Romero's world of *Dawn of the Dead*, this utopian transcendence fails to take place as the surviving humans are frozen in their dialectical development. Even though they have all their material needs fulfilled by the bounties of the mall, they cannot move beyond their perception of the world in terms of commodities. They find no joy in their activities and relative freedoms because of their overwhelming obsession with possessions. In fact, they cannot see anything around them — including each other — in terms other than those of commodification. From the beginning of the film, Fran and Stephen are perceived as *belonging* to each other, and their unborn child is even portrayed as an object belonging to Stephen; in fact, the men discuss whether the pregnancy should be aborted by Peter without Fran's participation or input. Although scholars such as Paffenroth demonstrate how *Dawn of the Dead* may be read as a progressive, "pro-female" text,[59] this key scene is a glaring example of misogynist stereotypes, emphasizing the age-old problem of women being depicted as mere commodities for men to use as objects of exchange.[60] Of course, Peter also acts as if *Roger* belongs to him: when Roger eventually dies from wounds he has received from a zombie bite and rises from the dead as a ghoul himself, Peter makes the choice to end that existence by shooting his former comrade in the head.

However, this act of euthanasia has more to do with releasing an enslaved loved one from a fate worse than death than it does with greedily protecting one's possessions, and the scene constitutes yet another link between *Dawn of the Dead* and the imperialist concerns of the early voodoo-themed zombie movies. Far more than *Night of the Living Dead*, this version of the zombie apocalypse reestablishes the zombies as a trope for colonialism and slavery, and mercy killings and suicide have a long-established tradition in slave narratives. Paul Gilroy argues that the writings and accounts of Frederick Douglass have provided a "metanarrative of emancipation" as an alternative to the master/slave allegory of Hegel.[61] For Douglass, the slave does not willingly submit to the whims of the master, and, in fact, "the slave actively prefers the possibility of death to the continuing condition of inhumanity."[62] Documented occurrences of slave suicide and representations of mercy killings in African-American fiction confirm this thesis that, for the slave, death is preferable to bondage, a paradigm that stands in opposition to the rational logic of Hegel's dialectic.[63] *Dawn of the Dead* introduces this drastic motif into the zombie genre, and by doing so, Romero reconfirms the allegory of the zombie as slave. In this case, zombies are not only slaves to modern-day consumerism; they are also slaves in the traditional, colonial sense, creatures with no free will or autonomy, aside from suicide, of course. Even though Roger could have continued to exist — at least in some form — as a ghoul, Peter cannot abide the absence of his friend's consciousness, and the act becomes a merciful one that will appear with increasing frequency in the zombie films that follow *Dawn of the Dead.*

With Roger gone, the other three become more and more isolated from each other. Although they have attempted to recreate the structural apparatuses of society — the mall has been carefully transformed into a fortress, a storehouse, a playground, a church,[64] and a home, with the three remaining survivors constituting a new family community — the institutions are mere fabrications, more "ghosts of the counterfeit." They fail to afford the survivors with a subjective identity and inclusion in a true society, and the three become increasingly unfulfilled and unhappy. Without the companionship of his close friend, Peter resorts to living in the past; he misses Roger and spends much of his time alone at his friend's grave, acting as if he has nothing left to live for. Stephen, on the other hand, seems to want to live only in the present. He, more than the other two, sees the mall as a utopian paradise and wants to keep things exactly the way they are. He even proposes to Fran, giving her an expensive ring that has lost all its exchange value; Fran, however, refuses the gesture, pointing out how the union wouldn't be real. She alone is living for the future. In fact, during Roger's makeshift funeral, Romero frames Fran sitting alone on a bench in front of a store called "Anticipation: Maternity." Indeed, the balance of the film is nothing *but* anticipation — especially for Fran — and while the other two waste their time playing games, activities reminiscent of the past, the expectant mother spends her time preparing meals, watering the mall's many plants, and looking forward to potential life and rebirth.

By the climax of the movie, the shopping mall of *Dawn of the Dead* has devolved into a static ecosystem that does little beyond preserving human life while maintaining a strange kind of status quo, and that stasis ultimately renders the three remaining survivors little more than caged animals. Marx identifies humans as "species beings," for whom "the productive life is the life of the species."[65] In contrast, animals are consumed by "life-activity" alone; lower beings have nothing beyond the activities that preserve and sustain life. Humans, however, are *conscious* of life-activity, giving their labor a purpose that transcends the *animal* and constitutes the *species*.[66] With nothing to work for, with no goal beyond survival, Peter, Fran, and Stephen are forced to focus on life-activity alone. They become increasingly more estranged from each other, and Romero's cinematographic framing emphasizes how many of their idle activities are conducted in isolation. Even Stephen and Fran, the representative "Adam and Eve" of this post-apocalypse society, grow increasingly distant from one another. When shown together in bed, for example, the two stare off listlessly in different directions. In fact, the only time the two do connect is when Stephen teaches Fran how to fly the helicopter — an activity that has obvious purpose and looks towards the future. Because the familiar systems of production, labor, and exchange values have been turned upside down, all of their attempts to recreate society and its comforting institutions prove futile. Their roughhewn society begins to fail, and the three surviving protagonists essentially cease to be "species beings," or, in other words, they become counterfeit ghosts themselves.

The unsuccessful utopian "dream" of Romero's consumerist fantasy most truly collapses when Peter, Fran, and Stephen are faced with yet another invasion — but this time the threat comes from other humans, not zombies. Eager to increase their collection of booty, a marauding army of militia and bikers descends upon the mall to rob it of its material goods. Confident in their numbers, they mostly ignore the zombies, allowing the eager creatures their long-awaited access to the mall when the human renegades move the trucks and open the loading dock doors. Instead of worrying about their own safety, these misguided humans focus on stealing money and jewelry — things with no real value in the new zombie economy — along with precious guns and ammunition. Although Peter pleads with Stephen to just lie low and wait until the heavily armed biker gang leave, the sight of all of their possessions being taken by others proves too much of a blow to the chopper pilot. In an irrational attempt to preserve the stagnant social system of the shopping mall, Stephen begins to shoot at the marauders, killing other humans — ironically the most valuable commodity left in the world — to protect the inert material goods of the mall. Chaos results: the zombies end up being far more of a threat than the bikers initially thought, and many of the gang are killed before they can escape the mall. Most tragically, Stephen is also attacked and killed by zombies. Before the dust settles from the invasion, he rises as a new conscript in the army of the walking dead, completing his transformation into a soulless being that cares for nothing beyond raw consumption.

The seemingly idyllic life raft of the mall is sinking fast, and the zombies — perhaps driven to a frenzy after all the long weeks of waiting outside the mall doors, just like holiday shoppers — quickly overrun the entire structure. Zombie Stephen, clearly retaining some lingering memory of his former life, leads the voracious ghouls to the hidden stairwell, breaking down the flimsy barricades and climbing up to the secret apartments above. Unfortunately, this version of Stephen cares nothing for the items on display in the stores below; he now only hungers for the flesh of his former lover and his one-time comrade. In an ironic twist indicative of all zombie narratives, the human characters have fully realized Henderson's conception of Gothic identity: they are now commodities with a specific use value. The last two survivors have no choice but to flee. Peter, having already lost his lust for life,

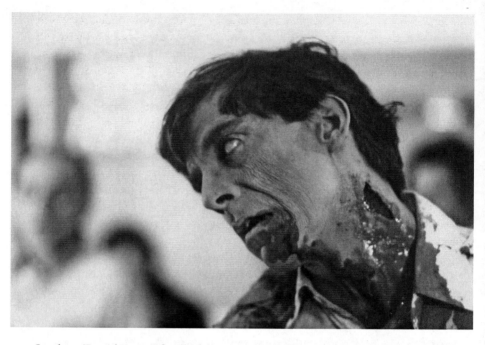

Stephen (David Emge) finally falls prey to the zombie plague, and his true consumer instincts are fully revealed at the end of *Dawn of the Dead* (United Film Distribution Company, 1978; Photofest Digital).

resolves to stay behind, distracting the horde so Fran and her unborn child can escape in the helicopter. Although Fran wastes no time getting to the roof, she lingers as long as she can, hoping Peter will change his mind. Having been abandoned by the feminine influence, the apartment now becomes a space given over to the id of the swarming zombies, and the former SWAT officer mercifully executes the zombie Stephen before preparing to kill himself in like fashion. Yet this need to fight, this need to struggle and work to survive, re-enflames Peter's sense of identity, his sense of subjective independence. According to Hegel, "The slave recovers his humanity, the humanity he lost on account of the fear of violent death, through *work*."[67] Fear of death shifts to the labor of survival, and, turning his gun once again on the zombies, Peter makes a daring dash to the roof to join Fran in the helicopter. Although they have little fuel and no plan, they at least have a chance to start over again — and they have regained their need to work for that survival.[68]

By creating such a bleak vision of the apocalypse, Romero increases the complexity of the zombie invasion narrative and cleverly presents a scathing criticism of his contemporary 1970s culture, making a mockery of the dehumanizing effects of late capitalism and rampant consumerism. He continues to emphasize the allegorical tropes of the Gothic space, but Romero also builds upon the established tropes of his subgenre to increase the narrative's power to do important cultural work. The new social order created by his four survivors at the rural shopping mall ends up being founded on hoarding and defense, not labor and production — and what labor does exist in this zombie economy is used not to *create* but merely to *preserve*. Even though the toils and rigor of capitalist society have virtually disappeared, and even though the survivors sequestered in the shopping mall have all of their material and even fantastic desires fulfilled, they ultimately cannot transcend the bonds of consumer ideology. By painfully illustrating the destruction of the social systems that have become so essential in the United States of the 1970s, Romero paints not a grim dystopian vision of how things *might* be, but rather the way things already *are*. Commodities and material possessions ultimately provide no happiness; true self-actualization comes only through labor, production, purpose, and community.

Chapter 5

HUMANIZING THE LIVING DEAD
The Evolution of the Zombie Protagonist

> But is he alive or dead? Well, that's the question nowadays, isn't it?
> — Dr. Logan, *Day of the Dead*

The phenomenal success of Romero's *Dawn of the Dead*—the film ended up grossing $55 million, approximately 85 times its meager production cost[1]— effectively assured the survival of the director's pet subgenre, resulting in a feast of imitators and knockoffs worldwide. Perhaps the most prolific production came not from Hollywood or through the independent channels of the United States, but rather via the low-budget film studios of Southern Europe. Italian filmmakers, having a long-established tradition of cheap knockoffs of American blockbusters, quickly jumped on the Romero bandwagon, producing a host of films about the reanimated dead. These films, some from such visionary directors as Fulci, unabashedly embrace the violent abuse of the human body, making their cannibals more brutal, more bloody, and more realistic than their American counterparts. In addition, the Italians diversified their methods of bodily objectification, infusing more nudity, titillation, and sex into the mix. In the United States, the zombies also enjoyed an increase in popularity, but after Romero's commercially disappointing *Day of the Dead*, the zombie phenomenon began its rapid descent into parody. Thanks largely to O'Bannon's much more successful *The Return of the Living Dead*, viewers began to see zombies as little more than comic figures, gross exaggerations of kitsch instead of telling social metaphors. Unless something could be done to revitalize or reinvent the subgenre, the cinematic zombie was destined for its own untimely demise.

Indeed, as I have said, in the years since Romero first established the tropes of the zombie invasion narrative, the cannibalistic walking dead have undergone surprisingly few alterations; however, recent developments in the subgenre have begun to bestow more personality, subjectivity, and even humanity upon the zombies. According to the protocols established by

Romero's *Night of the Living Dead*, zombies are dumb and unintelligent creatures, dead humans that have somehow risen from their graves to relentlessly feast upon the flesh of the living. Unlike the more prolific and arguably more popular vampires, zombies are unequivocally *dead* monsters, lacking any intellectual capacity beyond basic instincts and motor response. Although some zombie comedies, parodies, and fan films have explored the idea of sentient and even articulate zombies, the mainstream and "serious" horror films, graphic novels, and video games featuring zombies have remained remarkably true to Romero's original formula. In recent years, though, these lumbering creatures have become increasingly sympathetic and complex characters in their own rights. Botting has recognized how the depiction of Gothic monsters in contemporary popular culture has shifted; in fact, monstrous figures, "once represented as malevolent, disturbed, or deviant," are now rendered as fascinating, attractive, and more humane.[2] This revisionist movement began for the vampire narrative in the late 1970s, launched primarily by Rice's *Interview with the Vampire* (1976). Vampires were no longer merely devious fiends to be feared and hunted, but rather romantic and tragic souls with human thoughts, feelings, and desires, creatures to be sympathized with and even emulated, most especially in the recent "teen vampire" craze ignited by Meyer's *Twilight* series of novels. With films such as *Day of the Dead* and *Land of the Dead*, Romero himself has apparently been following this relatively new lead and paving the way for a fully realized zombie protagonist as well.

The gradual evolution of the cinematic depiction of the zombie can be most easily tracked by focusing primarily on Romero's canonical "Dead" movies. In the first two films, *Night of the Living Dead* and *Dawn of the Dead*, Romero's monsters are primarily "othered" creatures, possessing virtually no subjective, human qualities and encouraging almost no psychological suture with the audience. Although viewers are horrified by the physical similarities between themselves and the onscreen ghouls, the human survivors remain the clear protagonists of these films. With *Day of the Dead*, however, Romero creates a moderately sympathetic zombie, giving one central ghoul a name and asking audiences to see it — him — as a fully formed character and an active participant in the story. By *Land of the Dead*, Romero's zombies appear to have their own identities, personalities, and motivations; in fact, their adventures constitute a separate plotline from the central action and conflict of the film. This conception of the "evolved" zombie might be considered antithetical to the generic protocols of the subgenre, protocols codified by Romero himself, but the film takes an important step in the presentation of the zombie in a post-millennial climate. In the world of *Land of the Dead*, the humans are not necessarily humane (admittedly no big departure from other zombie movies), but neither are the zombies necessarily monstrous. Instead, Romero uses his command of cinematic language and editing techniques to encourage audience identification with the very monsters he had formerly taught them to fear. The zombie narratives of tomorrow must once again follow Romero's example and explore this idea of sentient and sympathetic ghouls if the subgenre is to remain fresh and relevant.

"Second Wave" Zombie Cinema and the Coming of Day

Romero's second zombie outing far surpassed *Night of the Living Dead* as both a financial successes and a prevailing cultural influence. Yet although *Dawn of the Dead* initiated what Dendle calls the "second wave" of zombie cinema,[3] the Italian zombie movies of the late 1970s and early '80s provide a better representation of this period. The envelope Romero had so deftly pushed with his allegorical shopping-mall zombies and their excesses of violence, blood, and gore was soon to be ripped open completely by low-budget directors working in Southern Europe. In Italy, where a film industry known for both Hollywood imitation and rampant productivity thrived, the zombie apocalypse came to be less about social and cultural criticism and more about unrelenting violence, overwhelming bodily abjection, and blatant sexuality. According to Russell, "What's so interesting about the Italian zombie movie is the way in which it frequently refutes any possibility of spiritual transcendence whatsoever, focusing instead on the collapse of the body, the unraveling of narrative meaning and an extensive revision of the genre's inherent racial politics."[4] In other words, while these films may care little about the human soul, they nevertheless challenge audience expectations about the way the subgenre depicts the human body, constructs its narratives, and addresses issues of racial difference. I will be focusing my investigation primarily on the way Italian filmmakers intensified corporeal abjection by inventing as many new ways as possible to disgrace, disfigure, and denigrate the human body. Because the Italians so unequivocally raised the bar on cinematic exploitation, they were able to give something back to American filmmaking, while at the same time paving the way for Romero's dark and sadistic *Day of the Dead*.

Because of the overwhelming commercial success of *Dawn of the Dead* in Italy — where it was released under the simple title *Zombi*— the Italian film industry was quick to exploit the subgenre with their own flood of "'spaghetti' rip-off[s]."[5] This relatively shocking movement began with Fulci's landmark *Zombi 2* (1979),[6] an unofficial sequel to Romero's film designed primarily, it seems, to take advantage of the commercial popularity of the name *Zombi*. However, *Zombi 2* ended up surpassing the box office receipts of its predecessor in Italy and launched a whole series of its own knock-offs and imitators. Much of the success of *Zombi 2* lies in the special effects work of make-up artist Giannetto De Rossi, who had also worked on *Non si deve profanare il sonno dei morti*. Thanks to De Rossi, the defining hallmark of the Italian zombie cycle became excessive violence and ultra-realistic gore, and a veritable tidal wave of blood followed in Fulci's wake. As Russell observes, "Taking the theme of bodily trauma that had become a genre staple in the hands of Romero, Grau, Rollin, and de Ossorio as their starting point, these distinctly marginal exploitation movies offered horror audiences an array of gruesome shock set-pieces. It was definitely a case of the gore the merrier."[7] Without a production code or the MPAA to worry about, Italian filmmakers such as Fulci were able to pursue the limits of their (often dark) imaginations, and audiences were soon exposed to not only a new level of gruesome violence, but also to inventive storylines and unexpected plot twists.

The main plot of *Zombi 2* is relatively simple and straightforward, with many elements taken directly from Romero, but Fulci transports the main action of his film to the isles of the Caribbean, re-embracing the voodoo roots of zombie mythology in a way Romero has yet to accomplish. After a mysterious cold opening, in which a disheveled man shoots a shrouded corpse, *Zombi 2* begins with a ghost ship entering New York harbor.[8] The Coast Guard takes the boat in to dock, but not before a mud- and blood-splattered zombie (Captain Haggerty) kills one of the men and falls overboard. The police trace the boat to Anne Bowles (Tisa Farrow), an unassuming and meek woman whose father has been missing in the West Indies for years. As she investigates the ship under the cover of darkness, Anne encounters the brash Peter West (Ian McCulloch), a reporter assigned to investigate the mystery surrounding the vessel. The two find a cryptic note from Anne's father, and soon they are on their way to the Antilles to investigate, enlisting the services of Brian Hull (Al Cliver) and Susan Barratt (Aurette Gay) to take them to the remote island of Matul by yacht. Once at the "cursed" island, the four meet David Menard (Richard Johnson), a half-crazed doctor who is attempting to cure the local population of an infection that first kills them and then reanimates their dead corpses. He sends his unexpected visitors up to his house to check on his wife Paola (Olga Karlatos), but they only find a gang of zombies feasting on the woman's bloody body. The action quickly escalates, with the few human survivors barricaded inside a missionary church against a relentless onslaught of slow-moving zombies.

One of the most notable aspects of Fulci's first zombie movie is his reintegration of voodoo folklore into the hordes of cannibalistic, infectious zombies. In other words, by turning to the past, *Zombi 2* infuses Romero's formula with new life — as it were — and reminds contemporary audiences of the true origins of the subgenre. However, in his treatment of both blacks and women, Fulci takes a decided step backwards, returning to the racism and misogyny *Dawn of the Dead* had so effectively eradicated. *Zombi 2* establishes an implicit racist tone early on, when a young, black coroner (James Sampson) is belittled and treated with disrespect by his white superior as he attempts to perform an autopsy on the victim of a zombie attack. Later, on the island of Matul, the preponderance of black zombies stands in stark contrast to the white protagonists; the former are depicted as primitive, superstitious, and dimwitted, and Dr. Menard both orders them about and executes them with equal impassivity. The climactic showdown in the missionary church, itself an obvious symbol of white imperialism and oppression, underscores the film's racism, with the three remaining whites frantically shooting black zombies and burning them with Molotov cocktails. Dendle notes this negative subtext, but argues in favor of Italian zombie cinema as a whole:

> There is sometimes an unfortunate colonial brutality implicit in the endless scenes of European survivalists gunning down native zombies, but on the whole these movies concentrate their energies precisely on those aspects of zombie film that have proven the most aesthetically powerful: provocative settings, the restrained appearance and blocking of the zombies, a mounting sense of claustrophobia and helplessness, and the careful pacing and rhythm of the escalating apocalypse.[9]

Aesthetically speaking, then, films such as *Zombi 2* fit quite seamlessly into the Hollywood zombie tradition, despite the dated racism and imperialist undertones. In fact, Fulci even manages both to transcend and to anticipate Romero on a number of stylistic and cinematic levels.

For one thing, Fulci audaciously explores the abjection of the female body. In this regard, the filmmaker pushes the established limits of cinematic taste and depictions of violence, but at the same time, Fulci also offers an intensely misogynistic view of his female characters. For starters, although her narrative drives the plot of *Zombi 2*, Anne seems unable to make any decisions on her own, relying instead on the hyper-manly Peter to tell her what to do. Yet Anne does manage to stay both clothed and alive throughout the film; the other two female characters are not as fortunate. Susan's role in the film appears to be simply providing eye-candy and titillation; for example, she insists on stopping the group's yacht off the coast of Matul long enough for her to go scuba diving wearing nothing but G-string underwear. Later, when confronted by the moldering corpse of a freshly risen zombie, Susan does nothing but stare, allowing the creature to rip her throat out with its badly decaying teeth. Paola proves to be the most stereotypically and negatively portrayed female character of all. Although she does talk back to her mad husband concerning his plans on the island, Dr. Menard quickly silences her into submission with a brutal slap to her face. Rather than retaliate or leave the doomed island on her own, Paola (naturally) takes a shower in a bathroom with two full-length mirrors, which insure the viewing audience a thorough voyeuristic experience. However, unlike Susan, Paola does try to fight off the zombies that soon invade her home, but to no avail.

Yet besides simply providing audiences with gratuitous female nudity, in itself a well-established method of objectification, Paola also stands at the center of *Zombi 2*'s most violent, bloody, and abject sequences. Having locked herself in the bathroom to hide from her unwanted guests, Paola presses both furniture and her body against the door hard enough to slice the fingers off a persistent zombie's hand. Unfortunately, one of the creatures proves preternaturally strong, smashing through the wooden planks of the door to grab the unfortunate woman by the hair. With relentless slowness, the zombie pulls Paola's head towards the splintered remains of the door, and Fulci's camera tracks her with equally methodical deliberateness. One eye, open wide with stark terror, gradually approaches a sharp splinter of wood, and the audience momentarily shares Paola's traumatic viewpoint with a subjective reverse-shot, the splinter growing ever larger in the frame as it approaches her eye. Rather than cutting away at the last moment, Fulci uses a merciless close-up shot to

Paola (Olga Karlatos) loses an eye in Fulci's *Zombi 2* (Variety Film Production, 1979; Jerry Ohlinger).

show the splinter entering Paola's juicy eye, accompanied by a gut-wrenching foley sound effect. This painfully long and evocatively memorable "rape" scene is indicative of the unflinching abjection of the body found in all Italian zombie cinema. In fact, Brad O'Brien points out how the sequence's duration is as telling as its visual content: "By emphasizing the manner in which Paola dies, and then allowing his camera to capture the visceral details of her death, Fulci revels in the violence, and the gore becomes much more sadistic than it would be if it took less screen time to portray."[10] The "feast scene" that soon follows only adds to Fulci's sadism, while further abjecting the female body. By the time the four visitors to Matul arrive at the Menards' house, Paola's body has been transformed from that of a living human into a macabre buffet table: a gang of muddy zombies, their heads hung low, take turns ripping bloody pieces of muscle and organs off the unrecognizable corpse. Paola has rapidly gone from being the object of male gaze to the object of biological sustenance — yet either way, she never transcends the status of a "thing" (see photograph on page 34).

Beyond his implicit racism, his explicit misogyny, and his excessive abjection, Fulci has also played an important role in the development of the cinematic zombie narrative with his innovative scenarios, scenes, and cinematography. One of the most unforgettable sequences in *Zombi 2* depicts an underwater battle between a zombie and a great white shark. Unlike anything that has been filmed before or since, at least to my knowledge, the extended scene explores the limits of a monster that neither requires air nor fears mortal danger.[11] Furthermore, Fulci allows his voodoo magic to affect more than just the recently dead; in a haunting sequence with no analogue in Romero, the skeletal remains of Spanish conquistadors slowly rise out of their graves, their bony fingers clawing the dirt like a panel from the E. C. Comics of the 1950s. Apparently, no dead are allowed to rest in peace in the world of *Zombi 2*, an extension of the typical scenario that enhances the gravity of the impending apocalypse by overwhelmingly increasing the numbers of the zombie army. Yet Fulci's most interesting and lasting development lies with his subjective camera perspective, by which he repeatedly aligns audience identification with the *zombies* instead of the human protagonists. For example, the camera often acts in the place of a zombie, jerkily tracking a human through the trees, surreptitiously viewing the disrobed Paola through a window, and even rising up from the grave, with grains of dirt sliding off the camera lens. By putting the audience so firmly in the place of the zombies, Fulci anticipates the development of zombie subjectivity Romero would explore so thoroughly in *Day of the Dead* and *Land of the Dead*.

Unfortunately, the majority of other Italian zombie films rely almost exclusively on bodily abjection alone as the source of their inherent terror.

Yet as demonstrated by *Zombi 2*, the human body is not only abjected through excessive violence in these movies; nudity and sex stand out as defining characteristics as well. Russell is quick to note that "rather than serving a purely titillating function, the nudity and sex in many of these films actually adds to their horror. Showing the female body in various states of undress and arousal adds an undeniable *frisson* to the zombie genre's inherent anxieties about the messy corporeality of the flesh."[12] This disturbing confluence of sex and death, pleasure and pain, arousal and repulsion — only hinted at by Fulci's voyeurism — is explored so thoroughly by other Italian filmmakers as to constitute a specialized subcategory of the zombie movie. For example, *Zombie Holocaust*,[13] written by *Zombie 2* producer Fabrizio De Angelis and directed by Girolami, combines the zombie narrative with both the cannibal film and the sexploitation movie — or, as Russell says, "If *Hustler* magazine merged with *Mortuary Management Monthly*, this might be the result."[14] Aside from the expected excesses of female flesh and bloody dismemberments, *Zombie Holocaust* primarily emphasizes *unnatural* penetration: cannibal hands reach into human wounds to see what lies insides the body, removing what they find for examination and consumption.[15] Once again, the body is reduced to a mere object, yet Girolami's film keeps any sexual intercourse at the level of unnatural metaphor.

Sex, in fact, pushes zombie infestation, cannibalism, and even violent death to the background in the short-lived micro-genre of Italian "zombie porn." Two of the more noteworthy examples come from prolific and long established pornography director Aristide Massaccesi, better known in the United States as Joe d'Amato. *Le notti erotiche dei morti viventi* (1980),[16] basically a "dated porno flick," disturbingly merges images of sex with those of horror.[17] D'Amato dispels any illusion that the human body is anything other than that of a mortal animal, repeatedly crosscutting between graphic sex scenes and images of zombies ripping people's throats out. *Porno holocaust* (1981) proves even less subtle in its intentions, featuring a lone, black zombie with a taste for living human flesh — for both sex and food. Endowed with a fatally large penis, the creature rapes the white visitors to its Caribbean island to death before eating them. Russell attempts to find a higher purpose to these films, and others like them, claiming, "Dark, depressingly grim and relentlessly nasty, these films seek to remind us that sex and death aren't laughing matters but are, instead, proof of our status as little more than meat."[18] Films such as *Porno holocaust*, Claude Pierson's *La Fille à la fourrure* (1977),[19] and Mario Siciliano's *Orgasmo esotico* (1982) therefore create "a different kind of pornography in which the body's surface is ruptured, exposing its inner mechanics to the audience's gaze. ... a frightening confrontation with the body's materiality and its status as an object."[20] By making sex an integral part of the horror, the Italian zombie porn cycle more graphically and dramatically depicts the extremes of bodily abjection than the films that emphasize physical violence and gore alone.

Although relatively short in its span, the Italian zombie cinema period thereby quickened the larger subgenre and infused zombie mythology with new concerns, emphases, and plot points that would even influence the Godfather himself. When Romero returned to the zombie scene in 1983 with what was then considered the conclusion of his opus zombie trilogy, *Day of the Dead*, he drew from both Italian innovations in abject imagery and the advancement of special effects to achieve a new level of visceral gore, although he left the titillation and pornography to other directors. Using Savini's innovative make-up effects to add an even greatest sense of realism to his latest zombie film, Romero chose to amplify his established allegorical purpose. This time, however, the zombie apocalypse has already occurred; *Day of the Dead* begins years after the events of both *Night of the Living Dead* and *Dawn of the Dead*, and a rag-tag alliance of soldiers, civilians, and doctors have established a new kind of society deep in an underground bunker and storage facility. This setting is inherently Gothic in nature, as the antiquated space has become little more than a tomb housing the remnants of a long-dead civilization, and the ensuing plot of *Day of the Dead* raises new questions about what it means to be alive and what it means to be a monster. Unlike the efforts of the Italian filmmakers, Romero's avoids any racist or sexist attacks, choosing instead to condemn all of humanity. Yet what *Day of the Dead* does adopt from the Italians is both a heightened level of bodily abjection and an attempt to align audience sympathy with the zombies instead of the rather inhuman humans. For the most part, Romero uses cinematography and editing techniques to achieve this subjective connection.

Humanizing the Zombie via Cinematic Suture

In his comprehensive survey of Romero's zombie movies, Paffenroth explores the physical similarities between humans and zombies — their essentially *Unheimlich*, or uncanny, nature. Because the walking dead look so much like their potential prey, the human protagonists in zombie narratives are both frightened and put at risk because they "identify and sympathize with [zombies] in a way that [they] never could with more powerful and demonic monsters."[21] Furthermore, because they basically look and act like living human beings, zombies can easily stalk their victims unawares, and when the zombie was once a beloved friend or family member, all precautionary defenses of the besieged humans can carelessly fall to the wayside. This uncanny correspondence between human and monster also represents the key point of such zombie films as *Dawn of the Dead*: the zombies are human and the humans are zombies.[22] Of course, on the narrative level of the films, the zombies are primarily and decidedly *inhuman*; they constitute a violation of the natural order of things and present a direct threat to the living. Even though doomed characters might sympathize with their monstrous attackers because of their resemblance to humans — as demonstrated by Peter's reaction to slaughtering a basement full of zombies in *Dawn of the Dead*— the viewers of zombie films are supposed to empathize with and relate to the human protagonists, not the invading hordes of the living dead.

Although such a rigid depiction of the cinematic zombie remains relatively constant throughout most examples of the genre, the nature and depiction of zombies has begun to shift in recent years. Paffenroth notes that traditional zombies are "completely imbecilic, incapable of making plans, coordinating their attacks, or learning from their mistakes"[23]; however, Romero begins to challenge this convention with *Day of the Dead*, exploring the idea of the increasing intelligence of zombies. Furthermore, audiences are being asked to relate to the zombies in a more direct way; instead of simply seeing their own potential death in the familiar visages of the walking dead foes, viewers are being encouraged to sympathize with the zombies, recognizing them as fully realized individual characters and even rooting for them in their narrative plights. In addition to deploying increasingly sophisticated storylines and creating more subjective zombie characters, Romero uses specific cinematic and editing techniques to foster audience identification with and sympathy for his army of the living dead. Christian Metz's theory of cinematic identification and Kaja Silverman's understanding of psychological "suture"[24] provide useful critical approaches to reading Romero's films and demonstrate how a steady increase in audience sympathy for zombies has been developed over the course of Romero's zombie films.

For an audience to connect and identify with the characters portrayed on the screen, they must first accept to some extent the reality of the cinematic fiction. This "suspension of disbelief" occurs when viewers willingly embrace the imaginary as the symbolically real, perceiving themselves as active participants in the depicted narrative. Metz explains that because the movie screen reflects light back at the viewing audience, it functions as a mirror, but because the bodies of the viewers are not literally reflected back as well, the mirror also works as a clear glass.[25] Thus rather than achieving actual subjectivity, as a child does during Lacan's mirror stage, the members of the viewing audience experience instead the subjectivity of perception for the characters who are supposedly experiencing the objective reality of the film. Through camera placement and the creation of each individual shot, film viewers identify themselves with the camera, assuming the perspective of the apparatus to be their own gaze.[26] This identification with the camera causes viewers to align themselves with characters whose visual point of view is represented by that cinematic perspective. Metz explains how the process of seeing a film therefore involves both the imaginary and the symbolic: viewers identify themselves with and see themselves as the characters whose gaze is replicated by the camera, thereby embracing the work of the imagination, and they willingly accept what they see to be real, outside of them, products of the cinema's symbolic discourse.[27]

The perspective of the camera therefore helps create subjective meaning, but Silverman emphasizes that this discursive process can work through editing as well. The nature of the shots and the method of their assembly cause audiences to identify with the fictional characters on the screen in a process called *suture*. According to Silverman, the "concept of suture attempts to account for the means by which subjects emerge within discourse," and French theoretician Jean-Pierre Oudart is credited with transporting this model into film studies.[28] Discursive subjectivity hinges on identification, and Silverman explains how one of the key operations of suture occurs because of the cuts between cinematic shots. In the shot/reverse shot construction, for example, viewers want to know who controls their perspective in a given shot — through whose eyes they are looking — and the reverse shot reveals to the audience the identity of the fictional character whose subjective point of view was represented by the initial shot. In a similar shot pairing, a character looks off frame in the first shot, and the second shot creates an "eyeline match," revealing the scope and object of that character's gaze.[29] The first shot dyad presents the gaze prior to the subject, and the second the subject prior to the gaze, but suture operates successfully in both cases because viewers identify themselves with the fictional character through these shared subjective points of view.[30]

Because an audience almost instinctively accepts the point of view of the camera as the perspective they are intended to share, the composition and editing of shots convey a sense of subjectivity and identification upon viewers and can encourage them, via psychological suture transferred from one shot to another, to feel genuine sympathy for the fictional characters on the screen. When these cinematic techniques are coupled with specific characterizations and plot elements, a director gains a level of manipulative control over the viewers of a film, forcing them to read the action of a film, and the depiction of the characters in that film, in a carefully intended way. Romero employs a variety of filmmaking techniques over the course of his zombie films to shift the loyalty of his viewers from character to character and ultimately from human to zombie, causing the audience to consider the role of the living dead in progressively different ways. In Barry Keith Grant's analysis of these films, he emphasizes how the zombies are depicted with increasing sympathy over the course of the series,[31] beginning with the almost exclusively human-centric *Night of the Living Dead* and culminating with the pitiable and almost heroic zombies of *Land of the Dead*, a film in which the walking dead have largely become victims instead of maniacal monsters. The methods of producing audience identification and suture prove invaluable tools in Romero's cinematic storytelling, resulting in a sympathetic viewing experience vastly different from most zombie films of the twentieth century.

The process of suture has always been a part of Romero's technique. His *Night of the Living Dead* opens fittingly enough with a trip to the cemetery, but both the camera perspective and editing are used to align viewer sympathy solely with the human characters. As bickering siblings Barbra and Johnny dutifully visit the grave of their father, Romero presents the majority of their conversation via standard two-shots. The first shot/reverse shot combination doesn't occur until Johnny looks off screen right, and the eyeline match that follows reveals a strange man shambling in the distance between the desolate headstones. This combination of Johnny's look and the subjective perspective of his gaze is immediately repeated, forcing audiences to identify with him despite his obnoxious behavior. An identical process of suturing occurs with Barbra when the mysterious man suddenly attacks her; her startled look up at the man is followed by a low-angle shot of his face in close up. In the struggle that follows, Johnny is ignominiously killed and the zombie rises from the ground to pursue Barbra. Although hunter and prey exchange looks,[32] the series of shots begins with Barbra's gaze, preserving her perspective as the one with which the audience is supposed to identify. Paffenroth points out that Romero could have filmed the stalking of Barbra that follows from the monster's point of view, as is typical of many horror films,[33] but he instead keeps the camera with her. After she locks herself insider her car, the zombie is shot primarily from Barbra's perspective, shown through the side windows as she locks the doors and again when she looks over her shoulder in another shot/reverse shot combination.

As Barbra flees to the perceived safety of a nearby farmhouse, a number of shot/reverse shot pairs occur, each beginning with her frightened stare off screen followed by a representation of what she subjectively sees. She becomes increasingly shocked and horrified by the sight of taxidermied animals heads displayed on the walls, the gathering crowd of zombies outside, and the partially eaten corpse of the home's former occupant; and because of the suture caused by the editing, audiences share these emotions as well, empathizing with Barbra and her plight as they share her experiences through her subjective gaze. In addition, cutting from Barbra's face in close up to these images of death and decay create what Sergei Eisenstein calls ideograms, shot pairs where each image separately "corresponds to an *object*, to a fact, but [whose] combination corresponds to a *concept*."[34] Barbra's ideograms emphasize her vulnerability and mortality and, as pointed out by Tony Williams, also foreshadow the film's tragic conclusion.[35] Stretched to the end of her emotional endurance, Barbra meets Ben, a man of action whose role in the film is quickly established by additional ideograms and shot/reverse shot combinations: a shot of Ben is followed by a close up of a crow bar, another shot matches Ben's off-screen look with a shot of tools and nails, and a particularly blatant rapid zoom couples Ben's eager gaze with an extreme close-up of a hunting rifle. As Barbra becomes increasingly catatonic and uninvolved in the film's action because of her fear, audience identification shifts to Ben, who is actively engaged in the necessary tasks of survival.[36]

As more and more zombies are featured visually, Romero emphasizes their human appearance as the fundamental connection between the monsters and the mortal protagonists. Steven Shaviro describes this visual analogue as the zombies' mimetic replication of humanity.[37] They look and act for the most part like normal humans, and, although the creatures have no individual personality, "they continue to *allude* to personal identity."[38] In *The Living and the Undead* (1986), Waller emphasizes how the zombies in *Night of the Living Dead* are each clearly differentiated individuals; their dress and appearance designates them as separate beings.[39] In addition, the zombies shy away from fire and use rudimentary tools, showing they retain some instinctual reflexes and basic memories.[40] However, Shaviro also emphasizes how the zombies' behavior has become "impersonal and indefinite, a vague solicitation to aimless movement."[41] Vestigial memories alone cannot turn the zombies into a sentient and organized force, as Ben's story of what happened before he found the farmhouse reveals. He explains to Barbra with confusion how the creatures had failed to get out of his way when he drove his truck right through a crowd of them, so zombies clearly make no efforts at self-preservation. Throughout *Night of the Living Dead*, Romero deliberately contrasts the zombies and humans, emphasizing the differences between the two camps and reminding viewers of the zombies' inhuman qualities, to illustrate that "the living dead are neither utterly alien, nonhuman monsters nor enviable creatures possessing superhuman powers."[42]

Although the majority of Romero's camera shots and editing choices in *Night of the Living Dead* clearly aligns audience perspective and sympathy with the struggling humans, one notable exception suggests the possibility of identifying with the zombies as well. As the living dead horde launches an attack on the farmhouse's weakening defenses, Helen Cooper retreats to the perceived safety of the basement to find that her daughter has risen from her sickbed as a zombie. The young girl methodically approaches her unbelieving mother, and for the most part, the sequence follows the human-centered cinematography established by the rest of the film: Karen is shot straight on from her mother's implied perspective, and reverse shots cut to Helen looking slightly off screen. However, after Karen takes a garden trowel off the wall, Romero resorts to a clichéd point-of-view (POV) shot, using a shaking hand-held camera to recreate and mimic the literal gaze of the child zombie. Nevertheless, although the audience clearly shares Karen's visual perspective for a moment, this device actually reinforces viewer sympathy for Helen — the living woman is the one menaced and in danger, and Karen no longer represents a tragic or sympathetic victim. Because the camera almost immediately adopts an objective position as the bloody trowel descends again and again across the screen, emphasis remains with Helen and her fate instead of asking viewers to consider the situation from the zombie's point of view. Almost unilaterally, therefore, Romero presents *Night of the Living Dead* as a story about humans, and the menacing zombies remain an unsympathetic and alien threat.

With *Dawn of the Dead*, Romero begins to blur the boundaries between the living and the dead more explicitly, presenting his overarching thesis that humans and zombies are essentially identical. Paffenroth claims the zombies in *Dawn of the Dead* are even more human in appearance than in *Night of the Living Dead* because they lack horrible wounds or signs of violence or decay.[43] By keeping makeup effects to a minimum and by completely forgoing rubber masks and other signs of fantastic monstrosity, Romero makes his zombies appear as if still alive. This visual depiction of the zombies alone makes them partially sympathetic creatures already, especially in the case of the ghouls who were once human protagonists, namely Roger and Steven. Furthermore, extended sequences featuring the senseless slaughter and abuse of zombies portray them as pathetic and even helpless victims. Nevertheless, as with his first zombie film, Romero continues to assert audience identification with the human protagonists who struggle to survive the horrors of the zombie apocalypse. Instead of challenging viewers to sympathize with the shambling monsters, any suture that does occur between the audience and the walking dead functions primarily to underscore Romero's proposition that humans are basically zombies already and that everyone can and will share their tragic fate.

In the opening sequences of *Dawn of the Dead*, Romero introduces his four human protagonists and employs his variegated cinematic techniques to ensure audience identification with them. The movie begins with a close-up of Fran waking from a nightmare to find herself already in the midst of a full-scale zombie infestation. Her experience mirrors that of the audience, who are similarly entering the terror of the narrative midstream, with no real exposition or setup. The next sequence, in which an urban SWAT team brutally infiltrates an ethnically diverse apartment complex, introduces viewers to Roger, a kind and sympathetic cop who tries to mentor a young rookie, to control the situation without using his gun, and to stop the uncontrolled violence of his racist superior. In addition, he is visibly sickened by the carnage going on around him, and the audience sees most of the sequence's action from his emotional, if not literal, perspective. Peter first appears on screen as an imposing and shadowy figure in a gas mask; it seems unclear if viewers are supposed to identify with Peter or distrust him completely, and the presentation of Fran's boyfriend Steven proves similarly ambiguous. However, when the four refugees stop to refuel at a rural airport, audiences see a different side of Peter. As he investigates the small airport terminal by himself, Peter is horrifically attacked by two zombie children. He must shoot them both, and the camera cuts between a close-up of Peter's shocked expression behind the sight of his rifle and images of the children writhing on a sofa. The eyeline match cuts suture the audience with Peter for the first time, but they also begin to suggest the pitiable nature of the zombies, creatures that really have no choice about what they have become.

The four survivors eventually discover the large suburban shopping center that will become their home, and as they work together to secure the mall as a defensible refuge, Romero continues to foster audience identification with and sympathy for the humans. During a risky game of cat and mouse, for example, the three men are repeatedly shown hiding from the zombies behind glass windows and doors, and the camera usually stays on the human side of the setup, once again giving audiences a prejudiced perspective of the situation.[44] Similarly, when a lone Hare Krishna zombie (Mike Christopher) attacks Fran, shots of the creature replicate her point of view instead of presenting viewers with the expected "monster POV" shot. Later, when the four protagonists attempt to block the entrances of the mall and eliminate the remaining threat within, multiple shot/reverse shot pairs emphasize the human perspective, and numerous bird's eye views recreate Steven's point of view from the helicopter. When Peter and Steven later loot a hunting store, shots of stuffed animal heads on the walls recreate Barbra's intellectual montage from *Night of the Living Dead*, equating the men with both the destruction they will soon unleash on the zombies and their own mortality. In addition, during the violent "ethnic cleansing" of the mall, Romero repeatedly masks the camera lens to resemble the crosshairs of a gun sight, associating the audience with the human hunters instead of their zombie prey.

Nevertheless, although the first zombies of *Dawn of the Dead* don't appear on screen until over nine minutes into the film, Romero almost immediately gives them a greater share of the camera's perspective than he does throughout the entirety of *Night of the Living Dead.* During the violent chaos of the apartment house sequence, a number of camera shots seem to be replicating the zombies' subjective visual perspectives; however, these shots usually depict guns being shot by police officers just below the camera frame as they exterminate the owners of the represented gaze. When Roger and Peter unite forces in the basement to liquidate the masses of zombies being stored there, the bloody sequence is shown almost exclusively from the low-angle perspective of the zombies. Other subjective shots later in the movie also recreate the point of view of the zombies, as in the scene in which Steven is caught alone in the maintenance corridors above the mall: a rickety hand-held camera lumbers around pipes and between machines, slowly stalking the ill-equipped pilot in the typical style of low-budget monster movies. Romero uses such subjective POV shots in *Dawn of the Dead* to equate the audience with the zombies, yet such POV shots always result in the destruction of the zombie, implying that the only way to share the point of view of a monster is to be killed immediately by the living since it remains paramount that the zombies must be destroyed. In other words, the subjective zombie shots in *Dawn of the Dead* merely represent the end of the monster's story, not the beginning.

Perhaps the most challenging parallels presented between the living and the dead by Romero in *Dawn of the Dead* occur when the one-time protagonists become zombies themselves. In Hamish Thompson's analysis of the ethical treatment of zombies, he emphasizes that "the sharpest moral challenge often arises when a character is faced with the realization of the altered state of a loved one and the choice of either terminating the loved one, who is thus transformed, or being transformed oneself."[45] In *Night of the Living Dead,* the audience never sees the destruction of zombie Johnny, nor do they really see Karen while she is alive. In *Dawn of the Dead,* however, Roger and Steven go from being fully realized, sympathetic protagonists to monstrous, inhuman zombies. Peter must reconcile his conflicting emotions of sentimental attachment with his instincts to survive, and the audience shares his plight; after over an hour of being conditioned to relate to and care for the two characters, viewers are suddenly expected to perceive them as monsters. When the survivors are watching the last remaining broadcasts on television, they see a Dr. Milliard Rausch (Richard France) explaining the physiological differences between humans and zombies, exhorting viewers that "we must not be lulled by the concept that these are our family members of friends. They are not.... They must be destroyed on sight." Although the living and the dead look physically similar, the latter are *not* human; instead, the zombies merely represent the unavoidable fate of all humans, film characters and audience members alike.

Romero's first two zombie movies represent a gradual development in the cinematic depiction of the zombie, and they demonstrate an increasing interest in both audience sympathy and zombie subjectivity. In *Night of the Living Dead*, Romero primarily focuses the audience's attention on the few surviving humans, placing viewers in the shoes of the besieged protagonists and making them the subject of the film's horror. Any camera work that does recreate the viewpoint of a zombie, such as that used in the scene of Karen's assault on her mother, remains at a relatively kitschy level. With *Dawn of the Dead*, however, Romero begins to position the zombies in the empathetic place of the victims, showing them at times to be tragic, helpless, and preyed upon. He uses suture techniques more frequently to align audience identification with the zombies as well as the humans, resorting to both shot-reverse shot pairs and subjective POV shots to call the true victims of *Dawn of the Dead*'s violence into question. Nevertheless, as much as we might empathize with the zombies, the creatures that overrun the Monroeville Mall remain unequivocally monsters, brainless corpses driven to hunt, kill, and eat the human population. *Day of the Dead*, on the other hand, dramatically changes the role of the zombie forever, establishing the creatures as not only victims of an unexplainable curse but also tragic figures capable of learning and limited evolution. With the creation of "Bub" (Howard Sherman), Romero takes the first shambling steps towards a fully realized zombie protagonist.

The Pathetic Dead of Day of the Dead

During the economic crises of the 1970s, Romero staged his morality play in a vast suburban shopping mall; it should come as no surprise then that the bulk of *Day of the Dead* takes place in an underground military bunker, a symbol for Cold War anxieties during the time of the United States' most excessive arms race. Yet this time around, the zombie apocalypse is not only in full swing; it looks as if the war is already over. A motley group of human survivors huddles in the dank depths of the cavernous bunker, themselves reduced to little more than the superannuated remnants of a lost civilization, the biological equivalent to the seemingly endless rows of stored files, records, and data. The target of Romero's social criticism becomes clear quickly: it's the industrial military complex of the United States, an overly bloated and arrogant arm of the government that cannot see the reality of the dire situation because of its own sense of supremacy. Captain Rhodes (Joseph Pilato) epitomizes this pessimistic characterization, being a megalomaniac who abuses his power by threatening those around him with revoked rights, bodily harm, and even rape and death. However, Romero has plenty of ire left over for the scientific establishment as well, depicting modern medicine as equally misguided and morally reprehensible. Dr. Logan (Richard Liberty), the man allegedly responsible for the salvation of the human race, comes across as an almost laughable caricature of Victor Frankenstein, yet the man's obsession with zombie physiology is nothing to snicker at. He butchers humans and zombies alike in his quest to redeem humanity, and devastating consequences soon follow. In the end, neither the military nor modern science can save the human race. The only thing left for a society so far gone is simply to start over.

Like the beginning of *Dawn of the Dead*, the opening sequence of *Day of the Dead* introduces the audience to a woman who will be the film's lead hero and the primary locus of viewer identification. The first shot of the movie shows Sarah (Lori Cardille) sitting with her back against a white, cinderblock wall. The second shot cuts to a close-up of her face looking directly at the camera, and the third shot cuts 180 degrees to reveal her subjective perspective: she is staring across the sterile room at a calendar showing the month of October with all the days crossed off. In other words, by the third shot of the film, Romero has already sutured the audience with Sarah and created a telling

John (Terry Alexander), Sarah (Lori Cardille), and William (Jarlath Conroy) constitute a diverse trio of protagonists in Romero's *Day of the Dead* (United Film Distribution Company, 1985; Jerry Ohlinger).

ideogram linking her with a sense of confinement, anticipation, and dread. She then approaches the wall, her subjective point of view reestablished via another shot/reverse shot dyad, and as she reaches out to touch the calendar, dozens of zombie arms suddenly break through the bricks. A jump cut shows Sarah waking from her dream to find herself riding in a helicopter. The parallels with *Dawn of the Dead*'s opening shot are obvious, but because the audience actually participates in Sarah's nightmare, the extent of this suture extends beyond that experienced with Fran. Romero continues to emphasize Sarah's gaze as she looks around the helicopter and down at the ground, with each shot of her looking off screen immediately followed by an eyeline match representing her perspective. In addition, she is singled out visually as one woman working with three men, and she gives orders and asserts herself as the one in charge of the operation.[46]

Despite the similarities between the female protagonists, the zombies of *Day of the Dead* prove to be quite different from the blue-faced and slightly comical stereotypes found in *Dawn of the Dead*.[47] Paffenroth emphasizes how these later zombies are "much more grotesque and mangled than in the previous two films,"[48] and this heavy use of gory makeup and prosthetics presents a new kind of zombie, one that looks far less familiar or human. When the helicopter lands in the middle of a large city so the team can look for possible human survivors, the audience gets its first look at the style of zombies in this latest of Romero's installments. As the first of the gruesome monsters shuffles slowly into frame, dramatically backlit by the sun, viewers are confronted by an obviously decomposing corpse, an oozing, bloody face that lacks a lower jaw and with it almost all ties to humanity. However, Tony Williams points out that "although *Day of the Dead*'s zombies are in a more advanced process of decay than their predecessors, they exhibit more basic patterns of thought, memory and intuition."[49] In fact, as many of the sequences featuring the zombies over the course of the film will show, these ghouls clearly learn from their experiences and can be conditioned to obey orders and replicate simple human behavior. This evolution of the cinematic depiction of the creatures makes the zombies of *Day of the Dead* both potentially more sympathetic to audiences and monstrously more dangerous to the characters in the film.

Once the reconnaissance crew returns to the safety of their underground bunker, Romero continues to favor Sarah's visual perspective, only occasionally including the other eleven male survivors in the suturing process. As Sarah accompanies three of the soldiers to extract two zombies from their cave-like holding cell, for instance, shot/reverse shot combinations recreate and favor the human viewpoint. Upon the group's arrival, however — and in stark contrast to the scenes in *Dawn of the Dead*'s mall — the camera is clearly placed on the zombie side of the fence: the audience sees the eyes of the humans peering through breaks in the wooden barricade, but shots of the zombies have no such visual impediments. Thus, despite the pervading alignment with the human point of view, the cinematography begins to offer the perspective of the walking dead more than just briefly. In fact, once the creatures approach the fence of their holding pen, low-angle shots directly recreate the visual POV of the zombies looking up at the menacing soldiers. Furthermore, the men verbally taunt and insult the essentially helpless creatures before lassoing them with collars and leading them out of the pen like livestock. Even more so than the mall zombies of *Dawn of the Dead*, Romero renders these creatures as pathetic and abused. For example, after two of the zombies are transported to another part of the facility and chained to the wall, the female creature cries out in what sounds like terror and even looks toward her male companion for support and guidance. By the end of the sequence, the humans appear to be the barbaric and monstrous ones, and Romero portrays the zombies as the helpless victims of an unjust incarceration.

Sympathy for the plight of the imprisoned zombies only increases when the audience is introduced to Dr. Logan and his macabre experiments. When Sarah enters Logan's abattoir of a lab, she is startled by a lunging male zombie that has been chained to the wall. She and the partially tame Bub exchange looks, the double reverse shots potentially suturing viewers with both of them by replicating both points of view. Sarah then turns to confront the wild-haired Logan, a clearly excessive and brutal man who rules over partially dissected corpses in his bloodstained lab coat. Viewers soon learn he has been performing a series of morbid and grisly experiments to determine how the zombie phenomenon works. According to Dendle's summary, "Logan determines that the R-complex of the brain core — the prehistoric reptile brain — is what drives the ghouls even after the outer brain has completely eroded."[50] However, this hypothesis, virtually proven by the doctor's series of experiments, would mean that "the brain begins to rot from the outside in, and the zombie, with increasingly reduced mental capacity, continues to function until the central core has wasted away."[51] Nevertheless, the mad scientist proposes that zombies can be trained and eventually "domesticated."[52] Logan's primary interest is therefore not seeking a cure to the zombie phenomenon but rather a way to train, condition, and control them. As Tony Williams emphasizes, this Frankenstein is a totalitarian who sees zombies as a compliant and subservient workforce or army,[53] much in the tradition of the early zombie films of the 1930s and '40s.

Romero's most revolutionary moment of *Day of the Dead*, however, occurs when he sutures audiences with the plight of the zombie Bub. Logan decides the key to the zombie problem is to condition them through a system of rewards and punishments, imitating the process of childrearing that he calls "being tricked into being good girls and boys." He focuses his grisly experiments on the Pavlovian conditioning of Bub, whom Romero himself describes as a "zombie with a soul."[54] With childlike enthusiasm, Logan takes Sarah and a third doctor (John Amplas) into a divided lab room, where Bub stands chained to the wall behind a one-way mirror. To prove his theory that zombies can remember and relearn the behaviors they exhibited when alive, Logan places a toothbrush, a shaving razor, and an appropriate copy of King's vampire novel 'Salem's Lot (1975) on a table in front of the remarkably docile creature before retreating to the other side of the room. Initially, the camera shows Bub through the one-way window, recreating the visual point of view of the three scientists. However, when the zombie picks up the razor, he looks straight ahead into the mirror, and the camera reverse shot recreates Bub's literal perspective, showing him looking at a reflection of himself. Proving Logan's psychoanalytic theory, the confused creature appears to recognize himself, roughly running the razor across his face as a sign of his newfound subjectivity. This remarkable shot provides the greatest degree of suture between the audience and a zombie of any of Romero's films, totally equating the viewers with the zombie by having them experience Bub's literal developmental mirror stage and his subjective self-identification.

Romero also presents Bub as a sympathetic subject by encouraging a more sophisticated and emotive acting style from actor Howard Sherman. For instance, when Captain Rhodes enters the room, Bub looks at the man's uniform, stands up straight, and throws him a formal salute. Logan

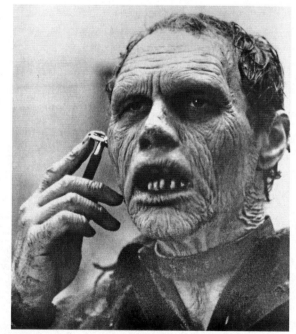

Bub (Howard Sherman) begins to remember his former life in *Day of the Dead* (United Film Distribution Company, 1985; Photofest Digital).

then provides the zombie with an unloaded pistol, and when Bub eventually figures out how to cock it, he looks slowly up at Rhodes (and the audience) with something akin to an evil gleam in his eye. Bub points the gun directly at the camera, the reverse shot reveals his view of Rhodes pointing a pistol back at him, and the third shot shows Bub pulling the ineffectual trigger. Realizing the new threat such a zombie poses, Rhodes cocks his own weapon, and in Bub's reaction shot, the zombie shows a clear look of fear on his face at the prospect of being attacked. Unlike Romero's usual stone-faced and deadpan zombies, Sherman deftly acts through his gray makeup and prosthetics, giving his zombie emotional expressions with which the audience can sympathize. Béla Balász describes this function of the close-up as "visual anthropomorphism," by which expressions represent "the most subjective manifestation of man, more subjective even than speech."[55] Such a description of emotional subjectivity certainly applies to Bub, a creature that (for the most part) lacks the power of speech entirely. In addition to camera angle, shot composition, and editing, this scene emphasizes how Romero also uses acting and the close-up to encourage audience sympathy and identification.

Although the zombies inevitably overrun the entire complex and brutally murder the remaining soldiers in the film's final reels, Romero never resorts to a shaky hand-held camera to replicate a marauding zombie's point of view directly, as he does briefly in both of his preceding zombie films. During this sequence of this film, Romero recreates the subjective perspective of the walking dead with the camera only when the zombie itself is being killed or destroyed. The audience never sees the murder or dismemberment of a human character from the direct POV of a zombie; instead, an omniscient third-person camera position shows the gruesome horror with some detachment. Romero is clearly willing to encourage audience identification with zombies when they represent human mortality or even pitiable victims, but not when they act as ravenous and violent beasts. Subjective camera shots are thus kept to a minimum during the destruction of the underground bunker; the exception, of course, lies with Bub. In an unexpected contrast to the film's irrational and cruel human characters, especially Rhodes, "Bub is shown to be capable of mercy, restraint, contemplation, and enjoying things other than shouting at or killing people."[56] Bub behaves towards Logan somewhat like a loyal puppy, even passing up the chance to take a bite out of his master's arm, although this behavior might have more to do with Bub's former military training — his remnant instinct memory — than any real emotional attachment to the doctor.[57]

Nevertheless, Bub's visible emotional reaction to Logan's murder appears to transcend mere instinct and provides the final sympathetic connection between the domesticated zombie and the viewing audience. After he has figured out how to undo his chains, Bub stumbles into the hallway and looks off screen. The following eyeline match recreates the zombie's vision of Logan lying on the floor. Aside from the suture created by the editing, this scene also exhibits the very human expressions of shock, disbelief, and sadness on Bub's face. Cleary distraught, Bub thrashes his chain around, cries and moans in grief, and looks around the room. Another shot/reverse shot pair links his gaze to a close-up of two pistols on the floor, a combination that further cements the identifying suture and also creates a foreshadowing ideogram. After picking up a gun, Bub turns to face Rhodes down a long hallway like an old–West cowboy preparing for a showdown. Bub points his gun directly at the camera and fires, and the reverse shot shows the bullet tear into a retreating Rhodes' shoulder. Romero depicts this act of revenge from the zombie's perspective, and the audience is clearly supposed to identify with this "just" execution of a violent criminal. After three replays of this literal "shot" and reverse shot dyad, a smug and satisfied looking Bub mockingly salutes the soldier as Rhodes is horribly ripped to pieces by the invading zombie horde. Bub then wanders off alone into the bowels of the shelter, foregoing the zombie slaughter and resulting feast.[58] Romero thus ends his third zombie film with a suggestion that the "enlightened" zombie can rise above instinct, adopting human drives such as sorrow and revenge instead of just raw hunger and consumption.

With *Day of the Dead*, Romero appears to be suggesting a haunting new trajectory for the subgenre, one that can increasingly cast humans in the roles of the monstrous antagonists and allow the zombies to take on more tragic and sympathetic roles. Unfortunately, the film performed far below expectations at the box office, grossing only $6 million after an estimated $3.5 million production budget.[59] The American public no longer seemed interested in serious investigations into the walking dead, preferring instead such campy and humorous interpretations as *The Return of the Living Dead*, a low-budget comedy that beat Romero's film to theaters by two months and outstripped it financially with $14 million in gross receipts.[60] Other zombie comedies inevitably followed, plunging the subgenre firmly into the parody phase of its development and leaving the gravitas of Romero far behind. The United States of the 1990s was perhaps too financially secure, too politically stable, to foster socially and culturally critical or fear-inducing films, and the allegorical zombie quickly suffered its own death at the hands of its brain-eating kin. Faced by the overwhelming force of such shallow fare, the zombie invasion narrative went underground, finding an incubating refuge in graphic novels and video games. It took the terrorist attacks of September 11, 2001, and George W. Bush's new America to change the cultural landscape enough to make the zombie's return not only inevitable but also vital to the culture.

The Rise of the "Zombedies" and "Splatstick" Cinema

During the 1980s, the decade of *Day of the Dead*, the zombie invasion narrative experienced something of a renaissance, with more zombie movies being produced in the United States than during any previous decade.[61] This cycle, characterized by low production values and self-parody, began with the release of Michael Jackson's 13-minutes long music video *Thriller*, a melodramatic, comedic, and self-referential spoof of established horror icons, including vampires, the wolf man, and zombies. The video became an instant sensation, but, of course, once the walking dead became the *dancing* dead, much of the "bite" left the genre, and people began to see the zombie as a "living room-friendly ghoul."[62] Nonetheless, a host of zombie movies followed Jackson's contribution, and most of these low budget, reductive, and generally unremarkable movies opted for cheap thrills, base humor, and sexual and racial exploitation. In other words, movies such as *The Gore-Met Zombie Chef from Hell* (1986), *I Was a Teenage Zombie, Redneck Zombies*, and *Zombie High* (1987) attempted to build on the Italian zombie cinema tradition while catering to a mass teenage audience.[63] As a result, most of the zombie fare from the 1980s and '90s is lackluster at best, attempting little to no cultural work and providing scholars with almost nothing of substance to analyze. However, the comedy films — the "zombedies" — became the ones that proved most able to explore the issue of zombie subjectivity. Because these films deflect the horror of the zombies through both humor and satire, they humanize the creatures and make it easier to relate to them. Furthermore, by making the zombies both humorous clowns and pathetic victims — and by giving them limited sentience, barely articulate speech, and the now ubiquitous hunger for human brains — those characters altered by the process of zombification can now take on more of a starring role. In fact, these parodic films helped keep the subgenre alive into the 1990s and marked a new direction for zombie cinema, one Romero would take up years later with *Land of the Dead*.

The most noteworthy and influential zombedy of the period is surely *The Return of the Living Dead*, a teenage comedy and sexploitation film with no pretensions. The movie began its existence with Russo, the co-screenwriter of *Night of the Living Dead*, who had devised his own zombie movie, a serious horror film designed as an unofficial sequel to Romero's 1968 success. Russo managed to sign Tobe Hooper as the director, but copyright disputes with Romero delayed production until 1984, and by that time both men were off the project, and O'Bannon had rewritten the script and stepped up to direct.[64] The movie was made for a modest $4 million budget,[65] but O'Bannon managed to attract established Hollywood and television actors such as Clu Gulager, James Karen, and Don Calfa. Of course, the title of the film and its similarity to Romero's cult classic certainly didn't hurt its reception either. Russell describes *The Return of the Living Dead* as "a breathless horror cartoon that aspires simply to make jaws drop to the floor through its sheer exuberant excesses."[66] Those excesses include plenty of slime and gore, buckets of blood, an overtly nihilistic ideology, a punk rock soundtrack, and gratuitous female nudity. However, the film holds an important spot in the lifecycle of the zombie subgenre because of its postmodern metatextuality; its introduction of sentient, fast moving, and brain-seeking zombies; and its mainstream commercial and popular success.

The entirety of *The Return of the Living Dead* takes place in perhaps the most Gothic and overtly antiquated space of any zombie film — a remote urban neighborhood that includes a medical supply warehouse, a mortuary, and a cemetery — and the action plays out in something close to real time. Frank (Karen) manages the UNEEDA Medical Supply warehouse, and on the fateful night of the film's narrative, he is endeavoring to train a newly hired teenager named Freddy (Thom Mathews). The building is filled with representations of death, from a rack of skeletons from India to a bizarre collection of "split dogs" used to train veterinarians to a cold-storage locker containing a male human corpse. Frank eagerly shows Freddy a number of mysterious vats stored in the basements, and he explains they are military containers that allegedly contain the remains of real-life zombies, the results of a misguided government experiment to destroy marijuana crops back in the 1960s. The bumbling Frank inadvertently ruptures one of the drums, releasing toxic gasses into both the warehouse and their own lungs. The strange fumes quickly render the two men unconscious, and the bald and strangely yellow cadaver upstairs (Terrence Houlihan) begins to move. When Frank and Freddy recover, their horrific discovery of the flailing half-bodies of the reanimated dogs convinces them to call in their boss, Burt (Gulager), whose chief concern upon arrival is to keep the authorities from finding out anything about the "accident." Frightened, bewildered, and confused, the three men turn to popular movies for help and guidance.

At this rather early point in the narrative of *The Return of the Living Dead*, the film reveals an unabashed postmodern metatextuality. Not only does Romero's *Night of the Living Dead* actually exist in the world of O'Bannon's film, but Frank also explains how that movie had been based on a true story.[67] He claims Romero had been inspired in 1969 when a number of corpses from a Pittsburgh VA hospital had become reanimated when a vat of the government's anti-drug pesticide had leaked onto their bodies. The military had quickly covered everything up, sealed the remaining creatures in storage vats, and sent them to a secure location. Frank explains further that due to an unsurprising SNAFU, some of the vats had been sent to UNEEDA instead. Now faced with a very real zombie of their own, the three men openly discuss *Night of the Living Dead*, eventually remembering how the creatures in the movie could only be destroyed by a blow to the head. Confident in their research, the men let the zombie out of the freezer, but it moves with unexpected speed and has unexpected strength. Frank and Freddy wrestle it to the ground, and Burt manages to impale a pickaxe into the back of the thing's head. However, the zombie continues to struggle — although now it is crying disturbingly — so Burt uses a hacksaw to remove the head completely. Unfortunately, even such extreme measures prove useless, as the headless corpse jumps up and begins to run amok around the warehouse. As the three men tackle and tie up the body, Frank moans, "It worked in the movie!" It seems *real* zombies, at least in this film, cannot be destroyed at all, and Romero had "really" been forced to change vital details about the Pittsburgh zombie outbreak to avoid a lawsuit from the United States government.

This overt lampooning and burlesquing of an established and expected tradition demonstrates yet another vital characteristic of the Gothic mode. When Walpole wrote *The Castle of Otranto*, he not only combined the supernatural elements of the romance with the realism of the novel,[68] he also adopted, appropriated, and deliberately altered narrative tropes from the past. For example, one of the most celebrated passages from Walpole's novel occurs when the portrait of Manfred's grandfather begins to move, stepping from its frame as a disapproving ghost. As in Shakespeare's *Hamlet*, the frightened scion humbly entreats the spirit for guidance and information, but Walpole's ghost, without uttering a single word, simply walks into another room and slams the door behind it.[69] In other words, the befuddled Manfred receives no admonition, no revelation, and no guidance. Another example of Walpole's deft manipulation of audience expectations concerns the giant ghost of Alfonso. Few moments in Gothic literature match the tragicomic death of Manfred's son Conrad, who is crushed by a giant helmet in the second paragraph of Walpole's novel. Additionally, the intermittent appearances of the ghost itself offer comedic moments in the story, not the least of which is the farcical report inexpertly delivered by Manfred's servants Diego and Jaquez. The most notable aspect of Alfonso's ghost, however, is the gradual revelation that the specter isn't a malevolent force at all; instead, the "much-injured Prince" has returned from the grave to punish the true villain of the novel, Manfred, and to restore the proper heir, Theodore, to the throne.[70] In other words, the ghost, usually the sinister monster of such macabre tales, is revealed to be not only a sympathetic victim but also the heroic savior of the novel.

Of course, the first zombie that appears in O'Bannon's film does attack the unsuspected protagonists, but *The Return of the Living Dead* wouldn't be much of a zombie movie with just the one monster. Faced with exposure, financial ruination, and possible jail time, Burt decides to take drastic measures, cutting the persistently animated body into pieces for immediate cremation at the neighboring mortuary, the ironically and self-referentially titled Resurrection Funeral Home. Ernie, the mortician (Calfa), is working late, and

A pair of tattered zombies rise from their graves in O'Bannon's campy *The Return of the Living Dead* (Fox Films Ltd., 1985; Jerry Ohlinger).

with some convincing and cajoling, he agrees to blast the zombie's remains in his superheated furnace. Meanwhile, Freddy's deadbeat friends, a group of seven punk teenagers seeking a place to party while they wait for Freddy to finish working, have overrun the neighboring cemetery. They play loud music and dance on the graves, and Trash (Linnea Quigley) ruminates on how she fantasizes about being eaten alive by old men before performing an erotic striptease atop a tombstone. The two storylines abruptly collide when it begins to rain, soaking the teenagers and the cemetery grounds with water that has been infused with the smoke and ashes from the recently cremated zombie. With alarming rapidity, all the corpses begin digging themselves out of their graves, revealing a host of gruesome creatures in various stages of decay. Once again, *The Return of the Living Dead* revels in its own irony as an army of zombies erupts from "Resurrection Cemetery" to pursue and kill a gang of young nihilists obsessed with anarchy and death. Some of the teenagers do make it to the relative safety of the funeral home, however, where Frank and Freddy are growing increasingly pale and ill.

Russell believes that "at the heart of *The Return of the Living Dead* is a savage kind of comedy, a nihilistic punk mentality that treats nothing as sacred."[71] Such a reductive overview accurately addresses the film's comedy and nihilism, but upon closer examination, O'Bannon's movie also offers a hauntingly sober look at the realities of death, and it presents a scathing criticism of the American military complex almost worthy of Romero's more thoroughgoing allegories. As Frank and Freddy's condition grows worse, the men complain of excruciating pain and intolerable chills.[72] Ernie calls for an ambulance, and when the two paramedics arrive, they diagnose the two poisoned men as clinically dead. Tina (Beverly Randolph), Freddy's distraught girlfriend, cradles the head of her suffering beloved in her lap as he describes the pain of feeling his organs fail, his blood pool in the muscles of his back, and his limbs stiffen from rigor mortis. At the same time, the zombies from the cemetery begin to assault the mortuary, forcing the few humans locked inside to board up the windows and doors in both reference to and imitation of *Night of the Living Dead*. Ernie manages to capture the desiccated torso of a dismembered female corpse (Cherry Davis) and tie it to his operating table for interrogation. With surprising lucidity, the monster explains how the overwhelming pain of decomposition drives zombies insane unless they can eat fresh human brains. This grim depiction of restoring the nervous system to a rotting body infuses *The Return of the Living Dead* with a horrific realism that might be overlooked because of the movie's many gags.

O'Bannon's film continues to parallel *Night of the Living Dead* when the local authorities prove to be useless, the defenses of the mortuary are eventually overrun, and nothing but a tragic and senseless outcome remains. Predictably, Freddy succumbs to the irresistible desires of his new condition; and although he drives Tina and Ernie into an attic, viewers cannot help but recognize the tragedy of the pathetic creature. Frank plays an even greater role in this development of the zombie protagonist. Showing substantially more control than Freddy, Frank chooses to incinerate himself in the crematory furnace rather than become a brain-eater himself. This curious move — although played somewhat for laughs — actually provides a revolutionary moment in the development of the subgenre, presenting viewers a zombie in a very empathetic light and demonstrating the cruel reality of such a fantastic situation from inside of it. No such emotional gravity exists in connection with the zombies swarming around outside the funeral home, however. They prove to be nothing more than clever monsters — both sentient and fast moving — that keep radioing for help to bring in fresh paramedics and police officers to eat. Meanwhile, Burt manages to return to the warehouse and calls the toll-free phone number printed on the side of the zombie canister, contacting the military and apprising them of the outlandish situation. The government of course has a contingency plan already in place; in a cynical move that both mirrors the anti-military sentiments of *Day of the Dead* and recalls the satire of Stanley Kubrick's *Dr. Strangelove* (1964), O'Bannon's film ends with a nuclear blast just outside of Louisville, one that vaporizes the hordes of zombies just in time for their smoke, dust, and ashes to infuse the gathering storm clouds. *The Return of the Living Dead* thus ends with the death of all its protagonists and the promise that the zombie invasion is really only beginning.

The Return of the Living Dead proved to be immensely popular with young viewers, a generation apparently far more interested in visual gags, exploitative nudity, and excessive cinematic gore than in cunning social commentary. In his brief discussion of the film, Russell focuses only on the negative contribution of O'Bannon's movie, writing that "although it remains a firm fan favourite, *The Return of the Living Dead* ultimately has very little to say. Perhaps if someone had listened to the zombies' repeated demands for 'Brains!' its legacy and influence might have matched its impressive box office returns."[73] Russell does have a point about the formal vacuity of the film, as O'Bannon's mechanical direction fails to provide any cinematic ingenuity or artistic innovation. Yet the film *does* have an important and lasting legacy: *The Return of the Living Dead* not only advanced the development of the genre, specifically through its exploration of zombie subjectivity and sentience — ideas that Romero himself was simultaneously investigating — but it also paved the way for an entirely new micro-genre, the "splatstick" comedy. By fusing the horrific with the comedic, O'Bannon opened the door for a host of films that were able to ratchet up the violence and the gore by shrouding their core narratives in a censor-defying coat of humor. The "serious" zombie narrative thus largely disappear into micro-budget shot-on-video (SOV) movies during the 1990s, being replaced in the mainstream by lighter fare such as the numerous *Return of the Living Dead* sequels, Sam Raimi's *Evil Dead* movies, and Peter Jackson's ultraviolent *Braindead*.

Even if Raimi's *Evil Dead* films feature demons and possessed corpses instead of traditional zombies, they mark an important turning point for the zombie subgenre because of Raimi's effective circumvention of the MPAA and other censorship organizations. After *The Evil Dead* (1981), a serious if excessively violent and bloody horror film, was effectively blocked by British censors, Raimi remade it entirely as a Three Stooges–inspired comedy, *Evil Dead II* (1987), and he thus can be said to have invented the splatstick film.[74] Rather than attempt any socio-political commentary, Raimi apparently just wanted extreme physical comedy, outrageous sight gags, and over-the-top special effects and gore. *Evil Dead II* certainly delivers on all counts, thanks primarily to the physical abilities of Bruce Campbell, whose portrayal of Ash launched the character to iconic cult status. Ash indefatigably combats a host of demons and reanimated corpses, pratfalling in mud and down stairs, bathing in showers of blood, dismembering dead bodies with shovels and a chainsaw, and even cutting off his own hand to fight with it like something out of a macabre *Tom and Jerry* cartoon. Thus *Evil Dead II*, like other splatstick efforts, "had a keen awareness of the horror of the body, [inviting] audiences to laugh or barf. In these movies, the human body becomes an object of ridicule rather than abjection, a faulty machine that doesn't seem to realize quite how ludicrously gross its mass of internal fluids and red matter actually is."[75] In other words, splatstick films continue to emphasize the objective nature of humanity, but their purpose is simply to make fun of it, entertaining audiences through sheer carnivalesque excess.[76]

Perhaps the most excessive, visually ludicrous zombie film to come out of the 1990s is Jackson's *Braindead*, released in the United States as *Dead Alive*— what Linda Badley calls a merger of "silent film slapstick with Monty Python routines."[77] After a diseased "rat-monkey" bites his mother (Elizabeth Moody) at a New Zealand zoo, the chief protagonist of *Braindead*— the hen-pecked "Momma's boy" Lionel (Timothy Balme)—finds himself struggling to care for his zombified "Mum," not unlike Norman Bates, while simultaneously keeping the infestation a secret. As more friends and family are infected, Lionel tries to feed and care for them in his house, a misguided attempt at filial duty that only escalates as the movie's outrageous plot moves forward. Soon, Lionel has a host of dangerous creatures under his roof— including a baby zombie and a pile of human organs that has developed into a surprisingly expressive creature all its own — and his mother continues to order him around; like the creatures in *The Return of the Living Dead*, Jackson's zombies maintain sentience, thought, and limited speech. Furthermore, the combination of the zombies' pathetic reliance on Lionel with their absurd and humorous behavior makes them more fully formed characters than the walking dead of films such as *Night of the Living Dead*. In fact, Lionel's gang of zombies takes on the semblance of a loveable, if understandably dysfunctional, family; but they unfortunately find the drive to eat human flesh irresistible. When things become too much for him to handle, Lionel finally decides to stand up to his mother and his increasingly demanding charges, and he eradicates the entire lot by strapping a lawn mower to his chest. As

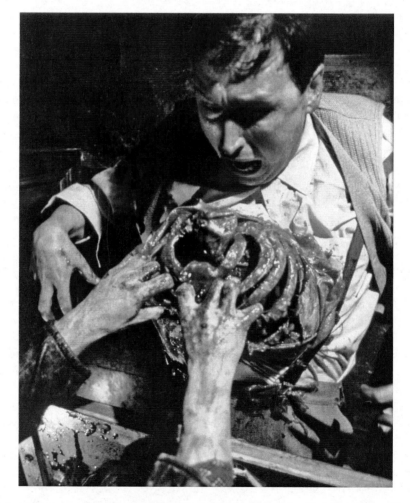

A drunken party guest loses his ribcage in the irreverently abject *Braindead* from Peter Jackson (WingNut Films, 1992; Jerry Ohlinger).

Lionel wades into a room filled with zombies, special effects wizard Richard Taylor holds nothing back as he demonstrates the human body to be nothing more than a loosely constructed system of flesh, organs, and blood — lots and lots of blood. Even though Jackson's film can be read as an Oedipal allegory,[78] *Braindead's* greatest significance and value lie with its inventive place at the pinnacle of the zombie splatstick period.

Ultimately, however, the closing decade of the twentieth century proved a tame one for zombie cinema, with Hollywood production plummeting into virtual insignificance. Although Savini attempted to restore the zombie to its place as a terror-inducing monster in the 1990s by directing a remake of *Night of the Living Dead*, the monster simply wasn't considered frightening any more. Not even Romero himself could find anyone in Hollywood to finance his planned fourth zombie film, initially titled *Twilight of the Dead* and later *Dead Reckoning*. The '90s clearly favored revisionist parodies and mainstream horror cinema, and "zombie movies were distinctly out of favour again."[79] The cinematic zombie invented by Romero inevitably retreated from the silver screen during this period to be replaced by much shallower fare, even though the subgenre found a home instead in SOV fan films and in video games. Nevertheless, as low-budget movies such as Andrew Parkinson's underground film *I, Zombie: The Chronicles of Pain* (1998) proved, the cinematic zombie still had a lot to offer the world. Not only would a new generation of viewers become interested in narratives that returned to the generic characteristics of Romero's early films, as in Snyder's innovative remake of *Dawn of the Dead*, but filmmakers would also continue to experiment with degrees of zombie subjectivity. And as in the past, one of the most successful of these latter examples is a clever parody, Wright's brilliant romantic comedy, *Shaun of the Dead*.

As a genre film, *Shaun of the Dead* defies simple classification, slipping easily from comedy to romance to satire to horror and back again, but it ultimately operates as part of the larger zombie tradition. Wright's movie begins as a standard, if slightly irreverent, romantic comedy, with Shaun (Pegg) arguing with his girlfriend Liz (Kate Ashfield) about Shaun's annoying roommate and intolerable third wheel Ed (Nick Frost). The title sequence that follows, however, presents viewers with a quick montage of people mindlessly working, answering their cell phones, and listening to portable music players as carefully orchestrated automatons. We learn that Shaun's days are similarly mundane and routine: he buys a Coke at the store down the street, he rides the bus to work with a crowd of glassy-eyed commuters, and he goes through the motions at his dead-end job. In this way, then, Wright's film clearly and deliberately embraces Romero's key trope from *Dawn of the Dead*: humans in this age of technology and routine labor are essentially zombies already. In fact, even as a zombie infestation is gradually overwhelming London's Crouch End, few people seem to notice the scattered news reports about a crashed space probe, increased incidents of violence, and unexplained military activity. Shaun begins the next day by obliviously following his long-established routine, ignoring numerous shuffling figures, clear signs of chaotic violence, and even a slippery puddle of blood. Later in the film, after he has grasped the gravity of the situation, Shaun leads a crew — including Ed, Liz, and his mother Barbara[80] (Penelope Wilton) — to the perceived safety of the Winchester pub. On their way, the human survivors must mimic the behavior of the shambling, moaning creatures to pass safely through a mob of zombies. Although the sequence is admittedly humorous, it reinforces the satire enacted by the film's opening scenes: virtually no difference exists between zombies and humans.

Shaun of the Dead is certainly both inventive and entertaining, and it builds on Romero's established allegorical project, but its greatest influence on the zombie subgenre lies not only in its comedic social commentary but also in its play with the idea of domesticating the "mobile deceased." As in the zombedies of the 1980s and '90s, Wright's film diminishes the threat of the walking dead by making its creatures decidedly clownish. For instance, when Shaun confronts his first zombies face to face, he ineffectually attacks them with kitchen appliances, utensils, and, as a last resort, his treasured vinyl records. He later fights his way through a series of the slow-moving, dimwitted foes, defeating them rather easily with unconventional weapons like a cricket bat and a tetherball pole. Yet at no time in Shaun of the Dead does the camera recreate the visual perspective of a zombie, so any connection or empathy a viewer might feel for the pathetic creatures comes either through comedy or via purely emotional, rather than cinematic, means. For example, despite the film's frequent levity, the moments in Shaun of the Dead when beloved protagonist are turned into zombies are both poignant and pathetic, such as with Shaun's antagonistic step-father Philip (Bill Nighy) and, even more tragically, his mother Barbara. However, when Ed becomes infected near the end of the film, Shaun simply cannot bring himself to euthanize his best friend. Instead, after the British military has finally managed to contain the chaos of "Z-Day," Shaun elects to chain the zombie Ed has become out in his garden shed, where the two can continue to play video games together. Of course, this development of Ed's character only occurs at the end of Shaun of the Dead, and the former protagonist is depicted as little more than a wild, untamed pet. Truly sympathetic zombie protagonists had still not yet made their way into a serious, big-budget horror film — until Romero was finally able to continue his vision of the zombie apocalypse with Land of the Dead.

The Zombie Protagonists of Land of the Dead

After movies such as Boyle's *28 Days Later* and Anderson's *Resident Evil* ushered in the zombie renaissance,[81] Romero returned to the subgenre that had established his filmmaking reputation with *Land of the Dead*. According to Tony Williams, Romero had based his first three zombie films on a three-act story he had written called "Anubis." In the story's second movement, a human extermination posse contends with a horde of zombies that have remembered how to use a variety of weapons and firearms, and in the third section, a megalomaniac succeeds in training zombies to fight for him as an organized army.[82] Although elements of the third act clearly appear in *Day of the Dead*, Romero had to wait for *Land of the Dead* to explore the idea of zombies organized into an armed assault force.[83] Moreover, in the latter film, Romero adjusts the protocols of the zombie subgenre, finally offering a serious consideration of the possibilities of zombie evolution. Thompson concludes his psychological investigation of zombie identity by claiming that what most distinguishes humans from zombies is the potential for the living to actualize "imaginative goal-directed action."[84] However, Romero clearly challenges this distinction in *Land of the Dead*, proposing a post-zombie-apocalypse world where such contrasts no longer hold true. The zombies of *Land of the Dead* clearly exhibit the ability to remember, to learn, and to act as an organized group, taking an active role in the film's storyline. In addition, Paffenroth points out how "*Land of the Dead* surprisingly and consistently puts the zombies in our shoes, making them more human than any of the other films, and therefore no longer the objects of our revulsion and fear, but of strange sympathy and respect."[85] By adjusting the very nature of the creature he had originally created, Romero presents viewers with zombies in the revolutionary role of sympathetic protagonists.

The initial sequence of *Land of the Dead* quickly establishes the new and unexpected nature of the film's zombies. After the opening credits, the camera passes slowly through the strangely idyllic community of Uniontown, where the walking dead are rather peacefully attempting to recreate the behaviors of their mortal lives. Romero thus shows audiences the zombies *before* he reveals any human characters, a marked departure from the pattern established by the first three films. Furthermore, although the creatures *appear* even less human and show more signs of disfigurement and decay, these zombies *act* human, trying to play musical instruments, attempting to pump gas, and even appearing to communicate with each other by grunting. A heavily armed human scavenging team, outfitted like combat soldiers, soon enters the town looking for supplies, launching fireworks into the night sky to distract the legions of walking dead. Acting for the most part like dumb animals, the

Big Daddy (Eugene Clark) can remember his old job, and soon he will lead a full-scale zombie revolt in Romero's *Land of the Dead* (Universal Studios, 2005; Photofest Digital).

zombies are initially entranced by the colorful display, and POV shots of the exploding pyrotechnics follow shots of multiple creatures looking upwards. However, Big Daddy (Eugene Clark), the gas station attendant, proves unaffected and emerges as a unique character and leader.[86] Contrary to expected zombie behavior, Big Daddy "tries to warn his fellow zombies, grunting, growling, and even courageously pushing zombies out of the way to save them from the humans' attack."[87] In addition, close-ups of Big Daddy show his rage and grief, and a number of subjective camera shots begin to suture him with the audience. By the end of the violent raid, Big Daddy has strapped on a machine gun and organized the zombies around him, so much so that the massed horde sluggishly follows him like some kind of macabre Moses out of Uniontown.

    Yet despite the various techniques Romero employs to ensure a greater level of audience identification with the zombie, humans remain the primary protagonists of *Land of the Dead*. The first set of shot/reverse shot edits of the movie recreate the visual perspectives of Riley (Simon Baker), establishing him as the hero of the narrative and the chief focus of audience identification. As leader of the team from Fiddler's Green, Riley worries about the increased abilities of the "walkers," explaining to his second-in-command Cholo (John

Leguizamo) that the creatures are apparently learning and adapting to their environment. As a foil for Riley, Cholo appears unconcerned about the threat posed by the zombies, and he shows little regard for the safety of the other men on the team; in fact, a rookie scavenger is killed by a zombie because of Cholo's reckless efforts to obtain alcohol for private monetary gain. Romero presents the undisputed and fascist leader of Fiddler's Green in an even more unsympathetic light; Kaufman, the "Donald Rumsfeld" of the Fiddler's Green tenants board,[88] has created a dystopian society in which the wealthy live in stylish opalescence while the masses barely eke out a pitiful existence on the streets. Furthermore, when Cholo and Kaufman meet to discuss the details of their crooked partnership, most of the conversation's reverse shots place the camera behind the shoulder of the person being spoken to, rather than replicating their subjective point of view. Essentially, audiences are supposed to identify with the noble human characters such as Riley but to recognize Cholo and Kaufman as unsympathetic villains. More than in any of Romero's other zombie films, then, *Land of the Dead* presents a world filled with wicked and selfish people who readily betray and even kill each other to get ahead or to stay on top.

Riley, however, visibly shows and repeatedly expresses understanding and sympathy for the zombies, recognizing that both the living and the dead communities are similarly struggling to survive in the new post-apocalyptic world. He sees little difference between the two groups, claiming both are simply "pretending to be alive." Riley is particularly sickened by the slaughter of the largely helpless zombies in Uniontown because, "for the first time in the movies, the violence done to the zombies not only seems mindless and grotesque, but downright cruel, as the zombies pose no threat and really are minding their own business."[89] The walking dead are indiscriminately exterminated, pitted against each other in cage fights, used for target practice, and even strung up for cheesy photo-ops like side-show attractions. In fact, the cruel behavior of the mercenaries shockingly mirrors the US military's inhumane treatment of Islamic prisoners at the Abu Ghraib prison in Iraq in 2004, emphasizing how one-time enemies can readily been seen as pathetic victims. Furthermore, when zombies occasionally approach the barbed-wire electric fences surrounding Fiddler's Green, the living soldiers take delight in the ghouls' electrocution and cavalierly riddle them with bullets as though they were the world's most undesirable immigrants. Because much of the film depicts the zombies being taunted, abused, and massacred,[90] audiences are willing to agree with Riley's perspective, sympathizing with the zombies as the victims of an even greater monstrosity: humanity. Nevertheless, the raw physical violence committed by the zombies against the humans in the film far exceeds anything done to them, and Riley himself is clearly justified when he never hesitates to kill the zombies to preserve human life.

As the zombie horde encounters various obstacles on its way to Fiddler's Green, Big Daddy communicates with the other ghouls through grunts and sign language and encourages them to evolve. He shows them how to use tools to break through fences and windows, how to walk across the bottom of the river to access the city, and how to use firearms and other weapons against the humans; they even cease to be distracted by the defensive firework displays. Although Paffenroth insists the majority of the zombies remain traditionally animalistic, primarily just responding to Big Daddy's leadership,[91] the handful of "featured zombies" that exhibit rational thinking remain noteworthy because of their ability to garner audience identification. For instance, after the butcher zombie (Boyd Banks) chops a hole in a wooden barricade, Big Daddy looks through the hole to see a mass of pitiful, writhing zombies hanging upside down with targets painted on their chests. Audiences experience this disturbing vista through Big Daddy's eyes, and they can perhaps understand his emotional wail at the injustices perpetrated against "his people." In addition, after the zombies have broken through the first line of the city's defenses, Big Daddy prevents his forces from feasting on the bodies of the dead soldiers; instead, he looks towards the illuminated tower of Fiddler's Green, with the audience sharing this subjective gaze, and gruntingly reminds the other zombies that the real prize still lies ahead. The creatures have clearly transcended their ravenous appetites; like humans, they can curb their hunger in favor of other motivations and drives — or at least delayed gratification.

Cholo's fate proves perhaps the most interesting of any human outcome in Romero's first four zombie films. After his attempts at blackmailing Kaufman have been thwarted by Riley, a vengeful Cholo is bitten by a zombie. Rather than resorting to suicide or allowing his companion to kill him, the pattern thoroughly established by this and the other zombie movies, Cholo consciously chooses to let the transformation take place, saying, "I always wanted to see how the other half lives." He then makes his way back to Fiddler's Green as he slowly dies from his infected wound, clearly attempting to place himself as close to Kaufman as possible before he becomes one of the walking dead completely. In an unexpected and novel twist, Cholo realizes the best way to get his revenge on the double-crossing Kaufman is to kill him as a zombie. In the parking garage below Fiddler's Green, Cholo emerges from the shadows and takes a shot at Kaufman with a harpoon gun. In an old–West standoff reminiscent of *Day of the Dead*'s confrontation between Bub and Rhodes, Kaufman fires back repeatedly with his pistol, but his one-time partner has just turned into a zombie and keeps coming. Yet Romero never recreates Cholo's visual perspective with the camera; instead, all the reverse shots are Kaufman's: seeing Cholo in the distance, witnessing Cholo being shot, and looking at Cholo's misshapen zombie face in close-up. However, when Big Daddy arrives with a flaming propane tank to destroy them both, the resulting conflagration is shown from the zombie's point of view.

By the end of the film, the roving horde of zombies more closely resembles a disciplined army than a mob of monsters; their violent actions appear to be serving a united purpose instead of merely slaking their base appetites. In fact, after the battle for Fiddler's Green has been more or less resolved, with the zombies once again proving to be an unstoppable supernatural force, "Riley and Big Daddy look at each other from a distance, and both seem to acknowledge that the bloody battles between zombies and humans are now over. Big Daddy and his zombies will be left alone by the humans, and vice versa."[92] The zombie masses turn and retreat into the depths of the city, and the remaining human survivors leave to try their luck elsewhere. In his philosophical analysis of the zombie monster, Simon Clark claims that, through their actions, communication, and organization, the zombies are creating a new kind of social structure, a civilization on their own terms.[93] He examines the inherent human dichotomy between civilization and instincts, claiming the majority of zombie films explore this conflict with the humans representing the former and zombies the latter.[94] *Land of the Dead* presents a possible resolution between these drives, with "the evolving zombies represent[ing] the beginnings of a pleasurable union between civilization and the instincts,"[95] and Paffenroth proposes the moral of *Land of the Dead* to be "if zombies can learn to be human and humane, then perhaps we can too."[96] At the end of his fourth zombie movie, therefore, Romero offers viewers an almost utopian future, one where the living and the dead can coexist peacefully because they have each found a way to curb their instincts within their disparate societies.

Land of the Dead may appear, at least at first glance, to violate the carefully crafted logic of Romero's initial trilogy, but a closer examination, such as this one, reveals how the movie is in fact a telling indicator of shifting cultural concerns. Although the zombies featured in *Land of the Dead* have clearly evolved in their mental capacities and their ability to communicate and organize, Romero never clearly explains how this process takes place. If the film truly belongs to the same narrative world of the other three films, as the title sequence and the appearance of Savini's character "Machete" from *Dawn of the Dead* imply, then the monsters should be following the trajectory laid out by Dr. Logan. That is, as the zombies age, their brains should decompose to the point where all motor function ceases. Instead, however, the creatures of *Land of the Dead* are shown becoming increasingly coordinated and even intelligent, almost as if their brains are growing or healing, not decaying. Furthermore, Riley's surprised behavior vis-à-vis the new threat indicates the zombies had been behaving in a very predictable manner for some time. In other words, the enlightened creatures of Uniontown appear to have evolved spontaneously, unexpectedly, and without any explanation. The internal logic of the subgenre would appear to preclude Romero's newly developed zombie protagonists; however, this partial revision of the fundamental tenets of the subgenre indicates a cultural shift that made possible, if not necessitated, a change in the way the zombies behave. Kaufman's iron fist and his repeated declarations that he won't negotiate with terrorists make his rule of Fiddler's Green an obvious analogue for the post–9/11 Bush administration. Yet the sympathetic portrayal of the zombies by Romero indicates a contrary and largely humane position: even terrorists have basic human rights and illegal immigrants may, like Big Daddy's wandering horde, just be looking for a better home. Once again, then, the zombies stand in as representatives for humanity, but in *Land of the Dead*, this analogue is a fundamentally empathetic and humane one.

The success of Romero's movies, and of most zombie films in general, ultimately lies in the human qualities manifested by the unnatural foes. Paffenroth emphasizes that "zombie movies will constantly have to change and adapt if they are to remain a powerful and popular force in the future,"[97] and over the course of forty years, the cinematic depictions of zombies, as with vampires, have drifted from monsters audiences should fear and loath to creatures they should sympathize with and even root for Shaviro attractively argues that Romero's zombie movies achieve "an overwhelming affective ambivalence by displacing, exceeding, and intensifying the conventional mechanisms of spectatorial identification, inflecting them in the direction of a dangerous, tactile, mimetic participation."[98] He also asserts that viewers "cannot in a conventional sense 'identify' with the zombies, but [audiences] are increasingly seduced by them, drawn into proximity with them."[99] Yet this proximity *does* encourage identification, as a systematic analysis of the Romero's cinematic process shows. Audiences can be taught to sympathize with the walking dead through increasingly complicated characterizations, empathetic and emotional acting, camera placement and shot choice, and the suturing process of montage. Although the creatures of Romero's first zombie movie may have merely acted as a stoic reminder of humanity's inevitable mortality, the later films continue to emphasize Romero's chief thesis: people and zombies are the same. The next step in the evolution of this highly specially subgenre will likely literalize the metaphor, presenting narratives in which the zombies tell their own stories, acting as true protagonists and even heroes.[100]

CONCLUSION—THE FUTURE SHOCK OF ZOMBIE CINEMA

There's gonna be more. There's got to be more.—Debra, *Diary of the Dead*

I began working on this cultural history of the zombie narrative in 2005, shortly after Romero released *Land of the Dead*. Of course, I had already noted a marked increase in zombie films following Boyle's *28 Days Later* and Anderson's *Resident Evil*, but it took the return of Romero himself, the "Shakespeare of zombie cinema,"[1] to convince me that here is a phenomenon worthy of further investigation. The subgenre clearly had its legs again — risen from the dead, as it were — and a completely new generation of fans was beginning to discover the visceral joys of reanimated corpses, beleaguered survivalists, and unmitigated screen violence. As I spent the next few years presenting my ideas at conferences and writing articles for publication in film and popular culture journals, I had an incessant fear that the zombie would play itself out before I had the chance to finish my examination. How far could this latest cycle of the subgenre go? Would the world lose interest in the cannibalistic walking dead in favor of the more sensational "torture porn" films such as *Saw* (2004) and *Hostel* (2005)? As events have unfolded, however, the zombie renaissance has continued to hold strong. In fact, in both 2008 and 2009, fans were treated to a wide variety of zombie movies, novels, short fiction collections, graphic novels, and video games, as well as an unexpected surge in production from Romero himself, who shows no signs of letting his subgenre return to a state of quiet incubation.

Nevertheless, although the immediate future looks bright for the zombie narrative, the question inevitably remains: Where does it go from here? Can the subgenre of the walking dead continue to survive without changing and adapting to new cultural concerns, new social anxieties, and the ever-shifting preferences of popular taste? As a fan of the subgenre, on both a personal and an academic level, I remain positive, and I see two primary directions in which zombie narratives will most likely develop. On the one hand, sto-

197

ries featuring zombies — be they on the screen, in the pages of books, or told through video games — will continue to fascinate and entertain new audiences by reviving the storylines, styles, and tropes of the past. Such "old school" outings such as remakes, sequels, and loving tributes to the days of the voodoo zombie and Romero's *Night of the Living Dead* will prove nostalgically popular with older fans and serve to introduce the next generation to the subgenre's roots. On the other hand, zombie narratives will also branch out and move forward. Tales following Boyle's lead will focus more on the contagious and violent nature of the zombies, disregarding their dead condition more and more (if not entirely) in favor of apocalyptic tales of infection and infestation. Revisionist parodies will also continue to thrive, as with any well-established genre, and these zombedies will push the subgenre into entirely unexpected directions, as we have seen in the past two decades. However, the most important potential development to the zombie subgenre will likely be the serialization of large-scope storylines, primarily through video games, graphic novels, and season-long television productions. Either way — looking backwards or looking ahead — I predict the zombie will remain an important and prevalent part of American popular and consumer culture for years to come.

Looking Backwards: The Revival of the Dead

Like any successful genre, the horror film has experienced notable increases and decreases in popularity, and the periods of greatest productivity can invariably be linked to the periods of greatest social unrest and political strife. For example, Magistrale points out how the films of the 1920s, such as Robert Wiene's *Das Cabinet des Dr. Caligari* (1920) and Murnau's *Nosferatu*, were "painfully realistic in recalling the unprecedented violence and trauma that occurred during World War I."[2] Then, thanks in large part to the Great Depression, Hollywood film production soared during the 1930s, particularly the creation of such monster movies as Browning's *Dracula* and Whale's *Frankenstein*, offering viewers what Skal calls "an instinctive, therapeutic escape."[3] The horror genre flourished again in the increasingly violent films of the 1970s as a barometric reaction to the horrors of the Vietnam War and the social tensions associated with the civil rights movement, and now, during the first decade of the twenty-first century, horror films have once again increased in popularity as we are faced with increasingly disturbing reports of terrorist attacks, global pandemics, and violations of human rights. However, these fluctuations in production also reveal the obsession horror cinema appears to have with reappropriation. For example, a host of classic films from the 1970s has recently been remade, including *The Last House on the Left* (1972 and 2009), *The Texas Chainsaw Massacre* (1974 and 2003), *The Hills Have Eyes* (1977 and 2006), *Dawn of the Dead* (1978 and 2004), *Halloween* (1978 and 2007), *The Amityville Horror* (1979 and 2005), and *Friday the 13th* (1980 and 2009). Such a list of paired texts should come as no surprise, for the tumultuous 2000s parallel the 1970s in many regards; not only is the United States currently grappling with an increasingly unpopular and destructive war, the country is also experiencing another polarizing struggle for social equality. With the decade so clearly looking to the past for narratives to express contemporary stresses and anxieties, it makes sense that Romero would take a similar path with the creation of his fifth zombie movie, *Diary of the Dead*.

Premiering in limited release in February of 2008, *Diary of the Dead* heralded Romero's return to the roots of his filmmaking career. Foregoing the large budget of the studio-backed, star-studded *Land of the Dead*, Romero instead reverted to the beginnings of his zombie invasion narrative, crafting a low-budget horror film with no-name actors and a small-scale narrative perspective. Although *Diary of the Dead* marks Romero's fifth zombie movie, it's not a sequel but rather a reboot: the zombie outbreak is only just beginning, and the bewildered protagonists do not live in a world where zombies are known (either in reality or through cinema). This revival of the narrative elements that made *Night of the Living Dead* such an unexpected success and sensation was hardly accidental. In a documentary included on the *Diary of the Dead* DVD, Romero explains his intentions behind the film:

> What's different about [*Diary of the Dead*] is that it goes back to the beginning. It's more like *Night of the Living Dead*. It's about a bunch of students that get caught up in this phenomenon as it just begins to happen, and they wind up documenting what happens to them over the first three days that the dead are coming back to life.... It's dissimilar from the later zombie films in that ... in those films everyone had already accepted the idea that the dead were coming back to life, and they were in greater numbers. So it's really a return to the roots for me.[4]

Instead of focusing on the apocalypse or the plight of society as a whole, *Diary of the Dead* focuses on a limited group of survivors who are just encountering the horrors of the living dead and must frantically figure out what is going on around them. In this way, *Diary of the Dead* recaptures the mystery, wonder, suspense, and terror of the earliest zombie movies, and it demonstrates how successful such a revivalist approach can be for the subgenre.

Looking to the past for recyclable images and tropes is hardly anything new; in fact, such reappropriation is a central tenet of the Gothic mode. When Walpole first set out to marry the fantasy of romance to the realism of the novel, he borrowed heavily from "ancient prose and verse romances" and from both Shakespearean tragedies and comedies to produce a "counterfeit medieval tale."[5] The resulting works — the novel *The Castle of Otranto* and the play *The Mysterious Mother* (1768) — mirror the artificial revival of Strawberry Hill, expressing "the new Romantic impulse to reclaim the strange, the exotic, the savage, the improbable, the mysterious, and the supernatural as legitimate zones of artistic pleasure."[6] Ann Radcliffe soon followed Walpole's lead, using her *The Mysteries of Udolpho* and *The Italian* (1797) to begin a new phase of the Gothic that, according to Robert Miles, emphasizes the sublimity and terror associated with tragedy and epic, "the two most prestigious literary forms."[7] Radcliffe thus established the founding principles of the "Female Gothic," including picturesque landscapes, ancient castles, and, according to Anne Williams, a decidedly curious heroine, suspenseful terror, and seemingly supernatural events that can be explained through rational means.[8] This popular mode of exploration and explanation would itself be revisited in works such as Brontë's *Jane Eyre*, du Maurier's *Rebecca*, and Gloria Naylor's *Linden Hills* (1985). In contrast, Matthew Lewis took the Gothic in an entirely different direction with *The Monk*, an explicitly violent novel that not only builds on the supernatural horror of Walpole but also borrows heavily from established legends, ghost stories, and oral traditions.[9] Lewis's use of abject horror has been repeatedly imitated by such Gothic authors as Stoker, Poe, H. P. Lovecraft, and Toni Morrison.

Recently produced Gothic narratives continue in this tradition of reappropriation and repetition. Botting argues, "Inured to Gothic shocks and terrors, contemporary culture recycles its images in the hope of finding a charge intense enough to stave off the black hole within and without, the one opened up by postmodernist fragmentation and plurality."[10] He cites the popularity of science fiction films such as Ridley Scott's *Alien* (1979) and Anderson's *Event Horizon* (1997), along with video games such as *Doom* and the *Silent Hill* series (1999–), as examples of recent Gothic narratives that grapple with anxieties concerning technology and social isolation against a backdrop of supernatural terror and suspense. Yet despite the seeming originality of these postmodern narratives, Botting emphasizes that "earlier forms and effects are never fully jettisoned"[11]; the essential tropes of these science fiction narratives deliberately recall Walpole, Shelley, Stevenson, and H. G. Wells. Bruhm describes the function of the Gothic, in Walpole's time as well as today, in psychoanalytic terms, for "it seems that we are caught in what Freud would call a repetition-compulsion, where we are compelled to consume the same stories (with minor variations), experience the same traumatic jolts, behold the same devastating sights.... [W]e need to consider that Gothic fiction in general can perform some kind of exorcism on us."[12] In other words, then,

Gothic fiction reworks past figures and formulae to suggest newer quandaries and problems, and Romero's fifth zombie film certainly operates in a similar fashion.

As in *Night of the Living Dead*, Romero's fifth zombie movie focuses as much on a disparate group of survivors as it does on the monsters themselves. In a cunning deployment of self-referential postmodernism, the protagonists of *Diary of the Dead* are film students engaged in making a low-budget horror movie about a mummy that has come back from the dead, a film fittingly titled *The Death of Death*. A stunning radio broadcast interrupts their efforts, however, when a newscaster — in the first of many obvious parallels to the tropes established by *Night of the Living Dead*— reports that corpses have begun to return to life to attack and eat the living. At first, no one believes it, but YouTube video feeds prove to be even more convincing than first-hand experience, and the gang of students soon load themselves into an old Winnebago to begin a harrowing journey away from Pittsburgh and back to their respective homes in Scranton. The characters are all panic-stricken and shocked by the violence and chaos unfolding around them; societal infrastructure quickly collapses, the police and military prove helpless, and humans begin looting and violently attacking each other. But Jason Creed (Joshua

Jason (Joshua Close) and Ridley (Philip Riccio) demonstrate that it's all about making the movie in Romero's *Diary of the Dead* (Weinstein Company, 2007; Photofest Digital).

Close), the director of *The Death of Death*, determines that the most important thing he can do is document the impending crises with his camera. Indeed, as the film progresses and as the characters find themselves in ever-increasing danger, Jason becomes more and more obsessed with his filmmaking duties. He even allows his friends to be attacked and killed in front of him, since he refuses to put the camera down for anything.

As I have shown, each of Romero's zombie films provides deliberate social and cultural criticism, using the zombies and the situations they create as allegories about the perils of modern life, and *Diary of the Dead* is no exception. Whereas his previous films attack the problems arising from decaying family values, rampant consumerism, Cold-War paranoia, and terrorism (respectively), *Diary of the Dead* functions as an indictment of postmodern media. In a world of 24/7 news, streaming internet video, and almost daily reports of terrorist attacks, natural disasters, and economic hardships, media culture itself can foment more fear and paranoia than the events themselves. Yet Debra Moynihan (Michelle Morgan), Jason's girlfriend and fellow director, points out how the media has also dangerously desensitized people to social injustice, violence, and human tragedy. While providing voice-over commentary to a montage of violent images,[13] Debra says,

> By now we've become part of it. Part of 24/7. It's strange how looking at things, seeing things through a lens, a glass, rose-colored or shaded black, you become immune. You're supposed to be affected, but you're not. I used to think it was just you out there, the viewers. But it's not. It's us as well, the shooters. We've become immune too, inoculated, so that whatever happens around us, no matter how horrible it is, we just wind up taking it all in stride. Just another day. Just another death.

The media can therefore cause two related problems: it can frighten people with things that are *not* real, but it can also prevent them from being aware of the problems that *are* real.

In addition, although *Diary of the Dead* largely follows the allegorical nature and narrative plot structure of Romero's early zombie movies, the film also attempts something new. Rather than simply reapplying the formula used in *Night of the Living Dead*, Romero employs a documentary conceit, presenting the whole of his film as actual footage taken exclusively by hand-held cameras or captured on the internet. In a frame narrative reminiscent of such Gothic novels as *Frankenstein* or *Dracula*, Debra claims in her opening voice over that the film the audience is watching, *Diary of the Dead*, is actually *her* film, a compilation of documentary footage and newsreel video that she has edited together to reveal what "really" happened. This first-person cinematic technique, clearly reminiscent of the wildly successful low-budget horror film *The Blair Witch Project* (1999), implies the invasion of the walking dead to be a reality, not a fantasy. Furthermore, this exclusive use of first-person perspective makes those in the audience feel as though they are part of the action, as if playing a video game, and not just passive observers. However, such a drastic approach also prevents any audience suture with the zombies. By so thoroughly and unequivocally aligning audience sympathy with the perspective and plight of the human protagonists, *Diary of the Dead* fails to follow through with the progression established by Romero's *Day of the Dead* and *Land of the Dead*. At no time does Romero attempt to present the zombies as sympathetic creatures or victims, even when they are former protagonists. Instead, *Dairy of the Dead* continues in its insistence on reviving the generic conventions of the older films that center on humans and leave zombies clearly the "other."

Diary of the Dead, though, represents just one of the recent zombie films that indicates a return to the fundamental roots of the subgenre, and other "traditional" or "classical" zombie narratives are in the works as well. For example, Rob Grant's *Yesterday*, released in 2009 in the UK, is described on *The Internet Movie Database* as a serious horror film about a group of human protagonists trying to survive the dangers of both a zombie infestation and each other while trapped inside a grocery store.[14] In fact, various production companies have already released or are currently developing remakes of a number of popular zombie movies, such as Steve Miner's recent *Day of the Dead* and the upcoming release of an *I Walked with a Zombie* remake by RKO Pictures and Twisted Pictures. Furthermore, Romero shows no signs of letting go of the subgenre that made him famous; the action of his latest film — titled *Survival of the Dead* and scheduled for DVD release in 2010 — takes place primarily on an island off the North American coast, perhaps indicating an embracing of the voodoo origins of the zombie mythology. In addition, Romero will use his sixth zombie movie to renew his exploration into and development of the subjective, sympathetic zombie, as the protagonists of *Survival of the Dead* will allegedly struggle to find a cure to save their infected comrades.[15] Clearly, the ideas explored by voodoo-centric zombie films and the early zombie invasion narratives remain interesting and worthy of further exploration, as does the creative genius of Romero himself.[16]

Looking Forward: The Future of the Dead

As long as audiences continue to be horrified, entertained, and amused by the traditional zombie cinema formula, filmmakers, authors, video game designers, and graphic novelists will continue to mine the genre's past in attempts to recapture the aesthetic and financial magic enjoyed by Romero and his immediate imitators. However, Botting reminds us that "once formulas become too repetitive and familiar, they are perceived as mechanical and boring. Without difference and variation, generic codes become obvious and predictable. Excitement, interest and affect wanes. Desire moves on, in search of innovation, stimulation and reinvigoration."[17] Texts that rely on generic revival alone will eventually cease to captivate oversaturated viewers; therefore, the creators of tomorrow's zombie narratives will either need to alter the key protocols of the subgenre or translate them to tales that are not technically about zombies at all. I have already explored the most promising development of the existing zombie subgenre in Chapter 5, the development of sympathetic zombie characters and full-blown zombie protagonists. In addition, however, the zombie comedy represents another tenacious and popular subgenre that holds (for the most part) to the tenets of Romero's formula, with minor alterations here and there and an increased interest in zombie subjectivity and intelligence. The adaptation of the zombie invasion subgenre into a different mode will likely focus on the contagion narrative, a subgenre of science fiction that has been around in one form or another since Shelley's 1826 novel *The Last Man*, and which has also enjoyed a recent resurgence in popularity. Ultimately, however, the future of the zombie narrative lies not in variation and transplantation but in a careful adaptation of the traditions of the past — taking the established zombie invasion narrative and playing it out on a larger scale and over a longer view, thereby tracking the development of the human protagonists over many years as they attempt to rebuild the post-apocalyptic world they now inhabit. I contend that this approach will likely prove the most rewarding, but such serialization will only work through graphic novels or an as-yet unproduced television series.

If current and scheduled production is any indication, the zombedy seems as healthy as ever, perhaps signaling another devolution of the subgenre into the depths of a parodic phase, as happened in the late 1980s and '90s. Played primarily for laughs, these irreverent films nevertheless explore the limits of zombie physiology and dare audiences to see the living dead as empathetic characters in their own right. The best of this subgenre has irrefutably been Wright's *Shaun of the Dead*, which actually uses enough of the traditional tropes to make it a rather effective horror film, although it is nearly matched by Andrew Currie's award-winning *Fido* (2006). Both films use sight gags and self-referential humor to lampoon the zombie subgenre, but, along the way, they ask probing questions about the plights and even rights of the infected walking dead. As I have shown, Wright's film concludes by introducing the idea of zombie domestication, a possibility, only hinted at by Romero in *Day of the Dead*, that exhibits obvious ties to the enslavement

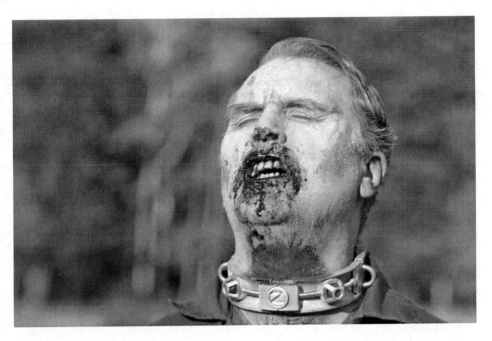

Fido (Billy Connolly) shows us the softer side of zombiism in Currie's *Fido* (Lions Gate Films, 2006; Photofest Digital).

tropes of the earliest zombie movies. *Fido*, however, takes this concept to the extreme, proposing a world in which zombie servants are not only a reality, but also a dangerous status symbol. Currie's zombies are abused and misused slaves, making them sympathetic victims as well as murderous monsters. Such comedic approaches provide endless variation on zombie elements, and, according to *The Internet Movie Database*, a number of zombedies began to be released in 2009, including *Office of the Dead* by Matthew Chung, Ryan Denmark's *Romeo & Juliet vs. The Living Dead*, the Woody Harrelson vehicle *Zombieland*, and J. T. Seaton's comedy *George's Intervention*, a film about a group of friends who try to dissuade their zombified friend from eating people.[18]

On the other hand, the contagion narrative has increasingly come to resemble the zombie invasion narrative in recent years, just without the reanimated corpses. These apocalyptic stories traditionally feature a virulent infection that quickly and thoroughly eradicates the majority of the human population, as in King's *The Stand*. Many of these narratives have the infected victims transform into bloodthirsty cannibals that behave very much like Romero's zombies, albeit very fast-moving ones. In fact, Romero helped pioneer this focus on the "murderous infected" with his film *The Crazies* (which he is, notably, remaking for 2010), and such tales understandably feature many of the characteristics of the zombie invasion narrative: an unexpected plague, the gradual collapse of societal infrastructure, struggling protagonists who must watch their loved ones turn into monsters, the pathetic destruction of those former loved ones, and the desperate hiding-out in hopes of rescue. Boyle firmly revived this subgenre with *28 Days Later*, and it has proven successful in mirroring the zombie renaissance with King's 2006 novel *Cell* and such notable films as Juan Carlos Fresnadillo's *28 Weeks Later*, Fernando Meirelles' 2008 adaptation of José Saramago's novel *Blindness* (1995), and John Erick Dowdle's *Quarantine* (2008), a remake of the Spanish film *[Rec]* (2007). Because post–9/11 anxieties about potential terrorist attacks via anthrax, avian influenza, swine flu, and other forms of biological warfare remain high, the contagion apocalyptic narrative might just outlast those stories that rely on zombies alone.

Zombedies and contagion narratives will certainly keep the basic thematic elements of the zombie invasion narrative popular and culturally relevant in the years to come, but the most insightful and revolutionary development in store for the zombie lies in its potential for serialization. One of the contentions I have presented in this study is that the human protagonists, and the post-apocalyptic world they are forced to inhabit, provide the greatest insight into the cultural value of the zombie narrative, and this exploration into the *human* can only be fully explored over the course of a long-term narrative form. Attempts have already been made to achieve this level of temporal scope, as in the first four zombie films from Romero (when viewed as a single story arc) and Brooks' *World War Z* (a film adaptation of which is currently in development), but only the graphic novel has managed so faithfully to track the plight of consistent characters over a long period of time. Kirkman's *The Walking Dead*, the most prolific and developed of the graphic serials, follows the struggles of Rick Grimes as he works with others to rebuild some kind of community after the world has collapsed around him. In essence, *The Walking Dead* isn't about the zombies at all; it's about human character — the chronicle of one man's life that has become, in the words of its creator, "the zombie movie that never ends."[19] I believe that the most rewarding exploration into a zombie apocalypse will follow Kirkman's lead, and the cinematic version of this "long-haul" approach will work best on television, in a way similar to Alan Ball's popular Showtime series *True Blood* (2007–). In fact, at the time of this writing, the American Movie Channel has just announced a development deal with director Frank Darabont to adapt *The Walking Dead* as a television series, a promising undertaking that will hopefully confirm my contentions regarding the zombie subgenre.[20] At the very least, such a production, if realized, would finally give the zombie narrative the time it needs to map out the complicated human relationships that would result from a zombie infestation that ends normal society.

Whether the zombie is merely enslaved or mysteriously reanimated, walking dead or infected living, horrific or comedic, fast moving or slow, this figure and the gripping narratives that surround it holds an important place in both the pantheon of supernatural horror and the cultural history of the United States. Zombie narratives are unique in that they developed directly from folklore, instead of following an established literary tradition (although they do heavily echo and replicate aspects of the Gothic), and because they constitute the only major monster — cinematic or otherwise — indigenous to the New World. Over the course of the last one hundred years, the zombie has developed from a misunderstood Haitian voodoo practice to a mainstream and bankable cinematic commodity, and the walking dead continue to both fascinate and terrify those curious enough to explore the rich stories they tell. Yet the zombie does its best cultural work not as mere entertainment or cheap thrill but instead as insightful and revelatory allegory. The zombie creature is, first and foremost, a metaphor that reflects prevailing social anxieties — such as oppression, violence, inequality, consumption, and war — that plague the contemporaneous culture that produces any given zombie narrative. In the 1930s and '40s, the zombie revealed fears the mainstream public harbored for Caribbean islands, black societies, and retaliation by the colonized. In the 1950s and '60s, zombies became an invading force, manifesting concerns about the Atomic Age, the Cold War, Communism, and modern warfare. With the help of Romero, zombie cinema also unearthed repressed social apprehensions regarding race relations, gender disparity, and the gradual erosion of the traditional family. Over the course of the last fifty years, zombie narratives have continued in this allegorical function, revealing additional uneasiness about violence, consumerism, paranoia, classism, immigration, infection, the power of the media, and the general end of the world. The zombie's work, it seems, will never be done.

Clearly, as this investigation has shown, the zombie is an important part of the modern cultural landscape of the United States, and viewers, fans, and scholars should have no fear that the subgenre will go away any time soon. However, the next monstrous renaissance might just belong to the werewolves instead of the zombies. According to *The Internet Movie Database*, a number of big-screen, large-budget werewolf pictures have either been released or are ready to roll out over the next two years, including Patrick Tatopoulos' *Underworld: Rise of the Lycans* (2009); Patrick Durham's revisionist take on the lycanthrope, *Cross* (2009); and Joe Johnston's remake of the 1941 classic *The Wolf Man* (2010). In addition, a number of vampire narratives that feature werewolves are also in vogue, such as *True Blood* and the next *Twilight* movies, especially *New Moon* (2009) and *Eclipse* (2010). Perhaps this new surge indicates an increase in cultural anxieties concerning split personalities, divided loyalties, or the struggle between the conscious human subject and our repressed animalistic instincts, but those narratives will require their own scholarly investigation. For the moment, however, the zombie continues to reign supreme in horror cinema and will continue to hold a special place in the hearts and minds of cinephiles with that special taste for the monstrous. And, of course, in a world where Seth Grahame-Smith's ultraviolent reappropriation novel *Pride and Prejudice and Zombies* (2009) makes the *New York Times* bestseller list, all bets, clearly, are off.

FILMOGRAPHY

Event Horizon (Paul W.S. Anderson, 1997)

The Evil Dead (Sam Raimi, 1981)

Evil Dead II (Sam Raimi, 1987)

Fear in the City of the Living Dead (see *Paura nella città dei morti viventi*)

Fido (Andrew Currie, 2006)

La Fille à la fourrure (Claude Pierson, 1977), also known as *Naked Lovers, Starship Eros, The Girl in the Fur Coat,* and *The Porno Zombies*

Frankenstein (James Whale, 1931)

Friday the 13th (Sean S. Cunningham, 1980)

Friday the 13th (Marcus Nispel, 2009)

Garden of the Dead (John Hayes, 1972)

The Gates of Hell (see *Paura nella città dei morti viventi*)

George's Intervention (J.T. Seaton, 2009)

The Ghost Breakers (George Marshall, 1940)

Ghost Ships of the Blind Dead (see *El buque maldito*)

The Ghoul (T. Hayes Hunter, 1933)

The Girl in the Fur Coat (see *La Fille à la fourrure*)

Godzilla (see *Gojira*)

Gojira (Ishirô Honda, 1954), also known as *Godzilla*

Gore-Met Zombie Chef from Hell (Don Swan, 1986)

The Grapes of Death (see *Les Raisins de la mort*)

Halloween (John Carpenter, 1978)

Halloween (Rob Zombie, 2007)

The Hills Have Eyes (Wes Craven, 1977)

The Hills Have Eyes (Alexandre Aja, 2006)

Horror of the Zombies (see *El buque maldito*)

Hostel (Eli Roth, 2005)

I Am Legend (Francis Lawrence, 2007)

I Walked with a Zombie (Jacques Tourneur, 1943)

I Walked with a Zombie (Adam Marcus, 2009)

I Was a Teenage Zombie (John Elias Michalakis, 1987)

I, Zombie: The Chronicles of Pain (Andrew Parkinson, 1998)

Invaders from Mars (William Cameron Menzies, 1953)

The Invasion (Oliver Hirschbiegel, 2007)

Invasion of the Body Snatchers (Don Siegel, 1956)

Invisible Invaders (Edward L. Cahn, 1959)

Island of the Flesh-Eaters (see *Zombie 2*)

Island of the Last Zombies (see *Zombie Holocaust*)

Island of the Living Dead (see *Zombie 2*)

Jaws (Steven Spielberg, 1975)

King of the Zombies (Jean Yarbrough, 1941)

Kung Fu Zombie (see *Wu long tian shi zhao ji gui*)

Le Lac des morts vivants (Jean Rollin, 1981), also known as *Zombie Lake* and *The Lake of the Living Dead*

The Lake of the Living Dead (see *Le Lac des morts vivants*)

Land of the Dead (George A. Romero, 2005)

The Last House on the Left (Wes Craven, 1972)

The Last House on the Left (Dennis Iliadis, 2009)

The Last Man on Earth (Ubaldo Ragona and Sidney Salkow, 1964)

Let Sleeping Corpses Lie (see *Non si deve profanare il sonno dei morti*)

The Living and the Dead (Simon Rumley, 2007)

The Living Dead at Manchester Morgue (see *Non si deve profanare il sonno dei morti*)

The Man They Could Not Hang (Nick Grinde, 1939)

La mansión de los muertos vivientes (Jesus Franco, 1982), also known as *Mansion of the Living Dead*

Mansion of the Living Dead (see *La mansión de los muertos vivientes*)

Martin (George A. Romero, 1977)

Metropolis (Fritz Lang, 1927)

Monster Island (Jack Perez, 2004)

Naked Lovers (see *La Fille à la fourrure*)

New Moon (Chris Weitz, 2009)

Night of the Comet (Thom Eberhardt, 1984)

Night of the Living Dead (George A. Romero, 1968)

Night of the Living Dead (Tom Savini, 1990)

Night of the Living Dead 3D (Jeff Broadstreet, 2006)

Night of the Zombies (Joel M. Reed, 1981)

La noche del terror ciego (Amando de Ossorio, 1971), also known as *Tombs of the Blind Dead*

Non si deve profanare il sonno dei morti (Jorge Grau, 1874), also known as *Don't Open the Window*, *Let Sleeping Corpses Lie*, and *The Living Dead at Manchester Morgue*

Nosferatu, eine Symphonie des Grauens (F. W. Murnau, 1922)

Le notti erotiche dei morti viventi (Joe D'Amato 1980), also known as *Erotic Nights of the Living Dead*, *Queen of the Zombies*, and *Sexy Nights of the Living Dead*

Oasis of the Zombies (see *L'Abîme des morts vivants*)

Office of the Dead (Matthew Chung, 2009)

The Omega Man (Boris Sagal, 1971)

Orgasmo esotico (Joe D'Amato and Mario Siciliano, 1982)

The Others (Alejandro Amenábar, 2001)

Ouanga (George Terwilliger, 1936)

Panic in Year Zero (Ray Milland, 1962)

Pater Thomas (see *Paura nella città dei morti viventi*)

Paura nella città dei morti viventi (Lucio Fulci, 1980), also known as *City of the Living Dead*, *Fear in the City of the Living Dead*, *Pater Thomas*, and *The Gates of Hell.*

The Plague of the Zombies (John Gilling, 1966)

Plan 9 from Outer Space (Edward D. Wood Jr., 1959)

Planet Terror (Robert Rodriguez, 2007)

Porno holocaust (Joe D'Amato, 1981)

The Porno Zombies (see *La Fille à la fourrure*)

The Poseidon Adventure (Ronald Neame, 1972)

Psycho (Alfred Hitchcock, 1960)

Quarantine (John Erick Dowdle, 2008)

Queen of the Zombies (see *Le notti erotiche dei morti viventi*)

Les Raisins de la mort (Jean Rollin, 1978), also known as *The Grapes of Death*

Rebecca (Alfred Hitchcock, 1940)

[Rec] (Jaume Balagueró and Paco Plaza, 2007)

Redneck Zombies (Pericles Lewnes, 1987)

La regina dei cannibali (see *Zombie Holocaust*)

Resident Evil (Paul W.S. Anderson, 2002)

Resident Evil: Extinction (Russell Mulcahy, 2007)

Return of the Blind Dead (see *El ataque de los muertos sin ojos*)

Return of the Evil Dead (see *El ataque de los muertos sin ojos*)

The Return of the Living Dead (Dan O'Bannon, 1985)

Revenge of the Zombies (Steve Sekely, 1943)

Revolt of the Zombies (Victor Halperin, 1936)

Romeo & Juliet vrs. The Living Dead (Ryan Denmark, 2009)

Saw (James Wan, 2004)

The Serpent and the Rainbow (Wes Craven, 1988)

Sexy Nights of the Living Dead (see *Le notti erotiche dei morti viventi*)

Shaun of the Dead (Edgar Wright, 2004)

Ship of Zombies (see *El buque maldito*)

Shock Waves (Ken Wiederhorn, 1977)

Silent Night, Zombie Night (Sean Cain, 2009)

The Signal (David Bruckner, Dan Bush, and Jacob Gentry, 2007)

The Sixth Sense (M. Night Shyamalan, 1999)

Slither (James Gunn, 2006)

Starship Eros (see *La Fille à la fourrure*)

Survival of the Dead (George A. Romero, 2009)

Svengali (Archie Mayo, 1931)

Tales from the Crypt (Freddie Francis, 1972)

The Texas Chainsaw Massacre (Tobe Hooper, 1974)

The Texas Chainsaw Massacre (Marcus Nispel, 2003)

Them! (Gordon Douglas, 1954)

The Thing from Another World (Christian Nyby, 1951)

Tombs of the Blind Dead (see *La noche del terror ciego*)

Trainspotting (Danny Boyle, 1996)

The Treasure of the Living Dead (see *L'Abîme des morts vivants*)

28 Days Later (Danny Boyle, 2002)

28 Weeks Later (Juan Carlos Fresnadillo, 2007)

Underworld (Len Wiseman, 2003)

Underworld: Rise of the Lycans (Patrick Tatopoulos, 2009)

The Walking Dead (Michael Curtiz, 1936)

War of the Worlds (Stephen Spielberg, 2005)

White Zombie (Victor Halperin, 1932)

The Wolf Man (George Waggner, 1941)

The Wolf Man (Joe Johnston, 2010)

Wu long tian shi zhao ji gui (I-Jung Hua, 1982), also known as *Kung Fu Zombie*

Yesterday (Rob Grant, 2009)

Zombie (1979) (see *Zombie 2*)

Zombie 2 (Lucio Fulci, 1979), also known as *Island of the Flesh-Eaters, Island of the Living Dead, Zombie Flesh Eaters,* and *Zombie*

Zombie 3 (see *Zombie Holocaust*)

Zombie Brigade (Carmelo Musca and Barrie Pattison, 1986)

Zombie Flesh Eaters (see *Zombie 2*)

Zombie High (Ron Link, 1987)

Zombie Holocaust (Marino Girolami, 1980), also known as *La Regina dei cannibali, Zombie 3, Island of the Last Zombies, Dr. Butcher M.D.,* and *Dr. Butcher, Medical Deviate*

Zombie Lake (see *Le Lac des morts vivants*)

Zombie Strippers (Jay Lee, 2008)

Zombieland (Ruben Fleischer, 2009)

Zombies of Mora-Tau (Edward L. Cahn, 1957)

CHAPTER NOTES

Introduction

1. Hall, "Cultural Identity," 211–212.
2. Magistrale, *Abject Terrors*, xiii.
3. Hogle, "Gothic in Western Culture," 4.
4. Jauss, *Aesthetic of Reception*, 19.
5. Andrew Currie's *Fido* (2006) was one of the hit Sundance films, and *The Signal* (2007) from the writing/directing team of David Bruckner, Dan Bush, and Jacob Gentry was the other. Although Currie's film is unarguably a "true" zombie movie, *The Signal* more closely resembles *28 Days Later* in that it addresses a violent, infectious apocalypse, if not the literal walking dead.
6. Oakes, "Movies." The *Zombie Movie Data-Base* website has a rather liberal definition of zombie movies, including in their numbers any feature film, short, or television show that features any undead or otherwise reanimated creatures (demonic possession, golems, mummies, etc.).
7. Most of the information I will present regarding movie titles, production personnel, and release dates comes from *The Internet Movie Database* (www.imdb.com), an invaluable resource for scholars and movie lovers alike.
8. Oxford English Dictionary, "Zombie," definition 1, and OED, "Zombie," definition 2.
9. Edward J. Kane first coined the term *Zombie S&L* in 1987 to describe toxic saving and loan firms as "institutional corpses capable of financial locomotion and various forms of malefic behavior." Kane, "Danger of Capital Forbearance," 78. Furthermore, *The Oxford English Dictionary* defines a *zombie computer* as "a computer of which another person has gained control without the knowledge of the user, usually as one of many used concertedly to send spam email or to bombard a targeted website with data so as to make the site inaccessible to other users." OED, "Zombie: Computing."

10. Dendle, *Zombie Movie Encyclopedia*, 2–3.
11. Dendle, *Zombie Movie Encyclopedia*, 217–221; Russell, *Book of the Dead*, 233–309; and Newitz, "Spikes in Zombie Movie Production." I have used three separate data sets to construct my graph, because not all scholars agree on what constitutes a "true" zombie movie or even in which year certain films were released. Furthermore, Dendle's chronology ends with 1998, and Jamie Russell's extensive filmography only goes through 2005. Annalee Newitz's web article provides the most current and the most liberal listing available, although she does admit "you have to correct somewhat for the fact that more movies are being made as we get closer to the present. ... there's [also] been a huge boom in indie and low-budget horror movies over the past ten years, and that undoubtedly accounts somewhat for the giant spike you see during the last 8 years or so." Newitz, "Spikes in Zombie Movie Production."
12. Maddrey, *Nightmares in Red, White and Blue*, 51.
13. Internet Movie Database, "*Night of the Living Dead* (1968)."
14. Internet Movie Database, "*Dawn of the Dead* (1978)."
15. Also known as *City of the Living Dead*, *Fear in the City of the Living Dead*, *Pater Thomas*, and *The Gates of Hell*.
16. Maddrey, *Nightmares in Red, White and Blue*, 129.
17. Dendle, *Zombie Movie Encyclopedia*, 10.
18. Internet Movie Database, "*28 Days Later* (2002)."
19. For a more detailed discussion of zombie video games and the presence of zombie avatars on the internet, see Krzywinska, "Zombies in Gamespace," 153–168; McIntosh, "Evolution of the Zombie," 11–15; and Scott, "Playing the Zombie Online," 172–174.
20. Wells, "Zombies Come Back," 2.

21. Ibid.

22. St. John, "Market for Zombies?" 1.

23. Ibid., 1 & 13.

24. Ibid., 1.

25. Dillard, "It's Not Like Just a Wind," 15.

26. Most scholars — such as Gregory Waller, Richard Greene, K. Silem Mohammad, Shawn McIntosh, and Marc Leverette — insist on labeling zombies as "undead" or even "(un)dead," but I contest such labels overlook important taxonomical distinctions that separate the zombie from its more romantic, rational kin.

27. Even though the Romero zombie is technically a dead, rotting creature, filmmakers have begun to push the logical limits of the monster's physiology to explore new narrative possibilities. In the non-canonical "zombedies," such as *The Return of the Living Dead* and *I Was a Teenage Zombie*, for example, the protagonists only gradually become zombies, and the plots of such films often revolve around feckless attempts to return the hapless heroes to normal. Additionally, Romero himself has been experimenting with the idea of zombie evolution, a concept progressing towards sentient ghouls and zombie protagonists, as in *Day of the Dead* and *Land of the Dead*. I will explore this relatively new development in the subgenre in more detail in Chapter 5.

28. Pegg, Afterword, 133.

29. Maddrey, *Nightmares in Red, White and Blue*, 122.

30. Skal, *Monster Show*, 311.

31. *Shaun of the Dead* is certainly the most thought-provoking and relevant of the zombedies, although the comedy is one of satire rather than just jokes and slapstick. Director Edgar Wright implies that a zombie infestation would probably go unnoticed by the average middle-class worker; as depicted by Pegg's Shaun, modern society has turned everyone into zombies already.

32. In fact, Romero considered filming a screen adaptation of *The Stand*, which Maddrey points out "would have been the one [of King's works] most suited to Romero's vision of America." Maddrey, *Nightmares in Red, White and Blue*, 127.

33. Yeats, "Second Coming," 1325.

34. Brooks, *Zombie Survival Guide*, 155.

35. This unpleasant possibility, that those hired to protect would actually cut and run, was manifested in New Orleans in the aftermath of Hurricane Katrina, when a number of local law-enforcement officers chose to flee the city with their families. "N. O. Police Fire 51."

36. Skal, *Monster Show*, 309.

37. Dillard, "It's Not Like Just a Wind," 22.

38. See Jones, *Horror: A Thematic History*, 161–162.

39. This is one of the more interesting aspects of the zombie scenario, but one that cannot be fully explored in a two-hour film. Romero's *Land of the Dead* shows the breakdown of social structure most fully, but, as I will discuss in my conclusion, it is best demonstrated by serialized narratives, such as Kirkman's *The Walking Dead*.

40. Jauss, *Aesthetic of Reception*, 20.

41. Ibid., 35.

42. Clery, "Genesis of 'Gothic' Fiction," 24.

43. Bruhm, "Contemporary Gothic," 260.

44. Ibid., 260–261.

45. Ibid., 259.

46. Botting, "Aftergothic," 280.

47. Boyle and Garland, "Commentary."

48. St. John, "Market for Zombies?" 13.

49. For example, Kevin Lair, who lived with his family near where the 17th Street levee burst, told reporters, "The whole thing looks like something out of a science fiction movie." "Like a Sci-Fi Movie." Additionally, John Graydon, who rode out the aftermath of the storm in the Superdome, called his father in England and said, "It's like a scene from *Mad Max* in there." Beard, "Horror of the Superdome."

50. James, *Pure Rage*.

51. Ibid.

52. Boyle and Garland, "Commentary."

53. Snyder and Newman, "Commentary."

54. Once again, a zombie movie eerily echoes contemporary headlines, as *Land of the Dead* was released the same summer America was debating the tragic case of Terri Schiavo, who ultimately was taken off life-support at the behest of her husband.

55. St. John, "Market for Zombies?" 13.

56. Mansi, *Undead Again*.

57. Ibid.

58. Goddu, *Gothic America*, 153.

59. Botting, "Aftergothic," 279.

Chapter 1

1. Métraux renders the term *voodoo* as *vaudou* in French Creole, Dayan writes *vodou*, and Wade Davis spells it *vodoun*; in this book, I will be using the more familiar westerniza-

tion *voodoo* for the sake of simplicity. I will also be using *zombie* instead of the (rather more accurate) Creole spelling *zombi*.

2. Dendle, *Zombie Movie Encyclopedia*, 2–3.

3. Northern Europe does have an established folkloric tradition of the "living corpse" or the "ghostly revenant" (see Koven, "Folklore of the Zombie Film," 24–26), but these legends are more akin to ghosts or even mummies than they are to zombies.

4. Bendix, *In Search of Authenticity*, 7.

5. Ibid., 53.

6. Toelken, *Dynamics of Folklore*, 37.

7. Ibid.

8. Kirshenblatt-Gimblett, "Folklore's Crisis," 286.

9. Ibid., 305 (emphasis mine).

10. Walz, *Fear Files: Zombies*.

11. Wylie, "Ro-Langs," 72–73.

12. Ackermann and Gauthier, "Ways and Nature of the Zombi," 478–79.

13. Ibid., 479.

14. Ibid., 489.

15. Mintz, "Introduction," 7–8.

16. Ibid., 8.

17. Dayan, *Haiti, History, and the Gods*, 29.

18. Ibid., 3.

19. Ibid., 16.

20. Ibid., 26.

21. Ibid., 281–82.

22. Ibid., 282 and 14.

23. Ibid., 10.

24. Ibid., 285–286.

25. Rhodes, *White Zombie*, 70–71.

26. Hurston, *Tell My Horse*, 91.

27. Métraux, *Voodoo in Haiti*, 15.

28. Hall, "Cultural Identity," 214.

29. Métraux, *Voodoo in Haiti*, 29.

30. Ibid., 30.

31. Ibid., 33.

32. Ibid., 323.

33. Ibid., 40.

34. Ibid., 327.

35. Ibid., 324.

36. Hurston, *Tell My Horse*, 114 and Métraux, *Voodoo in Haiti*, 324.

37. Hurston, *Tell My Horse*, 114.

38. Ibid., 116.

39. Ibid., 119.

40. See Hurston, *Tell My Horse*, 124–125, 153, and 171.

41. Toelken, *Dynamics of Folklore*, 30.

42. Davis, *Serpent and the Rainbow*, 12.

43. Ackermann and Gauthier, "Ways and Nature of the Zombi," 468.

44. Hurston, *Tell My Horse*, 179.

45. Ackermann and Gauthier, "Ways and Nature of the Zombi," 474.

46. Ibid., 747.

47. Rhodes, *White Zombie*, 78.

48. Ibid., 79.

49. Seabrook, *Magic Island*, 93.

50. Ibid.

51. Ibid., 95–100.

52. Ibid., 101.

53. Ibid., 101–102.

54. Hurston, *Tell My Horse*, 182.

55. Ibid., 182–183.

56. Ibid., 183.

57. Ibid., 196–97.

58. Ibid., 195.

59. Ibid., 197.

60. Ibid., 196.

61. Davis' scientific text was quickly adapted by Wes Craven into a more mainstream horror movie in 1988. Although the first half of the film is partially loyal to Davis' actual experiences, Craven soon departs from the anthropological sphere and presents a much more supernatural, violent, and spectacular version of Haiti.

62. Davis, *Serpent and the Rainbow*, 83.

63. Ibid., 213.

64. Ibid., 117.

65. Ibid., 123.

66. Ibid., 187.

67. Ibid., 29.

68. Ackermann and Gauthier, "Ways and Nature of the Zombi," 491.

69. Ibid., 490.

70. It's worth noting that Ackermann and Gauthier spend the bulk of their article discussing and investigating the little-understood "spirit zombie," or the "soul without a body." Although the West has sensationalized the corporeal zombie (reanimated corpses *lacking* a soul), voodoo belief considers the human being to possess two souls; thus, there exist two kinds of zombies. They encourage further research in this area, but my study focuses on the more traditional and familiar "body without a soul" variety of zombies and their depiction in popular narratives.

71. Toelken, *Dynamics of Folklore*, 39.

72. Ibid., 40.

73. Bing, "Entretiens avec Alfred Métraux," 29.

74. Métraux, *Voodoo in Haiti*, 15.

75. Hurston, *Tell My Horse*, 179.

76. Davis, *Serpent and the Rainbow*, 187.

77. Seabrook, *Magic Island*, 100.

78. Eagleton, *Ideology*, 9.

79. Ibid., 47.
80. Althusser, *Lenin and Philosophy*, 136.
81. Ibid., 136–137.
82. Ibid., 138.
83. Eagleton, *Ideology*, 6.
84. Seabrook, *Magic Island*, 103.
85. Ibid., 94.
86. Hurston, *Tell My Horse*, 191.
87. Ibid., 181.
88. Taussig, *Devil and Commodity Fetishism*, 109.
89. Ibid., xi.
90. Ibid., 94.
91. Ibid., 95.
92. Métraux, *Voodoo in Haiti*, 55.
93. Hurston, *Tell My Horse*, 184.
94. Althusser, *Lenin and Philosophy*, 146.
95. Ackermann and Gauthier, "Ways and Nature of the Zombi," 475.
96. Hurston, *Tell My Horse*, 197–98.
97. Eagleton, *Ideology*, 5.
98. Davis, *Serpent and the Rainbow*, 213.
99. See Hurston, *Tell My Horse*, 199–203.
100. Davis, *Serpent and the Rainbow*, 250.
101. The seven transgressions (not unlike the European "Seven Deadly Sins") for which one could be sold to a society are listed by Leophin as
"1. Ambition — excessive material advancement at the obvious expense of family and dependents.
"2. Displaying lack of respect for one's fellows.
"3. Denigrating the Bizango society.
"4. Stealing another man's woman.
"5. Spreading loose talk that slanders and affects the well-being of others.
"6. Harming members of one's family.
"7. Land issues — any action that unjustly keeps another from working the land."
Davis, *Serpent and the Rainbow*, 253.
102. Ibid., 255.
103. Rhodes, *White Zombie*, 72 and Métraux, *Voodoo in Haiti*, 16.
104. See Rhodes, *White Zombie*, 74.
105. Walz, *Fear Files: Zombies*.
106. Rhodes, *White Zombie*, 75.
107. See Dayan, *Haiti, History, and the Gods*, 37.
108. Rhodes, *White Zombie*, 75.
109. Ibid., 76.
110. Ibid., 77.
111. Ibid., 78.
112. Ibid., 77–78.
113. Ibid., 83.
114. Ibid., 82.
115. Ibid., 84.
116. See Dorson, *Folklore and Fakelore*, 5 and 28.
117. Moser, "Folklorismus in unserer Zeit," 185.
118. Ibid., 199.
119. Métraux, *Voodoo in Haiti*, 57.
120. Toelken, *Dynamics of Folklore*, 48.
121. Kirshenblatt-Gimblett, "Folklore's Crisis," 307.

Chapter 2

1. Russell, *Book of the Dead*, 9.
2. See Russell, *Book of the Dead*, 19–20, for a detailed discussion of Webb's stage production.
3. Rhodes, *White Zombie*, 161.
4. Russell, *Book of the Dead*, 21.
5. Ibid., 42.
6. Young, "Cinema of Difference," 114.
7. See Dendle's *The Zombie Movie Encyclopedia* for a thorough description of all the major twentieth-century zombie films and Russell's exhaustive *Book of the Dead* for a detailed cultural survey of the entire zombie phenomenon.
8. Aizenberg, "Pleasures and Perils of Postcolonial Hybridity," 462.
9. Berliner, *Ambivalent Desire*, 4.
10. Ibid., 5.
11. Ibid., 236.
12. Aizenberg, "Pleasures and Perils of Postcolonial Hybridity," 462.
13. Lizabeth Paravisini-Gebert (40) concisely summarizes the elements prevalent in these accounts: "...the coveting of a beautiful, light-skinned or white upper-class girl by an older, dark-skinned man who is of lower class and is adept at sorcery; the intimations of necromantic sexuality with a girl who has lost her volition; the wedding night ... as the preferred setting for the administration of the zombie poison; the girl's eventual escape from the bokor in her soiled wedding clothes (the garment of preference for white or light-skinned zombie women); [and] her ultimate madness and confinement in a convent or mental asylum."
14. Ibid., 42.
15. Of course, the black populations of the Caribbean in general, and of Haiti in particular, are not technically "native" at all. In

fact, the key ideological concerns of the zombie allegory stem from how the current inhabitants of the Caribbean descended from races initially enslaved by imperialism and unjustly relocated to the islands of the West Indies (as I discuss in Chapter 1). I am using the problematic designation of "native" both in the sense that those descended from slaves are now, essentially, the indigenous race of many Caribbean islands, and to recreate the way contemporary whites in the United States would have perceived those races and cultures.

16. Dendle, *Zombie Movie Encyclopedia*, 3.

17. Aizenberg, "Pleasures and Perils of Postcolonial Hybridity," 462.

18. Dayan, *Haiti, History, and the Gods*, 37.

19. Herskovits, *Dahomey*, 243.

20. Dayan, *Haiti, History, and the Gods*, 37.

21. See Hegel, *Phenomenology of the Mind*, 228–240.

22. Fanon, *Black Skin, White Masks*, 217.

23. Ibid., 220.

24. Ibid., 221.

25. Césaire, *Discourse on Colonialism*, 41.

26. Ibid., 42.

27. Depestre, *Change*, 20.

28. Métraux describes the zombie as "a beast of burden which his master exploits without mercy, making him work in the fields, weighing him down with labour, whipping him freely and feeding him on meager, tasteless food." Métraux, *Voodoo in Haiti*, 282.

29. Césaire, *Discourse on Colonialism*, 76.

30. Spivak, "Can the Subaltern Speak?" 284.

31. Yet there is nonetheless a relationship between the sub-subaltern and the rest of the class hierarchy. Because members from all levels of this hierarchy can potentially become zombies, the structure faces possible inversion through which "slaves" become masters of other "slaves." As I shall illustrate later, this inversion becomes a key element in analyzing *White Zombie*.

32. Bing, "Entretiens avec Alfred Métraux," 28.

33. Russell, *Book of the Dead*, 21.

34. Rhodes, *White Zombie*, 21.

35. Ibid., 22, 26, and 30.

36. *Trilby* had been adapted numerous times for the stage and screen prior to 1932, with an influential Warner Brothers film version titled *Svengali* appearing in 1931 (see Kinnard, *Horror in Silent Films,* 51, 68, and 141), and it was a primary inspiration for Gaston Leroux's *Le Fantôme de l'Opéra* (1909–10) (see

Hogle, *Undergrounds of the Phantom of the Opera*, 22–24).

37. I would argue the primary visual antecedent of the shambling zombie to be the somnambulist from Robert Wiene's *Das Cabinet des Dr. Caligari* (1920), but Rhodes makes just a passing reference to this landmark film.

38. Vivian Meik's short story "White Zombie" (1933) should not be mistaken for either Weston's source text or as a novelization of the 1932 film; it is instead a semi-ethnographic account of native magic and the walking dead in Africa (see Haining, Introduction, 15).

39. Rhodes, *White Zombie*, 17.

40. It remains unclear if the zombies in Halperin's movie are alive or dead. Rhodes emphasizes how that in spite of the zombies' obvious breathing, bullets fail to stop them; furthermore, although Legendre speaks of the zombies as dead, his own death releases Madeleine from her trance (see Rhodes, *White Zombie*, 23). The ambiguities about what Legendre's zombies really are simply reiterates Western ignorance of the subtleties of voodoo and Haitian occultism — modern audiences simply don't need (or perhaps want) to know the details.

41. Russell, *Book of the Dead*, 23.

42. Ibid.

43. Said, *Culture and Imperialism*, 223.

44. Marx, "Klassenkämpfe in Frankreich," 15.

45. Lugosi himself presents a larger problem; as a white, European actor, he is ill chosen to portray a native Haitian voodoo priest. Instead, he embodies the West — and more importantly, the legacy of the Austro-Hungary Empire.

46. Rhodes, *White Zombie*, 45.

47 See Rhodes, *White Zombie*, 15–18.

48. Rhodes, *White Zombie*, 47.

49. Ibid., 48.

50. Césaire, *Discourse on Colonialism*, 36.

51. See my Chapter 1 and Davis, *Serpent and the Rainbow*, 162–167 and 187–188 for a more detailed discussion of the possible scientific explanation of the zombie ritual.

52. Critical response to *White Zombie* was mixed at best, but the film enjoyed more popular and financial success than Halperin had expected. Part of the draw was certainly Lugosi's personal fame and popularity, but even African Americans embraced the film despite its fundamentally racist overtones (although they may have simply been supporting Muse's minor — yet credible — role as the carriage driver). See Rhodes, *White Zombie*, 115–160,

for an extensive survey of the film's critical and popular reception.

53. Russell, *Book of the Dead*, 27.

54. See Dendle, *Zombie Movie Encyclopedia*, 130–132.

55. See Russell, *Book of the Dead*, 33–41.

56. Ibid., 42.

57. Young, "Cinema of Difference," 106.

58. Wallace, "I Walked with a Zombie," 97–99. As we have seen, most ethnographic accounts of the Haitian zombie — including Seabrook's, Weston's, and Wallace's — emphasize how the taste of salt will break the zombie curse and return the living dead to truly dead; nonetheless, few of the voodoo-based films take this seemingly important plot point into account.

59. Russell, *Book of the Dead*, 42.

60. In fact, Young points out how "in its exploration of the notion of difference, and in its complexity of narrative, [*I Walked with a Zombie*] … anticipates Jean Rhys' novel *Wide Sargasso Sea* (1966)." Young, "Cinema of Difference," 106.

61. Brontë, *Jane Eyre*, 287.

62. Russell, *Book of the Dead*, 42.

63. Young, "Cinema of Difference," 108.

64. Ibid., 105.

65. Russell, *Book of the Dead*, 46.

66. Young, "Cinema of Difference," 104.

67. See Paravisini-Gebert, "Women Possessed," 46.

68. Ibid., 44.

69. Young, "Cinema of Difference," 110–111.

70. The folk song also reveals the truth of Jessica's condition and illustrates that the locals on Saint Sebastian are keeping a close eye on Betsy:

> The wife fall down,
> and the evil came,
> and it burned her mind
> in the fever flame….
> Her eyes are empty,
> and she cannot talk,
> and the nurse has come
> to make her walk.
> The brothers are lonely,
> and the nurse is young….
> Shame and sorrow for the family.

71. Paravisini-Gebert, "Women Possessed," 42.

72. Althusser, *Lenin and Philosophy*, 136.

73. Césaire, *Discourse on Colonialism*, 41.

74. Young, "Cinema of Difference," 114.

75. Ibid., 116.

Chapter 3

1. Jauss, *Aesthetic of Reception*, 20.

2. Dendle, *Zombie Movie Encyclopedia*, 6.

3. Halberstam, *Skin Shows*, 57.

4. Ibid., 59.

5. LoLordo, "Possessed by the Gothic," 35.

6. Crane, "Monster," 406.

7. Ibid., 413.

8. See LoLordo, "Possessed by the Gothic," 48.

9. Crane, "Monster," 418–419.

10. Ibid., 429.

11. Ibid., 414.

12. LoLordo, "Possessed by the Gothic," 48.

13. Ibid., 51.

14. James, "Jolly Corner," 396.

15. Ibid., 397.

16. Diehl, *Tales from the Crypt*, 28.

17. Wells, *Horror Genre*, 82.

18. Frumke, *Document of the Dead*.

19. See Dendle, *Zombie Movie Encyclopedia*, 89–91 and 63–64.

20. Ibid., 135–36.

21. See Dendle, *Zombie Movie Encyclopedia*, 211–12.

22. Frumke, *Document of the Dead*.

23. Waller, *Living and the Undead*, 3.

24. Dillard, "It's Not Like Just a Wind," 26.

25. Wood, "Neglected Nightmares," 126.

26. King, *Danse Macabre*, 308.

27. Martin, *Dead Will Walk*.

28. Perhaps the first novel to explore this idea of global annihilation fully is Shelley's *The Last Man* (1826); yet whereas that novel primarily chronicles the gradual destruction of humanity by an incurable plague, Matheson's picks up months after a similar chain of events. In addition, while Shelley's Lionel Verney is well and truly left alone, Neville has hordes of vampires to contend with.

29. Most apocalyptic narratives have rather obvious ties to Daniel Defoe's 1719 *Robinson Crusoe*, where the protagonist attempts to rebuild the enlightened world when he is faced with a situation void of such comforts. Such a utopian view of society will become even more blatant and important, as we shall see, in Romero's *Dawn of the Dead*.

30. Savoy, "Face of the Tenant," 9.

31. Cather, *Professor's House*, 12.

32. Matheson, *I Am Legend*, 31.

33. Although Francis Lawrence's 2007 film version of *I Am Legend* starring Will Smith

preserves Neville's immunity, his domestic fortifications, and his scientific investigations, the movie completely abandons the idea of two distinct versions of vampirism. Furthermore, Smith's Neville is *not* the last man on earth, and he dies as a heroic martyr who saves the old human race instead of as a legendary monster who attempts to destroy the new race of human/vampire hybrids.

34. Freud, "Uncanny," 147.

35. Freud, "Uncanny," 124. I prefer Freud's German term because of the direct connection with the home as the comfortingly familiar — literally translated into English, the *Unheimlich* is the "un-home-like," which has obvious relevance to this discussion of *Night of the Living Dead.*

36. See Freud, "Uncanny," 148.

37. Dillard, "It's Not Like Just a Wind," 20–21.

38. Freud, "Uncanny," 148.

39. The mummy might be considered a sub-class of the zombie; however, unlike its mindless cousins, a mummy is usually brought back to life by a curse, operates by itself, doesn't infect its victims or reproduce, single-mindedly pursues a specific task, shows some intelligence and possibly even speech, and eventually returns to its slumber.

40. See Stoker, *Dracula*, 31.

41. Freud, *Ego and the Id*, 19.

42. Romero defies this assumption in *Day of the Dead*, which features a zombie named Bub that has been somewhat domesticated by an irrational scientist. With *Land of the Dead*, Romero takes things to the next level, featuring zombies that have evolved intellectually, making them much more sympathetic and posing them against humans as the true antagonists of the film. I will explore this aspect of both films in more detail in Chapter 5.

43. See Mori, "Uncanny Valley." I have recreated Mori's original graph here as adapted by Karl F. MacDorman for an online version of the article at the *Android Science* website (http://www.androidscience.com/theuncanny valley/proceedings2005/uncannyvalley.html). Use of this figure is approved by the GNU Free Documentation License as described by the Creative Commons Corporation (http://creativecommons.org/licenses/by-sa/3.0/legal code).

44. See Freud, *Beyond the Pleasure Principle*, 37.

45. Freud, "Uncanny," 148.

46. Freud, *Beyond the Pleasure Principle*, 46.

47. Matheson, *I Am Legend*, 77.

48. Matheson realizes the narrowly averted climax of W. W. Jacob's 1902 short story "The Monkey's Paw," in which the return of the son from the grave is prevented by the expenditure of the last of three wishes.

49. Russell, *Book of the Dead*, 65.

50 For a detailed discussion of the apocalypse as rendered in Romero's zombie films, see Pagano, "Space of Apocalypse," 71–80.

51 Russell, *Book of the Dead*, 69.

52. In yet another example of the current pervasiveness of all things zombie, Mark Strauss has published a mock non-fiction exposé on the science behind zombie brain function. See Strauss, "Harvard Psychiatrist Explains Zombie Neurobiology."

53. Stephen Spielberg's 2005 version of *War of the Worlds* is a notable exception. Although it embraces the spectacular conventions of the alien-invasion picture, the film tells the story in a decidedly mundane way, focusing on average citizens in rural locations — exactly like the classic zombie invasion movie.

54. Russell, *Book of the Dead*, 68.

55. Dillard, "It's Not Like Just a Wind," 20.

56. Pegg, Afterword, 133.

57. Russell, *Book of the Dead*, 67.

58. Ibid., 70.

59. Dillard, "It's Not Like Just a Wind," 22.

60. King, *Danse Macabre*, 134.

61. Bruhm, "Contemporary Gothic," 267.

62. This is a problematic scene; Romero's zombies almost always attack their victims with their hands and teeth, not tools. Karen's murder of her father is clearly driven by the desire to eat his flesh; however, her subsequent attack on her mother appears to be driven simply by the desire to kill. In addition, the trowel is an obvious phallus, allowing this scene to be read as an extreme manifestation of the Oedipal complex — the girl has already murdered her father and now penetrates her mother with a phallic representation.

63. Pegg, Afterword, 133.

64. Russell, *Book of the Dead*, 68.

65. Hogle, "Gothic in Western Culture," 2.

66. Ibid., 4.

67. Punter, *Literature of Terror*, 354.

68. Bruhm, "Contemporary Gothic," 264 and Williams, *Art of Darkness*, 46.

69. Williams, *Art of Darkness*, 44.

70. Freud, "The Uncanny," 126 and 129.

71. Ibid., 132.

72. Waller, *Living and the Undead*, 285.

73. Savoy, "Rise of American Gothic," 168.
74. Williams, *Art of Darkness*, 39.
75. Savoy, "Face of the Tenant," 9.
76. Ibid., 10.
77. Ibid., 13.
78. This confrontational shot in *Night of the Living Dead* reveals Romero's debt to the filmic style of Hitchcock, specifically to *Psycho* (1960), a movie that features not one, but two shots of dead eyes starring accusatorily at the audience: the wide eye of Marion Crane (Janet Leigh), whose recently murdered body lies on the floor of a hotel bathroom, and the desiccated corpse of Mrs. Bates, a dramatic literalization of Savoy's prosopopoeia hidden in the heart of Norman Bates's (Anthony Perkins) "haunted" house.
79. Williams, *Art of Darkness*, 47.
80. Ibid., 41.
81. In fact, all the women of *Night of the Living Dead* are placed in such subservient roles. Judy questions Tom about the wisdom of leaving the safety of the house, but her concerns and intuition go unheard by her boyfriend, who is blindly following the advice of Ben, who is in turn acting on the suggested course of action offered by the reporters and scientists on the television — all men. Helen repeatedly challenges the actions of her husband, but she is mostly ignored and spends the bulk of the film relegated to the cellar. The women of *Night of the Living Dead* prove to be the wise ones, but they are ignored to the ultimate detriment of all. For a more detailed investigation into the role of women in Romero's first three zombie films, see Patterson, "Cannibalizing Gender and Genre," 108–115.
82. Fiedler, *Love and Death*, 132.
83. Dillard, "It's Not Like Just a Wind," 15.

Chapter 4

1. See Hegel, *Phenomenology of Mind*, 238–239.
2. Césaire, *Discourse on Colonialism*, 42.
3. Kristeva, *Powers of Horror*, 4.
4. Russell, *Book of the Dead*, 67.
5. Ibid., 68.
6. According to *The Internet Movie Database*, *L'Abîme des morts vivants* was also released and later reissued under such titles as *Oasis of the Zombies, The Treasure of the Living Dead*, and *Bloodsucking Nazi Zombies*; *Le Lac des morts vivants* was released similarly as both *Zombie Lake* and *The Lake of the Living Dead*.

7. Russell, *Book of the Dead*, 71.
8. Ibid., 74.
9. Dendle, *Zombie Movie Encyclopedia*, 54.
10. Russell, *Book of the Dead*, 81.
11. Grau's film was released and re-released under a variety of different titles, including *Don't Open the Window* and *Let Sleeping Corpses Lie* in the United States and *The Living Dead at Manchester Morgue* in Great Britain.
12. Grau is clearly playing with Freudian psychology here, taking the male desire for the breast as a longing for the lost milk of the mother to an almost ludicrous extreme: feasting on her lifeblood instead.
13. *Non si deve profanare il sonno dei morti*, however, offers audiences a catharsis missing from Romero's first film: having been unjustly murdered, George returns as a zombie to kill police chief Kinsey (Aldo Massasso). Although the emotionally satisfying turn lacks evidence of conscious intent on the part of the zombie, this plot development anticipates Romero's own experiments with zombie subjectivity, which I will explore in Chapter 5.
14. The mannequins that populate Betty's (Lone Fleming) workshop clearly prefigure those found in the mall of *Dawn of the Dead*. Whereas they primarily function as uncanny representations of unclothed women in de Ossario's film, they nonetheless represent additional parallels to shallow consumption and human objectification.
15. Russell, *Book of the Dead*, 84.
16. Ibid., 91.
17. Skal, *Monster Show*, 311.
18. The only explanation for the zombie infestation in *Dawn of the Dead* comes from Peter (Ken Foree), who quotes his voodoo-priest grandfather as having said, "When there is no more room in hell, the dead shall walk the earth." The film thus implies that the human race and modern society as a whole have become so wicked and corrupt that hell cannot accommodate any more tenants.
19. Shaviro, *Cinematic Body*, 85.
20. Latham, "Consuming Youth," 131.
21. Paffenroth, *Gospel of the Living Dead*, 57.
22. Ibid., 23.
23. Botting, *Limits of Horror*, 135.
24. Walker, "Romero and Aristotle on Zombies," 84.
25. Horne, "I Shopped with a Zombie," 97.
26. Ibid.

27. The irony of Romero's social criticism becomes all the more potent for those viewers who saw *Dawn of the Dead* in a shopping mall movie theater. Although severely critical of capitalism, the film is clearly a commodity itself (see Loudermilk, "Eating *Dawn* in the Dark," 85).

28. Kirkman, *Best Defense*, 86.

29. Loudermilk, "Eating *Dawn* in the Dark," 85.

30. As I discuss in Chapter 1, Althusser calls such specialized institutions Ideological State Apparatuses (ISAs). He criticizes such things as the family, the legal system, the trade-union, the communications industry, and culture in general as being tools of a repressive state system. These ISAs are employed by the state to maintain the status quo and preserve the means of production in a capitalist society. See Althusser, *Lenin and Philosophy*, 136–137.

31. Because it has already been treated quite thoroughly elsewhere, I am deliberately avoiding any lengthy discussion of the gender issues presented in *Dawn of the Dead*; for a critical reading of Fran's role as a woman in the movie, see Paffenroth, *Gospel of the Living Dead*, 59–66.

32. Russell, *Book of the Dead*, 93.

33. I am once again using *uncanny* here in the psychoanalytical sense of the *Unheimlich*; see my discussion of Freud's *The Uncanny* in Chapter 3.

34. Peter is played by an African American, and much has been written about his racial role in the film (see Paffenroth, *Gospel of the Living Dead*, 62–66 in particular). As with the issue of Fran's gender, I am avoiding any direct discussion of Peter's race; his importance to my analysis stems from his role as a consumer.

35. Rick Grimes, the tragic protagonist of The Walking Dead graphic novel series, succinctly describes the structural collapse resulting from a zombie apocalypse: "It's bad — near as we can tell anyway. From the looks of it, our government has crumbled. There's no communication, no organization, no resistance, I've not even seen any military presence, which I'll admit seems odd. It appears civilization is pretty well screwed." Kirkman, *Safety Behind Bars*, 24.

36. Loudermilk, "Eating *Dawn* in the Dark," 89.

37. Wright, "Church of George," 41.

38. The recreational pleasures of the shopping mall recall Shelley's *The Last Man*, for, in the wake of a global pandemic, "the student

left his books, the artist his study: the occupations of life were gone, but the amusements remained; enjoyment might be protracted to the verge of the grave." Shelley, *Last Man*, 273.

39. Loudermilk, "Eating *Dawn* in the Dark," 93.

40. Wright, "Church of George," 42.

41. Botting, *Limits of Horror*, 36.

42. Frank, "Appendix A," 280.

43. Friends of Strawberry Hill, "The House."

44. Hogle, "Ghost of the Counterfeit," 25.

45. Hogle, "Gothic in Western Culture," 15.

46. Hogle, "Ghost of the Counterfeit," 30.

47. Savoy, "Face of the Tenant," 14.

48. Dendle emphasizes, "The zombies are cleverly blended with the mannequins abounding in the mall, as well — thus the complex teems with glassy stares and detached limbs; humans and plastic are one and the same." Dendle, *Zombie Movie Encyclopedia*, 44.

49. Paffenroth, *Gospel of the Living Dead*, 59.

50. Walker, "Romero and Aristotle on Zombies," 87.

51. Henderson, *Romantic Identities*, 49.

52. Hegel, *Phenomenology of Mind*, 238.

53. According to Fukuyama (xii), "Both Hegel and Marx believed that the evolution of human societies was not open-ended, but would end when mankind had achieved a form of society that satisfied its deepest and most fundamental longings. Both thinkers thus posited an 'end of history': for Hegel this was the liberal state, while for Marx it was a communist society. This did not mean that the natural cycle of birth, life, and death would end.... It meant, rather, that there would be no further progress in the development of underlying principles and institutions, because all of the really big questions would be settled."

54. Ibid., xxi.

55. Nietzsche, *Thus Spoke Zarathustra*, 130.

56. Fukuyama, *End of History*, xxiii.

57. Paffenroth, *Gospel of the Living Dead*, 53.

58. Kojève, *Phenomenology of Right*, 473.

59. Paffenroth, *Gospel of the Living Dead*, 61.

60. See Irigaray, *Sex Which Is Not One*, 84–85.

61. Gilroy, *Black Atlantic*, 60.

62. Ibid., 63.

63. Ibid., 68.

64. Romero's shooting script for *Dawn of*

the Dead describes the mall as a "cathedral," with the pair of two-story department stores at each end representing the altars. Horne, "I Shopped with a Zombie," 98.

65. Marx, "Manuscripts of 1844," 75–76.
66. Ibid., 76.
67. Fukuyama, *End of History*, 194.
68. Loudermilk points out that Peter and Fran are the only survivors because they have best resisted the lure of the mall—"the consumption of comforts that can never solve their real problems." Loudermilk, "Eating *Dawn* in the Dark," 92.

Chapter 5

1. Internet Movie Database, "*Dawn of the Dead* (1978)."
2. Botting, "Aftergothic," 286.
3. Dendle identifies *Night of the Living Dead* as the beginning of the "First Wave" of zombie cinema, spanning 1968–1978, with the "Second Wave" beginning with *Dawn of the Dead* and lasting until 1985. He proposes that *Day of the Dead* actually failed to begin a third wave, as zombie comedies and "splatstick" took over in both production and popularity (see Dendle, *Zombie Movie Encyclopedia*, 8). I argue that the zombie renaissance has accomplished this long-awaited "Third Wave," beginning with *28 Days Later* and continuing into today.
4. Russell, *Book of the Dead*, 131.
5. Ibid., 129.
6. Also known as *Island of the Flesh-Eaters, Island of the Living Dead, Zombie Flesh Eaters*, or, in the United States, as simply *Zombie*.
7. Russell, *Book of the Dead*, 132.
8. The abandoned vessel brings with it a plague that will decimate the human population, a plot point that is both reminiscent of Dracula's ghost ship, the *Demeter*, and a cunning play on the colonialism that similarly infected the indigenous tribes of North America.
9. Dendle, *Zombie Movie Encyclopedia*, 8.
10. O'Brien, "*Vita, Amore, e Morte*," 63.
11. The scene can also be read as a trump of Spielberg's *Jaws* (1975)—Fulci's zombie literally takes a bite out of the great white, after all.
12. Russell, *Book of the Dead*, 132–133.
13. Also known as *La regina dei cannibali, Zombie 3, Island of the Last Zombies*, and *Dr. Butcher, Medical Deviate*.

14. Russell, *Book of the Dead*, 134.
15. Despite its relatively low production values, *Zombie Holocaust* remains an interesting film, mostly because Girolami splits the apocalyptic zombie figure into both living, aboriginal cannibals and dead, subservient zombies. If anything, the movie constitutes a throwback to the pre–1968 zombie films, with Dr. Obrero (Donald O'Brien) acting as a cross between Victor Frankenstein and Doctor Moreau who transplants brains and reanimates dead tissue to create his own army of macabre servants. In *Zombie Holocaust*, the zombies refrain from dismembering and eating the living, and, at one point, they even rescue the white protagonists from the bloodthirsty cannibals.
16. Also known as *Erotic Nights of the Living Dead, Queen of the Zombies*, and *Sexy Nights of the Living Dead*.
17. Russell, *Book of the Dead*, 134.
18. Ibid., 136.
19. Also known as *Naked Lovers, Starship Eros, The Girl in the Fur Coat*, and *The Porno Zombies*.
20. Russell, *Book of the Dead*, 136.
21. Paffenroth, *Gospel of the Living Dead*, 9.
22. Ibid., 10.
23. Ibid., 6.
24. Silverman, *Subject of Semiotics*, 195.
25. Metz, "Imaginary Signifier," 802.
26. Ibid., 804. I use *gaze* in the literal sense of a visual perspective or look, one that fosters identification with the viewer, rather than the objectification of the one being looked at.
27. Ibid., 807.
28. Silverman, *Subject of Semiotics*, 199–200. See also Oudart, "Cinema and Suture."
29. Ibid., 202.
30. Ibid., 205.
31. Grant, "Taking Back the *Night of the Living Dead*," 210.
32. According to Tony Williams, "the looks often exchanged between hunters and hunted hints at some deep, unconscious connection between the living and the dead," a connection that will prove essential in the development of shifting audience sympathies. Williams, *Cinema of George A. Romero*, 27.
33. Paffenroth, *Gospel of the Living Dead*, 35.
34. Eisenstein, *Film Form*, 30.
35. Williams, *Cinema of George A. Romero*, 26.
36. However, as we have already seen, Ben becomes increasingly violent and irrational towards the other humans in the narrative,

knocking a hysterical Barbra into unconsciousness, beating the obstinate Harry Cooper, and eventually shooting Cooper in cold blood, character traits and behaviors that likely alienate audiences and limit the scope of their sympathy.

37. Shaviro, *Cinematic Body*, 85.
38. Ibid., 86.
39. Waller, *Living and the Undead*, 273.
40. Dendle, *Zombie Movie Encyclopedia*, 122.
41. Shaviro, *Cinematic Body*, 86.
42. Waller, *Living and the Undead*, 291.
43. Paffenroth, *Gospel of the Living Dead*, 68.
44. This setup is curiously challenged later when Fran and a lone zombie sit on either side of a sliding glass door, each apparently contemplating the other, for the camera shows both figures through the glass, shooting over their shoulders to recreate their mirrored perspective. Of all the human characters in *Dawn of the Dead*, Fran consistently proves to be the most empathetic towards others.
45. Thompson, "Zombies, Values, and Personal Identity," 29.
46. These elements of Sarah's presentation and character also recall *Dawn of the Dead*, from Fran's demarcated place in the news studio, to her position in a group consisting of one woman, two white men, and a black man.
47. For an insightful discussion of the role of humor in *Dawn of the Dead*, see Badley, "Zombie Splatter Comedy," 36–41.
48. Paffenroth, *Gospel of the Living Dead*, 73.
49. Williams, *Cinema of George A. Romero*, 134.
50. Dendle, *Zombie Movie Encyclopedia*, 47.
51. Ibid.
52. Paffenroth, *Gospel of the Living Dead*, 74.
53. Williams, *Cinema of George A. Romero*, 135.
54. Grant, "Taking Back the *Night of the Living Dead*," 210.
55. Balász, "Close-Up," 306.
56. Paffenroth, *Gospel of the Living Dead*, 82.
57. See Williams, *Cinema of George A. Romero*, 136.
58. See Paffenroth, *Gospel of the Living Dead*, 82.
59. Internet Movie Database, "*Day of the Dead* (1985)."
60. Internet Movie Database, "*Return of the Living Dead* (1985)."

61. Russell, *Book of the Dead*, 151. Although Russell calls this period a "renaissance," I see it more as the continuation of a productivity curve that had begun with *Night of the Living Dead*. The 1980s indeed saw more zombie movies than before, but there had been no discernible lull since 1968. Not until the zombie film had virtually disappeared in the 1990s could a true renaissance — a true "rebirth" — of them take place.
62. Ibid., 153.
63. Ibid., 151.
64. Ibid., 154.
65. Internet Movie Database, "*Return of the Living Dead* (1985)."
66. Russell, *Book of the Dead*, 154.
67. The opening title screen of *The Return of the Living Dead* offers another layer to this postmodern self-reflection, declaring that O'Bannon based *his* film on a true story as well — a metatextual move that, by extension, claims *Night of the Living Dead* is really a true story and that zombies do, in fact, exist.
68. Clery, "Genesis of 'Gothic' Fiction," 24.
69. Walpole, *Castle of Otranto*, 81.
70. Ibid., 145.
71. Russell, *Book of the Dead*, 155.
72. Frank and Freddy play off each other in a comic pairing reminiscent of both Rosencrantz and Guildenstern from *Hamlet* and Diego and Jaquez from *The Castle of Otranto*, although the zombie duo proves substantially more pathetic and tragic.
73. Russell, *Book of the Dead*, 155.
74. Ibid., 157.
75. Ibid.
76. For more on *Evil Dead II*, the spatstick subgenre, and the role of the carnivalesque in such horrorcomedy films, see Badley, "Zombie Splatter Comedy," 43–44.
77. Ibid., 44.
78. Indeed, at *Braindead*'s climax, Mum becomes a giant, mutant zombie that devours Lionel with a vaginal opening, thus literally returning the son to the womb. To escape, Lionel must fight his way out of his mother's body, physically destroying her to obtain his freedom.
79. Russell, *Book of the Dead*, 164.
80. The name of Shaun's mother is just one of many intentional references to Romero's zombie movies, and Ed makes this allusion even clearer with his version of a famous line from *Night of the Living Dead*, "We're coming to get you, Barbara!" Other homage elements include the names of incidental characters, the

dialogue spoken by news broadcasters, and various songs featured on the film's soundtrack. In other words, Wright's film is unabashedly intertextual and thoroughly self-aware.

81. For a thorough critical discussion of the zombie renaissance, see my introduction; for the sake of space, I will refrain from repeating that investigation here.

82. Williams, *Cinema of George A. Romero*, 128.

83. Furthermore, the first draft of Romero's *Day of the Dead* screenplay featured a survivalist society with a strict and unjust class system ruled by a tyrannical political leader, with Governor Henry Dickerson living in affluent luxury while the rest of the population languishes in the squalor of ghettos (see Williams, *Cinema of George A. Romero*, 130). These elements of Romero's social criticism of the Reagan administration resurface in *Land of the Dead* as an updated critique of George W. Bush (see Mansi, *Undead Again*).

84. Thompson, "Zombies, Values, and Personal Identity," 36.

85. Paffenroth, *Gospel of the Living Dead*, 115.

86. Big Daddy's position as protagonist also follows the pattern of Romero's other zombie films because like Ben, Peter, and *Day of the Dead*'s John (Terry Alexander), the actor who plays the zombie leader is African American. All four movies feature a sympathetic black leader who, at least to some extent, survives the horrors of the narrative.

87. Paffenroth, *Gospel of the Living Dead*, 117.

88. Mansi, *Undead Again*.

89. Paffenroth, *Gospel of the Living Dead*, 130.

90. Clark, "Undead Martyr," 208.

91. Paffenroth, *Gospel of the Living Dead*, 128.

92. Ibid., 124.

93. Clark, "Undead Martyr," 208.

94. Ibid., 198.

95. Ibid., 209.

96. Paffenroth, *Gospel of the Living Dead*, 132.

97. Ibid., 133.

98. Shaviro, *Cinematic Body*, 96.

99. Ibid., 96–97.

100. Marc Price's *Colin* (2008), produced for only £45 and shot entirely on a camcorder, takes viewers in just this direction. According to Simon Crerar, this microbudget film "puts an unusual slant on the zombie genre, telling the story from the point of view of a zombie trying to understand what has happened to him, rather than a human trying to escape and survive." Crerar, "Colin the Movie." With the film achieving critical attention at the 2009 Cannes Film Festival, a studio-backed release seems inevitable, and future Hollywood productions will likely follow its lead, as I will propose in my conclusion.

Conclusion

1. Dendle, *Zombie Movie Encyclopedia*, 121.

2. Magistrale, *Abject Terrors*, xiii.

3. Skal, *Monster Show*, 115.

4. "Roots."

5. Hogle, "Gothic in Western Culture," 1.

6. Frank, "Introduction," 11.

7. Miles, "Effulgence of Gothic," 43.

8. See Williams, *Art of Darkness*, 101–104.

9. See Miles, "Effulgence of Gothic," 52–53.

10. Botting, "Aftergothic," 298.

11. Botting, *Gothic Romanced*, 16.

12. Bruhm, "Contemporary Gothic," 272.

13. *Diary of the Dead* repeatedly features file footage and news clips showing various kinds of violence from all over the globe, but it's never clear if these images were produced for Romero's film or if they were taken from actual, real-life news broadcasts. This intertextual ambiguity emphasizes the way the media deftly — and perhaps dangerously — blurs the line between reality and fiction.

14. Internet Movie Database, "Plot Summary for *Yesterday* (2009)."

15. Internet Movie Database, "*Survival of the Dead* (2009)."

16. An additional revival pattern appears in the "zombiesque" films about alien-possession, such as James Gunn's *Slither* (2006) and Oliver Hirschbiegel's 2007 remake of *Invasion of the Body Snatchers*, *The Invasion*.

17. Botting, *Gothic Romanced*, 22.

18. Internet Movie Database, "Plot Summary for *George's Intervention* (2009)."

19. Kirkman, *Days Gone Bye*, 7.

20. See Littleton, "Frank Darabont Circles Zombies."

BIBLIOGRAPHY

Ackermann, Hans W., and Jeanine Gauthier. "The Ways and Nature of the Zombi." *Journal of American Folklore* 104.414 (1991): 466–494.

Aizenberg, Edna. "'I Walked with a Zombie': The Pleasures and Perils of Postcolonial Hybridity." *World Literature Today* 73.3 (1999): 461–466.

Althusser, Louis. *Lenin and Philosophy and Other Essays*. Translated by Ben Brewster. London: New Left Books, 1971.

Badley, Linda. "Zombie Splatter Comedy from *Dawn* to *Shaun*: Cannibal Carnivalesque." In McIntosh and Leverette, *Zombie Culture*, 35–53.

Balász, Béla. "The Close-Up." In Braudy and Cohen, *Film Theory and Criticism*, 304–311.

Beard, Matthew. "'A Scene from Mad Max': Britons Reveal Horror of the Superdome." *The Independent*, 3 September 2005. http://www.independent.co.uk/news/world/americas/a-scene-from-mad-max-britons-reveal-horror-of-the-superdome-505300.html.

Bendix, Regina. *In Search of Authenticity*. Madison: University of Wisconsin Press, 1997.

Berliner, Brett A. *Ambivalent Desire: The Exotic Black Other in Jazz-Age France*. Boston: University of Massachusetts Press, 2002.

Bing, Fernande. "Entretiens avec Alfred Métraux." *L'homme* 4.2 (1964): 23–32.

Bishop, Kyle. "Dead Man *Still* Walking: Explaining the Zombie Renaissance." *Journal of Popular Film and Television* 37.1 (2009): 16–25.

_____. "The Idle Proletariat: *Dawn of the Dead*, Consumer Ideology, and the Loss of Productive Labor." *The Journal of Popular Culture* 43.2 (forthcoming).

_____. "Raising the Dead: Unearthing the Non-Literary Origins of Zombie Cinema." *Journal of Popular Film and Television* 33.4 (2006): 196–205.

_____. "The Sub-Subaltern Monster: Imperialist Hegemony and the Cinematic Voodoo Zombie." *The Journal of American Culture* 31.2 (2008): 141–152.

Botting, Fred. "Aftergothic: Consumption, Machines, and Black Holes." In Hogle, *The Cambridge Companion to Gothic Fiction*, 277–300.

_____. *Gothic Romanced: Consumption, Gender and Technology in Contemporary Fictions*. New York: Routledge, 2008.

_____. *Limits of Horror: Technology, Bodies, Gothic*. New York: Manchester University Press, 2008.

Boyle, Danny, and Alex Garland. "Commentary." *28 Days Later*, special ed. DVD. Directed by Danny Boyle. Beverly Hills: Twentieth Century–Fox Home Entertainment, 2003.

Braudy, Leo, and Marshall Cohen, eds. *Film Theory and Criticism*. 5th ed. New York: Oxford University Press, 1999.

Brontë, Charlotte. *Jane Eyre*. New York: Signet Classic, 1997.

Brooks, Max. *The Zombie Survival Guide*. New York: Three Rivers Press, 2003.

Bruhm, Steven. "The Contemporary Gothic: Why We Need It." In Hogle, *The Cambridge Companion to Gothic Fiction*, 259–276.

Campbell, John W., Jr. "Who Goes There?" In *Who Goes There? Seven Tales of Science*

Fiction, 7–75. Cutchogue, NY: Buccaneer Books, 1948.

Cather, Willa. *The Professor's House*. New York: Vintage Books, 1990.

Césaire, Aimé. *Discourse on Colonialism*. Translated by Joan Pinkham. New York: Monthly Review Press, 2000.

Clark, Simon. "The Undead Martyr: Sex, Death, and Revolution in George Romero's Zombie Films." In Greene and Mohammad, *The Undead and Philosophy*, 197–209.

Clery, E. J. "The Genesis of 'Gothic' Fiction." In Hogle, *The Cambridge Companion to Gothic Fiction*, 21–39.

Crane, Stephen. "The Monster." In *Crane: Prose and Poetry*, 391–448. New York: Library of America, 1984.

Crerar, Simon. "Colin the Movie, Made by Marc Price for £45, Typified Cannes Spirit." *Times Online*, 17 May 2009. http://entertainment.timesonline.co.uk/tol/arts_and_entertainment/film/cannes/article6306149.ece.

Davis, Wade. *The Serpent and the Rainbow*. New York: Simon and Schuster, 1985.

Dayan, Joan. *Haiti, History, and the Gods*. Berkeley: University of California Press, 1995.

Dendle, Peter. *The Zombie Movie Encyclopedia*. Jefferson, NC: McFarland, 2001.

Depestre, René. *Change*. Paris: Editions du Seuil, 1971.

Diehl, Digby. *Tales from the Crypt: The Official Archives*. New York: St. Martin's Press, 1996.

Dillard, R. H. W. "*Night of the Living Dead*: It's Not Like Just a Wind That's Passing Through." In *American Horrors*, edited by Gregory A. Waller, 14–29. Chicago: University of Illinois Press, 1987.

Dorson, Richard M. *Folklore and Fakelore*. Cambridge, MA: Harvard University Press, 1976.

Du Maurier, Daphne. "The Birds." In *You and Science Fiction*, edited by Bernard Hollister, 281–299. Lincolnwood, IL: National Textbook Company, 1995.

Eagleton, Terry. *Ideology: An Introduction*. London: Verso, 1991.

Eisenstein, Sergei. *Film Form: Essays in Film Theory*. Edited and translated by Jay Leyda. New York: Harcourt, 1977.

Fanon, Frantz. *Black Skin, White Masks*. Translated by Charles Lam Markmann. New York: Grove Press, 1967.

Fiedler, Leslie A. *Love and Death in the American Novel*. Champaign, IL: Dalkey Archive Press, 1997.

Finney, Jack. *Invasion of the Body Snatchers*. New York: Scribner, 1998.

Flint, David. *Zombie Holocaust: How the Living Dead Devoured Pop Culture*. London: Plexus, 2009.

Frank, Frederick S. "Appendix A: Walpole's Correspondence and Strawberry Hill." In Frank, *The Castle of Otranto and The Mysterious Mother*, 257–287.

_____. "Introduction." In Frank, *The Castle of Otranto and The Mysterious Mother*, 11–34.

_____, ed. *The Castle of Otranto and The Mysterious Mother*. Peterborough, Ontario: Broadview Press, 2003.

Freud, Sigmund. *Beyond the Pleasure Principle*. Translated by James Strachey. New York: Norton, 1961.

_____. *The Ego and the Id*. Translated by Joan Riviere. New York: Norton, 1960.

_____. "The Uncanny." In *The Uncanny*, translated by David McLintock, 123–162. New York: Penguin Books, 2003.

Friends of Strawberry Hill. "The House." *Friends of Strawberry Hill*. 7 Apr. 2009. http://www.friendsofstrawberryhill.org.

Frumke, Roy, dir. *Roy Frumke's Document of the Dead*. 1989. Disc 4. *Dawn of the Dead*, ultimate ed. DVD. Directed by George A. Romero. Troy, MI: Anchor Bay Entertainment, 2004.

Fukuyama, Francis. *The End of History and the Last Man*. New York: Avon Books, 1992.

Gilroy, Paul. *The Black Atlantic: Modernity and Double Consciousness*. Cambridge: Harvard University Press, 1993.

Goddu, Teresa A. *Gothic America: Narrative, History, and Nation*. New York: Columbia University Press, 1997.

Grant, Barry Keith. "Taking Back the *Night of the Living Dead*: George Romero, Feminism, and the Horror Film." In Grant *The*

Dread of Difference: Gender and the Horror Film, edited by Barry Keith Grant, 200–212. Austin: University of Texas Press, 1996.

Greene, Richard, and K. Silem Mohammad, eds. *The Undead and Philosophy*. Popular Culture and Philosophy. Chicago: Open Court, 2006.

Haining, Peter. Introduction to Haining, *Zombie!*, 7–20.

_____, ed. *Zombie! Stories of the Walking Dead*. London: Target, 1985.

Halberstam, Judith. *Skin Shows: Gothic Horror and the Technology of Monsters*. Durham: Duke University Press, 1995.

Hall, Stuart. "Cultural Identity and Cinematic Representation." In *Black British Cultural Studies: A Reader*, edited by Houston A. Baker Jr., Manthia Diawara, and Ruth H. Lindeborg, 210–222. Chicago: University Chicago Press, 1996.

Hegel, Georg Wilhelm Friedrich. *The Phenomenology of Mind*. 2d ed. Translated by J. B. Baillie. New York: Humanities Press, 1966.

Henderson, Andrea K. *Romantic Identities: Varieties of Subjectivity, 1774–1830*. Cambridge: Cambridge University Press, 1996.

Herskovits, Melville J. *Dahomey, an Ancient West African Kingdom*. New York: J. J. Augustin, 1938.

Hogle, Jerrold E. "The Ghost of the Counterfeit in the Genesis of the Gothic." In *Gothic Origins and Innovations*, edited by Allan Lloyd Smith and Victor Sage, 23–33. Atlanta: Rodopi, 1994.

_____. "Introduction: The Gothic in Western Culture." In Hogle, *The Cambridge Companion to Gothic Fiction*, 1–20.

_____. *The Undergrounds of the Phantom of the Opera: Sublimation and the Gothic in Leroux's Novel and its Progeny*. New York: Palgrave Macmillan, 2002.

_____, ed. *The Cambridge Companion to Gothic Fiction*. Cambridge: Cambridge University Press, 2002.

Horne, Philip. "I Shopped with a Zombie." *Critical Quarterly* 34.4 (1992): 97–110.

Hurston, Zora Neale. *Tell My Horse: Voodoo and Life in Haiti and Jamaica*. New York: Harper and Row, 1938.

The Internet Movie Database. "Box Office/Business for *Dawn of the Dead* (1978)." *The Internet Movie Database*. http://www.imdb.com/title/tt0077402/business.

_____. "Box Office/Business for *Day of the Dead* (1985)." *The Internet Movie Database*. http://www.imdb.com/title/tt0088993/business.

_____. "Box Office/Business for *Night of the Living Dead* (1968)." *The Internet Movie Database*. http://imdb.com/title/tt0063350/business.

_____. "Box Office/Business for *The Return of the Living Dead* (1985)." *The Internet Movie Database*. http://www.imdb.com/title/tt0089907/business.

_____. "Box Office/Business for *28 Days Later* (2002)." *The Internet Movie Database*. http://www.imdb.com/title/tt0289043/business.

_____. "Plot Summary for *George's Intervention* (2009)." *The Internet Movie Database*. http://www.imdb.com/title/tt1310641/plotsummary.

_____. "Plot Summary for *Yesterday* (2009)." *The Internet Movie Database* http://www.imdb.com/title/tt1326278/plotsummary.

_____. "*Survival of the Dead* (2009)." *The Internet Movie Database*. http://www.imdb.com/title/tt1134854/.

Irigaray, Luce. *This Sex Which Is Not One*. Translated by Catherine Porter. Ithaca: Cornell University Press, 1985.

"It's Like a Sci-Fi Movie." *News 24* 10 January 2005. http://www.news24.com/News24/World/Hurricane/0,,2-10-1942_1809596,00.html.

Jacobs, W. W. "The Monkey's Paw." In *Lady of the Barge and Other Stories*, 23–34. Charleston, SC: BiblioBazaar, 2007.

James, Henry. "The Jolly Corner." In *The Turn of the Screw and Other Short Fiction by Henry James*, 369–403. New York: Bantam Books, 1981.

James, Toby, dir. *Pure Rage: The Making of 28 Days Later*. 2002. *28 Days Later*, special ed. DVD. Directed by Danny Boyle. Beverly Hills: Twentieth Century–Fox Home Entertainment, 2003.

Jauss, Hans Robert. *Toward an Aesthetic of Reception*. Translated by Timothy Bahti.

Theory and History of Literature 2. Minneapolis: University Minnesota Press, 1982.

Jones, Darryl. *Horror: A Thematic History in Fiction and Film*. London: Arnold, 2002.

Kane, Edward J. "Dangers of Capital Forbearance: The Case of the FSLIC and 'Zombie' S&Ls." *Contemporary Policy Issues* 5.1 (1987): 77–83.

Kay, Glenn. *Zombie Movies: The Ultimate Guide*. Chicago: Chicago Review Press, 2008.

King, Stephen. *Danse Macabre*. New York: Berkley Books, 1981.

_____. *The Stand*. New York: Doubleday, 1990.

Kinnard, Roy. *Horror in Silent Films: A Filmography, 1869–1929*. Jefferson, NC: McFarland, 1995.

Kirkman, Robert. *The Best Defense*. The Walking Dead 5. Orange, CA: Image Comics, 2006.

_____. *Days Gone Bye*. The Walking Dead 1. Orange, CA: Image Comics, 2004.

_____. *Safety Behind Bars*. The Walking Dead 3. Orange, CA: Image Comics, 2005.

Kirshenblatt-Gimblett, Barbara. "Folklore's Crisis." *Journal of American Folklore* 111.441 (1998): 281–327.

Kojève, Alexadre. *Outline of a Phenomenology of Right*. Edited by Bryan-Paul Frost. Translated by Bryan-Paul Frost and Robert Howse. Oxford: Rowman & Littlefield, 2000.

Koven, Mikel J. "The Folklore of the Zombie Film." In McIntosh and Leverette, *Zombie Culture*, 19–34.

Kristeva, Julia. *Powers of Horror: An Essay on Abjection*. Translated by Leon S. Roudiez. New York: Columbia University Press, 1982.

Krzywinska, Tanya. "Zombies in Gamespace: Form, Context, and Meaning in Zombie-Based Video Games." In McIntosh and Leverette, *Zombie Culture*, 153–168.

Latham, Rob. "Consuming Youth: The Lost Boys Cruise Mallworld." In *Blood Read: The Vampire as Metaphor in Contemporary Culture*, edited by Joan Gordon and

Veronica Hollinger, 129–150. Philadelphia: University of Pennsylvania Press, 1997.

Littleton, Cynthia. "Frank Darabont Circles Zombies." *Variety* 11 August 2009. http://www.variety.com/article/VR1118007161.html?categoryid=14&cs=1.

LoLordo, Nick. "Possessed by the Gothic: Stephen Crane's 'The Monster.'" *Arizona Quarterly* 57.2 (2001): 33–56.

Loudermilk, A. "Eating *Dawn* in the Dark." *Journal of Consumer Culture* 3.1 (2003): 83–108.

Maddrey, Joseph. *Nightmares in Red, White and Blue: The Evolution of the American Horror Film*. Jefferson, NC: McFarland, 2004.

Magistrale, Tony. *Abject Terrors: Surveying the Modern and Postmodern Horror Film*. New York: Peter Lang, 2005.

Mansi, Marian, dir. *Undead Again: The Making of* Land of the Dead. 2005. *Land of the Dead*, unrated director's cut. DVD. Directed by George A. Romero. Universal City, CA: Universal Studios, 2005.

Martin, Perry, dir. *The Dead Will Walk*. 2004. Disc 4. *Dawn of the Dead* ultimate ed. DVD. Directed by George A. Romero. Troy, MI: Anchor Bay Entertainment, 2004.

Marx, Karl. "Economic and Philosophical Manuscripts of 1844." In *The Marx-Engels Reader*, 2d ed., edited by Robert C. Tucker, 66–125. New York: Norton, 1978.

_____. "Die Klassenkämpfe in Frankreich 1848–1850." In Vol. 7, *Marx Engels Werke*, 12–34. Berlin: Dietz Verlag, 1960.

Matheson, Richard. *I Am Legend*. New York: Tom Doherty Associates, 1995.

McIntosh, Shawn. "The *Evolution of the Zombie*: The Monster That Keeps Coming Back." In McIntosh and Leverette, *Zombie Culture*, 1–17.

_____, and Marc Leverette, eds. *Zombie Culture: Autopsies of the Living Dead*. Lanham, MD: Scarecrow Press, 2008.

Métraux, Alfred. *Voodoo in Haiti*. Translated by Hugo Charteris. New York: Schocken Books, 1972.

Metz, Christian. "The Imaginary Signifier." In Braudy and Cohen, *Film Theory and Criticism*, 800–817.

Miles, Robert. "The 1790s: The Effulgence of Gothic." In Hogle, *The Cambridge Companion to Gothic Fiction*, 41–62.

Mintz, Sidney W. "Introduction to the Second English Edition." In Métraux, *Voodoo in Haiti*, 1–15.

Mori, Masahiro. "The Uncanny Valley." Translated by Karl F. MacDorman and Takashi Minato. *Energy* 7.4 (1970): 33–35.

Moser, Hans. "Vom Folklorismus in unserer Zeit." *Zeitschrift für Volkskunde* 58 (1962): 177–209.

"N. O. Police Fire 51 for Desertion." *Fox News*, 30 October 2005. http://www.fox news.com/story/0,2933,173879,00.html.

Newitz, Annalee. "War and Social Upheaval Cause Spikes in Zombie Movie Production." *io9: Strung out on Science Fiction* 29 October 2008. http://io9.com/5070243/war-and-social-upheaval-cause-spikes-in-zombie-movie-production.

Nietzsche, Friedrich. *Thus Spoke Zarathustra: A Book for All and None.* In *The Portable Nietzsche*, edited and translated by Walter Kaufmann, 103–439. New York: Penguin Books, 1982.

Oakes, David, ed. "Movies." *Zombie Movie Data-Base* 2007. http://www.trashvideo. org/zmdb/view/index.php?page=list&type=&mode=&key=& start=.

O'Brien, Brad. "*Vita, Amore, e Morte*—and Lots of Gore: The Italian Zombie Film." In McIntosh and Leverette, *Zombie Culture*, 55–70.

Oudart, Pierre. "Cinema and Suture." Translated by Kari Hanet. *The Symptom* 8 (Winter 2007). http://www.lacan. com/symptom8_articles/oudart8.html.

The Oxford English Dictionary. "Zombie." *OED Online.* 2d ed. 1989. http://diction ary.oed.com.

_____. "Zombie: Computing." *OED Online.* September 2006. http://dictionary. oed.com.

Paffenroth, Kim. *Gospel of the Living Dead: George Romero's Visions of Hell on Earth.* Waco: Baylor University Press, 2006.

Pagano, David. "The Space of Apocalypse in Zombie Cinema." In McIntosh and Leverette, *Zombie Culture*, 71–86.

Paravisini-Gebert, Lizabeth. "Women Possessed: Eroticism and Exoticism in the Representation of Women as Zombie." In *Sacred Passessions: Vodou, Santeria, Obeah and the Caribbean*, edited by Margarite Fernández Olmos and Lizabeth Paravisini-Gebert, 37–58. New Brunswick, NJ: Rutgers University Press, 1997.

Patterson, Natasha. "Cannibalizing Gender and Genre: A Feminist Re-Vision of George Romero's Zombie Films." In McIntosh and Leverette, *Zombie Culture*, 103–118.

Pegg, Simon. Afterword. *Miles Behind Us*, The Walking Dead 2, by Robert Kirkman, 133. Orange, CA: Image Comics, 2004.

Punter, David. *The Literature of Terror: A History of Gothic Fictions from 1765 to the Present Day.* New York: Longman, 1980.

Rhodes, Gary D. *White Zombie: Anatomy of a Horror Film.* Jefferson, NC: McFarland, 2001.

"The Roots." 2008. *George A. Romero's Diary of the Dead.* DVD. Directed by George A. Romero. Santa Monica: Dimension Extreme, 2008.

Russell, Jamie. *Book of the Dead: The Complete History of Zombie Cinema.* Godalming, Surrey: FAB Press, 2006.

Said, Edward W. *Culture and Imperialism.* New York: Vintage Books, 1994.

St. John, Warren. "Market for Zombies? It's Undead (Aaahhh!)." *New York Times* 26 March 2006, sec. 9: 1+.

Savoy, Eric. "The Face of the Tenant: A Theory of American Gothic." In *American Gothic: New Interventions in a National Narrative*, edited by Robert K. Martin and Eric Savoy, 3–19. Iowa City: University of Iowa Press, 1998.

_____. "The Rise of American Gothic." In Hogle, *The Cambridge Companion to Gothic Fiction*, 167–188.

Scott, Ron. "'Now I'm Feeling Zombified': Playing the Zombie Online." In McIntosh and Leverette, *Zombie Culture*, 169–184.

Seabrook, W. B. *The Magic Island.* New York: The Literary Guild of America, 1929.

Shaviro, Steven. *The Cinematic Body.* Theory Out of Bounds 2. Minneapolis: University of Minnesota Press, 1993.

Shelley, Mary. *Frankenstein*. Edited by Johanna M. Smith. Boston: Bedford Books, 1992.

_____. *The Last Man*. Edited by Morton D. Paley. London: Oxford University Press, 1998.

Silverman, Kaja. *The Subject of Semiotics*. New York: Oxford University Press, 1983.

Skal, David J. *The Monster Show*. New York: Faber and Faber, 1993.

Snyder, Zach, and Eric Newman. "Commentary." *Dawn of the Dead*, unrated director's cut. DVD. Directed by Zach Snyder. Universal City, CA: Universal Studios, 2004.

Spivak, Gayatri Chakravorty. "Can the Subaltern Speak?" In *Marxism and the Interpretation of Culture*, edited by Cary Nelson and Lawrence Grossberg, 271–313. Urbana: University of Illinois Press, 1988.

Stevenson, Robert Louis. *Dr. Jekyll and Mr. Hyde*. New York: Signet Classic, 2003.

Stoker, Bram. *Dracula*. Edited by Nina Auerbach and David J. Skal. Norton Critical Edition. New York: Norton, 1997.

Strauss, Mark. "A Harvard Psychiatrist Explains Zombie Neurobiology." *io9: Mad Neuroscience* 10 June 2009. http://io9.com/5286145/a-harvard-psychiatrist-explains-zombie-neurobiology.

Taussig, Michael T. *The Devil and Commodity Fetishism in South America*. Chapel Hill: University of North Carolina Press, 1980.

Thompson, Hamish. "'She's Not Your Mother Anymore, She's a Zombie!': Zombies, Value, and Personal Identity." In Greene and Mohammad, *The Undead and Philosophy*, 27–37.

Toelken, Barre. *The Dynamics of Folklore*. Logan: Utah State University Press, 1996.

Walker, Matthew. "When There's No More Room in Hell, the Death Will Shop the Earth: Romero and Aristotle on Zombies, Happiness, and Consumption." In Greene and Mohammad, *The Undead and Philosophy*, 81–89.

Wallace, Inez. "I Walked with a Zombie." In Haining, *Zombie!*, 95–102.

Waller, Gregory A. *The Living and the Undead*. Chicago: University of Illinois Press, 1986.

Walpole, Horace. *The Castle of Otranto*. In Frank, *The Castle of Otranto and The Mysterious Mother*, 56–165.

Walz, Jon Alon, dir. *Fear Files: Zombies*. The History Channel. 24 Oct. 2006.

Wells, Paul. *The Horror Genre: From Beelzebub to Blair Witch*. Short Cuts: Introductions to Film Studies 1. New York: Wallflower Press, 2002.

Wells, Steven. "G2: Shortcuts: Zombies Come Back from the Dead." *Guardian* [London] 2 January 2006, Features: 2.

Williams, Anne. *Art of Darkness: A Poetics of Gothic*. Chicago: University of Chicago Press, 1995.

Williams, Tony. *The Cinema of George A. Romero: Knight of the Living Dead*. Directors' Cuts. London: Wallflower Press, 2003.

Wood, Robin. "Neglected Nightmares." In *Horror Film Reader*, edited by Alain Silver and James Ursini, 111–127. New York: Limelight Editions, 2000.

Wright, Edgar. "The Church of George." *Virginia Quarterly Review* 81.1 (2005): 40–43.

Wylie, Turrell V. "Ro-Langs: The Tibetan Zombie." *History of Religions* 4.1 (1964): 69–80.

Yeats, William Butler. "The Second Coming." In *The Norton Introduction to Literature*, 8th ed., edited by Jerome Beaty, et al., 1325. New York: Norton: 2002.

Young, Gwenda. "The Cinema of Difference: Jacques Tourneur, Race and *I Walked with a Zombie* (1943)." *Irish Journal of American Studies* 7 (1998): 101–119.

INDEX

Numbers in **bold italics** indicate pages with illustrations.

231